# A VICTORIAN REBEL

*From a drawing by Cosmo Rowe, by permission of the artist.*

WILLIAM MORRIS

# A VICTORIAN REBEL

# REBEL

*The Life of William Morris*

❖

By LLOYD WENDELL ESHLEMAN

*Author of Moulders of Destiny:
Renaissance Lives and Times*

❖

We who once were fools and dreamers then shall be the great and wise;
There amidst the world new builded shall our earthly deeds abide,
Though our names be all forgotten, and the tale of how we died.

NEW YORK
*CHARLES SCRIBNER'S SONS*
1940

*For*

## WALTER PHELPS HALL
*Professor of History*
*Princeton University*

# CONTENTS

vii

## BOOK III

## DAYS OF THOUGHT

## BOOK IV

## THE S. D. F.—AND REVOLUTION

BOOK V

## THE SOCIALIST LEAGUE—AND BLOODSHED

BOOK VI

## THE HAMMERSMITH SOCIALIST SOCIETY—AND VICTORY IN SIGHT

EPILOGUE

## "THE SINGERS HAVE SUNG AND THE BUILDERS HAVE BUILDED"

# ILLUSTRATIONS

# ACKNOWLEDGMENTS

FOR THE KINDNESS and generosity displayed by numerous correspondents in answering letters, supplying information, making suggestions, recounting personal reminiscences and in sending to the author copies and originals of otherwise unprocurable clippings, letters, articles, periodicals, pamphlets, booklets and books, together with their good wishes for the success of the enterprise, the author is deeply grateful. From among the many correspondents the author is deeply and particularly indebted to Miss May Morris, Mrs. Katherine Bruce Glasier, Mrs. H. H. Champion, Mr. George Bateman, Mr. Robert Blatchford, Mr. G. D. H. Cole, Mr. Holbrook Jackson, Professor Karl Litzenberg of the University of Michigan, Mr. Arthur Mackmurdo, Mr. J. S. Middleton, Mr. Henry W. Nevinson, Sir Charles Oman of Oxford University, Mr. John Paton, Mr. George Roebuck, Mr. Cosmo Rowe and Mr. Eustace A. Stedman. For assistance in procuring copyright privileges he is especially indebted to the late Miss May Morris, daughter of William Morris; Sir Sydney Cockerell, former trustee of the Morris estate, and Mr. Walter Jefferay of the publishing firm of Longmans, Green & Company.

For permission to reproduce the Burne-Jones drawings a very special indebtedness is acknowledged to the late Miss May Morris; to Mrs. Mackail, the daughter of Edward Burne-Jones; to the authorities of the British Museum; and to the publishing firms of the Macmillan Company and Basil Blackwell, both of which hitherto had reproduced some of them. For Mr. New's drawing of the Merton Abbey Works and the mill pond I am indebted to Longmans, Green & Company. For the frontispiece and the Morris lecture notes I am indebted to Mr. Rowe, the artist. I am also indebted to the librarians of Princeton University, Yale University, the New York Public Library, the Columbia University Library, the Pierpont Morgan Memorial Library, and to the officials of the British Museum for courtesies extended to me for purposes of research.

Above all, I must express my very great indebtedness to Professor Walter Phelps Hall of Princeton University and to the late Professor Henry R. Shipman of Princeton University. These men made the initial suggestions and helped me with the plan of my original study, *William Morris: Artist-Philosopher and Practical-Socialist,* which was a dissertation offered in candidacy for a doctorate at Princeton University some years ago. The present volume, of course, represents a development of the earlier work, and I trust that the gist of the findings are now available in a style that the average reader may not find objectionable. I trust also that I have not departed far from the kindly and patient criticisms of my original work as they were offered by Professor W. P. Hall and Professor Willard Thorp, both of whom saved me from a number of slips.

Besides furnishing much valuable information, Mrs. Katherine Bruce Glasier and the late Miss May Morris were especially generous in waiving copyrights in the works of Bruce Glasier, William Morris and May Morris: a procedure that was followed also by Messrs. Longmans, Green & Company, publishers of most of their works. To Henry Holt & Company I am indebted for permission to quote two brief passages from the work of Arthur Clutton-Brock; to Houghton, Mifflin Company for permission to abstract a passage from the works of Peter Kropotkin, and to The Macmillan Company for permission to quote from *The Memorials of Edward Burne-Jones.* These passages are listed in the notes.

THE AUTHOR

New York City,
August 20, 1940.

# I

## DAYS OF YOUTH

*But lo, another, how shall he have praise?*
*Through flame and thorns I led him many days*
*And nought he shrank, but smiled and followed*
    *close,*
*Till in his path the shade of hate arose*
*'Twixt him and his desire: with heart that burned*
*For very love, back through the thorns he turned,*
*His wounds, his tears, his prayers without avail*
*Forgotten now, nor e'en for him a tale,*
*Because for love's sake love he cast aside.*

## CHAPTER I

### THE FAMILY

THE time at which this story begins was just about one hundred years ago. The place was England, and Queen Victoria, aged twenty-one, was enduring the third year of her long and virtuous reign. Everywhere, in city and countryside alike, the air was full of change, the kind of change that was to make England look familiar to the modern eye. Then, the change was just beginning. People still rode in stagecoaches, although paved roads and railroads were beginning to appear. The city of London was slowly taking on the aspect of a modern metropolis.

In our own time the Morden-Edgware Line of the London Underground Transport has built an escalator connection from the Bank of England station to join the District Line at the Monument. This makes easy transport connections for people who work in London's financial district and who come and go between their distant homes and their offices on the Central London, the District, and the Morden-Edgware underground lines. For in our own time London has expanded in all directions, and its inhabitants usually live far from "the old city." Now one can jump upon an ever-moving London bus (for in London every one jumps upon buses, even in the midst of the financial district) and be in Walthamstow, on the edges of the green and fertile land—some five miles as the crow flies, but not as the London streets run—within less than an hour.

A century ago, however, one had to take a stagecoach which left the city at a point near Cannon Street Station and travelled north on Moorgate, past Finsbury Square and Islington to Dalston, where it turned eastward, north of the Hackney

Marshes, to Walthamstow and Woodford, on the edges of what was then the formidable Epping Forest. Or one could travel eastward past the Fenchurch Street Station and Stepney to Bow, thence north and west of West Ham, Forest Gate and the Wanstead Flats to the same destination. At no point on either route could the horses have travelled at more than ten miles per hour.

In such a manner did William Morris's father go back and forth to his work at 83 King William Street, in the "City." For in those days the Morris home was in Walthamstow, on the near side of Epping Forest.

William Morris's father was a rather small, darkish man, of neat habits: a businessman who inspired respect. His head was cool and his judgment shrewd. He lived a regular, quiet life, keeping very much to himself whatever thoughts he may have had. It is needless to add that he always prospered, and that at the time this story begins he was a very wealthy man.

As was not uncommon among middle-class businessmen of his time, William Morris's father looked back upon his family tree with pride; and in view of his own rising position as a partner in the rich brokerage firm of Sanderson and Company, he could look forward to the day when he, like many another middle-class man, might be granted a family coat-of-arms. Certainly that would do no harm, and it might do a lot of good.

And what had Mr. Morris, by way of a family, to be proud of?

His own family came from respectable gentry who had lived for a number of generations in the upper Severn valley of western England. His father—who was named William like him and like his own youngest child at this particular moment—had been a prosperous burgess in the city of Worcester. And his father, like him, had made a very good marriage. His mother had been Elizabeth Stanley in her youth, daughter of a retired naval surgeon of Nottingham. His mother had brought new force and vigour into the Morris family; for the Stanleys, unlike the Morrises, were of tough and vigorous stock, that type of Englander who, perhaps descended from Danish Vikings, takes naturally to the sea. Possibly that was why Elizabeth's famous grandson came to resemble a sea captain more than anything else, and why every one thought that he seemed like a latter-day Viking. In any event, Elizabeth Stanley Morris was a beautiful, tall, strongly built personage; and she lived vigorously to the age of eighty-five, long after the period at which our story begins.

Shortly after his admission into the firm of Sanderson and Company, William Morris II followed in his father's footsteps and made a very excellent marriage. He also married a woman who was strong, beautiful and fair: one Emma Shelton, a childhood friend, daughter of Joseph Shelton of Worcester. The Sheltons also were an eminently respectable and accomplished family: they traced their ancestry at least as far back as one Henry Shelton, who had been a mercer of Birmingham in the reign of Henry VII. Throughout the Tudor and Stuart periods most of the Sheltons had been merchants and landed proprietors, but a number of their sons throve in the Church and at the bar. They were no ordinary people, by any means, and although not noble they had always possessed a fine æsthetic sense and been exceedingly musical. Emma Shelton's father had been a music teacher in Worcester and her two elder brothers were singing canons in Worcester Cathedral and Westminster Abbey. Moreover, the Sheltons, like the Stanleys, were descended from long-lived, vigorous English stock of strong frame and rugged constitution. Emma herself, the mother of William Morris—our "Victorian Rebel"—was to live to the age of ninety, her death preceding that of her famous son by only two years.

In 1833 William Morris's father, with Emma and their two young daughters, had moved from the city of London to Elm House on Clay Hill, in Walthamstow, Essex. The family, under the wise financial guidance of the father, was prospering to the point at which it could look forward to the delightful life of a typical country gentleman's household, if only business and social prestige kept increasing. And here in Elm House, on March 24, 1834, the third William Morris had been born.

The estate lay close to Epping Forest on what was then pleasant, rolling land overlooking the Lea valley. Every morning the horses of an old-fashioned stagecoach carried William Morris's father across the little valley of the Lea, past the East London slums of Hackney and Bethnal Green, down into the heart of the financial district on the Thames, not far from London Bridge.

William's father usually emerged from his office soon after tea time, and as he stepped upon the street he could feel himself to be in the midst of a noble historic setting. Below him, near the lower end of the street, stood the Monument, symbol of the Great Fire of London. At the upper end, on the corner of Princes and Threadneedle Streets, stood the Bank of England, gaunt guardian of British financial interests. Opposite it was the Mansion House, where the Lord Mayor of London resided during his year of office.

Turning at the corner of Swithin's Lane, William Morris's father passed behind the Mansion, past its Egyptian Hall and the City Police Court, down Victoria Street to Cannon. On the way, and it was only a few steps, he crossed Watling Street, built in Roman times, where Roman paving blocks still persisted, supposedly, and on to the coaching inn from which his stage departed for Walthamstow. Unlike some other travellers and commuters he did not stop to sample the ale in the taproom, for he was a thrifty man, and he knew, with perhaps a slight feeling of superiority, that the home-brewed ale of Elm House was indescribably better than that which was handed out in any city tavern.

So he rode home on almost every week day, well satisfied with his lot in life and knowing that in a house he loved, out in the fresh, green countryside, he would find an excellent warm dinner awaiting him.

As he neared Clay Hill his thoughts turned to his wife and his three children: the two girls, born in the city, and six-year-old, tousle-headed William, born at Elm House, and who, sickly at first, as if resentful of his masculine entry into a family of feminine children, was now turning into a restless little trouble-maker, constantly investigating everything, and usually completing his investigation by falling on his head and then running to his mother with dirty hands, torn clothes and tears in his eyes.

William Morris's father may have wondered to himself if William would be his only son, and whether God would grant more offspring to this so blesséd union. For he did not know, at this time, that six younger children were still to come: four more boys and two more girls, increasing the Morris family to eleven.

Little William, as his father always thought of him, was the third Morris in a row to bear that name. During infancy he had been such a sensitive and delicate little boy that almost every one, even the father, had despaired not only of his future, but, indeed, of his life. Only the mother had refused to give up hope. She herself said in after years that she kept the little fellow alive on beef tea and calves-foot jelly, and that as time went on he grew strong and handsome, tending more and more to resemble his maternal ancestors. In any event, Emma was very proud of her first boy.

The Morris family lived a happy life on week days and on Sundays they all attended a Low Anglican Church, for which they were always attired most suitably, as befitted respectable Victorian families. One and all, without exception, they loved the joys of country life and detested city life. They kept their own horses, cows, pigs, chickens and rabbits, baked their own bread, made their own cheeses, and brewed their own beer.

Holidays in the Morris home were always the occasions of glamorous festivities. Both parents gloried in old traditions and in the necessity of maintaining a feeling of historical immanence. Christmas, Hallowe'en and Twelfth Night were specially celebrated, and the spirit that prevailed was more ancient and pagan than Christian and Victorian. The late Miss

May Morris, William's second daughter, said that "delicious rum punch was brewed and given to every one, children and all—half a tumbler of it! (Surely we don't know how to drink now!) They had jolly eleven o'clock lunches, too: cake and cheese, and a glass of small beer brewed at home. My father often said that that cake 'was nicer than anything of the kind that he ever tasted afterward.' "

It was a complete and wholly happy world into which young William Morris was born: a world that has handed down to us some nostalgic memories of a lingering past. And it was a happy and good family into which young William was born and amidst which he was reared. Even if it was just a trifle "too" respectable we should not hold that against it—even if William sometimes did—for that was the way of families in Victorian days. Yet since his was the only genius which has given to that family any great and special prominence, we can afford to leave the family, for the most part, and pass on into the world of that little boy who was forever investigating and turning upside down or inside out almost everything with which his own little world of private happiness brought him into contact.

## CHAPTER II

---

A LITTLE BOY QUESTIONS HIS SMALL WORLD

WILLIAM, aged six, and Jennie, about two years his senior, were waiting patiently behind a clump of lilac bushes for their father's return. The little girl felt a very intense and girlish-maternal interest in her younger brother; she adored him and loved to watch his every step and his every breath—to the boy's intense discomfiture and childish disgust. She it was who had been responsible for those reading lessons which the girls' governess had been required to bestow upon the childish lad for the past two years. He was a genius, the governess had declared: "To think of any child of four learning to read those long, difficult novels of his own accord; and he's so eager about it, too!"

The statement was true. For almost two years "Little William" had been wading avidly through the Waverley novels, one of the few sets of readable books which graced the library of Elm House. At six his mind was filled with thoughts of chivalry and noble deeds, with fragments of muddled history and countless acts of bright and daring bravado. Already he had been pestering his father for a suit of toy armour (real armour was what he really wanted) and his father had at last begun to look around for some one who could provide armour and a pony that would be suitable for a small lad of six. For the time being, however, William had to content his soul as best he could with a silver bow that shot bright red arrows tipped with gilt and feathers. The bow and two of the bright arrows were now clutched in his left hand, in true warrior fashion.

As William's father neared the long, winding path which led to the low, rambling structure that was Elm House and home to him, Jennie gripped her brother's arm with intensely suppressed excitement. "Hush," she whispered, "Father is coming now; don't dare to breathe."

"Hush yourself, Jennie," retorted the small boy. "That is Saladin, the Turkish heretic, and I am Richard of the Lion Heart, waiting to fell him with my strong iron sword and good long bow."

"Father!" cried the little girl, rushing forth from their ambush, "here we are," while her "dear little William" came scrambling after her, his tousled yellow hair waving in all directions, his bow and arrows thrown aside, and his feet tripping over one another at every third step, until he went tumbling head over heels on the greensward.

Such was a welcome home which William Morris's father was more than half expecting, now that new and great gifts for his children were in order.

"Why, I believe it's Miss Morris! What a charming surprise!" exclaimed their father, while he grasped Jennie with one arm. Extending his cane with his free hand, he helped little William to his feet, mockingly rebuking him: "Now, now, my dear boy; you should learn to walk in a dignified manner, like a gentleman!"

They went talking and laughing into the long, low living room of Elm House, there to await the warm dinner which had been in slow and savoury preparation for the past two hours over a wood and charcoal fire. In the Morris home, food was always cooked in the most thorough of time-honoured fashions: there was never any harmful time-saving about that! Indeed, everything about this household was as irreproachable as the food, for Mrs. Morris was a zealous housekeeper.

While the rest of the family prepared for dinner, little William went dashing toward his bedroom; he usually dashed, but seldom reached the top of a flight of stairs without falling, for his eagerness to get things done in a hurry often caused his undoing.

In the bedroom, across two chairs set slightly apart, was his model of London Bridge. This was the closest approach to a mechanical toy which the child ever possessed. On the pillow of his bed there lay a woolly lamb that squeaked.

The child paused to examine the replicas of old houses on his bridge with an admiring eye, looked at the carpet below to see that his imaginary Thames was still flowing smoothly along its banks, and then turned to the lamb. He decided that he liked the lamb better, picked it up and hugged it until it cried, then set it carefully back on the pillow, pulled up the covers around its neck, kissed it once, and then ran off to wash his hands in the briefest and most superficial of fashions. By the time he got downstairs again and had seated himself at the dinner table, one would have thought that he had not washed them at all.

His elder sisters always regarded little William's escapades with particular misgivings. They had watched him go; and now they watched him come back. They glanced at their mother, then at him, then at their mother again with meaningful eyes, and then exclaimed in unison: "What a naughty, wicked boy! He hasn't washed for dinner!"

For it should be understood that the evangelical attitude ran through many middle-class families of the early Victorian era; and the Morris family was no exception. Thus it was that, according to Miss May Morris, "William was frequently 'naughty and wicked' in their eyes." And the girls, extremely dutiful little creatures that they were, had picked up the "naughty and wicked" expression from their mother, after which anything that William did was most likely to be "naughty and wicked" in their eyes, too. But they loved him just the same.

It is needless to state that little William disagreed with them profoundly. He did not know it, but he was rapidly becoming a latent individualist. Indeed, he was even learning to develop a temper; had he not already assigned his nurse to hell?[1] After he had been rebuked and nagged by his mother and sisters for the hundredth time or more, he could look at them with fire in his eyes; and one might have thought—if one remembered the "psychology" of a "naughty and wicked" child of six—that he would have loved to kill them outright with the leg of a chair.

The fiery look that he now bestowed upon them was not lost upon his fond and loving parents. It was very apparent, remarked his father, that little William was not becoming "a young gentleman." Instead, he was developing capacities for getting into mischief.

"So upstairs, young man, and wash those hands!"

[1]Morris's earliest poem, written in early childhood, is as follows:

> Where have you been so long to-day?
> Tell me true, sweet Step-daughter.
> To my brother's house I went to play:
> Something hurts me, Step-mother.
>
> What did you eat for your dinner there?
> Roasted eels and black pepper.
>
> What did you do with the broken meat?
> I gave them to my dogs to eat.
>
> What then did to your dogs betide?
> The flesh fell from them that they died.
>
> What do you leave to your father dear?
> My barn of wheat to make good cheer.
>
> And what will you leave to your brother dear?
> My great ship that sails everywhere.
>
> And what will you leave to your sister dear?
> My gold that shineth red and clear.
>
> And what will you leave to your Step-mother?
> The flames of Hell I leave to her.
>
> And what then will you leave your nurse?
> Mother, what could I wish her worse?

So upstairs it is; there is no other alternative.

So upstairs William went, feeling very certain that there was no justice in his world.

He washed very dutifully, this time, and returned to eat his dinner in silent moodiness.

Soon after dinner the children were sent to bed. But for a long time that night little William brooded over his inability to make other people understand his awkwardness, his words, his intentions, his inmost thoughts and feelings. Certainly he had washed twice that evening; and certainly he had done nothing and said nothing to offend any one.

Labouring mind and hot blood made the child grow feverish on such a night as this, and he tossed and kicked beneath the warm blankets and comforter (just as he was to do, and to have some reasons for doing, upon so many later occasions in his life) until at last he tore the sheets of his bed. For having done that he might very well receive adequate reprimands and punishment on the morrow.

It was a long time before the little boy relaxed and softly cried himself to sleep. Only in his dreams could he realize to the full his mental and physical prowess, and ride forth, a noble knight in shining armour, to help right the injustices of the world.

## CHAPTER III

## A CHILD'S "UTOPIA"

FURTHER disillusionment was in store for him. It came the next morning at breakfast as he came strolling manfully into the breakfast room. But his steps faltered and his face fell as he heard the conversation of his parents.

"Really, my dear, you know that William is altogether too young to be riding around on a pony," he heard his mother declare with her accustomed clarity and definiteness. "We should much rather be thinking of placing him in school, where he will soon belong, instead of encouraging his propensity for falling down and damaging his knees and clothes. Besides, what would people think, round about us, if they saw him dressed in a coat-of-mail in this day and age? Here there is scarcely room enough for the children to play as it is—you know how much they need the outdoor exercise and the sunshine—and most certainly the child could not ride a pony in this neighbourhood without running down his sisters or getting run over himself by some galloping stage. No, I don't like the idea at all; we should wait until he is eight or nine years old at least before we even think of such a thing! And just what are we to do, William, about the child's education?"

He heard his father hesitate and cough. His father was a man who, unlike his mother, made decisions slowly and cautiously; but when he acted, caution was thrown to the winds. So little William approached respectfully, tip-toeing in his agony of mind, and waited for them to notice him.

His father picked him up and sat him down upon the chair at his right, all the while looking at him in a most penetrating fashion.

"I believe," his father hazarded, "that the estate of Woodford Hall can soon be had rather advantageously. At Woodford there would be plenty of room for the children to play. Would you like to be a big, strong man?" he added, looking at his son.

"Yes, Father," the boy answered with more than usual respect; for he had visions of what fun might be had on the other side of Epping Forest, where the countryside was beautiful, and the hornbeam thickets grew thick and deep.

"And school!" cried his mother. "I think it may be just the place! Isn't the Misses Arundels' Academy for Young Gentlemen in Woodford?"

"Perhaps it is," answered Mr. Morris. "If that is so, we might at last produce a young gentleman as well as a hale and hearty man. I'll look into the matter further."

So it came about that in the spring of 1840 the Morris family purchased Woodford Hall.

Woodford Hall was a fine mansion on a large estate of about one hundred acres, a mile or two away, on the other side of Epping Forest. The huge dwelling stood in about fifty acres of park. Behind it the farm land spread gently down to the little stream called Roding. Here the Morris family was to live happily enough, for the most part, until the father's death in 1847. And it was no mean feat that during the intervening seven and a half years the Morris family should have been increased by the addition of six more children. Moving into a larger estate and a less populous region was certainly a move worth making, in more ways than one.

At Woodford Hall the young William spent his most formative years. Here he completed his reading of the Waverley novels, and here he was sent to the Misses Arundels' Academy for Young Gentlemen, in George's Lane, just as his parents had planned. Afterward, he attended for a short time Doctor Greg's Boarding School. But that is looking several years ahead.

At Woodford Hall, when he had reached the age of eight, he received the long-promised pony and the suit of toy armour, complete with lance and trappings, in which he could be seen galloping about the park almost every fine day. Of the imaginary battles that he fought, one can only guess; and many a neighbour wondered what manner of youth this might be.

There were only two difficulties connected with the small boy's life at the Hall: his brothers were infants, always infants to him; and there were no other playmates except certain lowly born youngsters whose parents did not send them to the right church. For his parents were especially desirous that their children should never associate with any but Church of England people—Quakers being the one exception to this rule. And Essex was not noted for its Quakers, although some Quaker relatives lived in far-away Worcestershire. Unitarians, his parents thought, were neither seemly nor good; Methodists, Baptists and Congregationalists were Calvinists to be shunned, usually not quite respectable; Papists also were to be shunned. In addition to these restrictions, the boy suffered, sometimes, because of an overabundance of disciplinary restrictions, both at home and at school.

There were stocks on a bit of wayside green in the village of Woodford, and beside them a *Cage* that dated from the days of the Fat George. "I remember," William wrote to his sister Jennie in after years, "that I used to look at these two threats with considerable terror, and decidedly preferred to walk on the opposite side of the road."

Very early in life the child was inspired with an intense interest in ancient places. On many a lonely walk he visited the near-by country houses and the old churches of the Essex neighbourhood. Sometimes these objects inspired a poetical outburst, as when he wrote in *The Abbey and the Palace*, at about the age of nine:

> Standing away from all men
>   In October weather
>   A grey tower lifting
>   Where the grey clouds are shifting,
>     Four great arches stood:

Beneath them lay the tall men
  Who have fought together,
    There the old monks lay
    And the wind moaned well-a-day
      For their chaunt through the wood.

Lying there in the choir
  By the ruined wall
    With his hands clasped together,
    Praying there forever,
      Look at the stone-carved Knight.

And about lies the shivered spire
  Once so tall, so tall;
    And the crow flies over
    The head of the lover,
      Of him was brave in fight.

Sometimes William and his favourite sister, Jennie, would seek seclusion with some fantastic story book. When they did not wish to be discovered they frequently concealed themselves in the rabbit warren. Here they pored wonderingly through a number of ghost stories and Gothic tales. *The Old English Baron* was among them. These tales so filled their young minds with fantastic imagery that when night came down upon them and it was too late to read longer, they were sometimes afraid to go home across the park. On these occasions it was a fearsome sort of protection which the young knight offered to his fair lady as they slipped along the side lane, and then ran pell-mell for the lighted kitchen of the Hall.

As a child, William must have come across many old ballads and songs of the Middle Ages, as well as tales of history and romance, if we are to judge from his own early productions. One of his earliest attempts to write poetry took the form of an excellent imitation of a short Scotch ballad, and it displayed his love for the mediæval scene in both its tragic and romantic aspects. It told how:

Malmston had a dream in the night
That harm had come to his heart's delight,

and of how he rode away to find his love, only to meet with her funeral bier and himself fall dead.

A longer poem of forty-nine stanzas displayed the early development of his gifts for sustained narrative and for sustained rhyming. It displayed also his quick and true perception of all that pertains to a vivid description of natural beauty. Withal, there is intertwined the half-articulate expression of his early religious training and concepts: his childhood philosophy of Nature, God, and the Universe; and his idea of humanity, Christianity, and human sacrifice—the essential ingredient and powerful renewer of Christianity. The following three excerpts will suffice to illustrate these trends of his childish thoughts, as he strove to put them into poetic language:

> O! love was round him like a sea,
> The love of all fair things that be,
> The love of every beauteous tree,
>
> The love of birds that skim along,
> The love of ringing olden song,
> The love of churches, where the long,
>
> Long sunbeam striketh down the nave
> Upon the place where banners wave
> Upon the ancient warrior's grave.
>
> . . . . . . .
>
> O me! the solemn East behind,
> The moon is coming up the wind,
> The light, calm, westward-blowing wind.
>
> The moon she goeth westernly,
> The woods look up entrancedly,
> In morning light the moon will die.
>
> Ah! all things die, and come again,
> Ah! all things, but the feet of men,
> They die, and never come again.
>
> . . . . . . .

I muttered low, "God needs me then,
I will go help you, brother men,
No single man I love again;

I will live, loving God alone,
Loving no one man, for the moan
That rises up in monotone:

And shrieks rise with it evermore,
And fiendish laughter; on the floor
Lie God's own chosen, and His poor.

O heart! my love I will out-tear,
It maketh me a coward—there!
It lyeth in the moonlight fair.

'Twill be a glorious destiny,
Ah! truly they shall hear of me,
The narrow world will ring with me."

Another youthful effort, based upon his mixed feelings with
regard to city life and humanity as they appeared to his boyish
eyes, is contained in his poem of thirty-three stanzas entitled
*The Night-Walk:*

Night lay upon the city
    Dull clouds upon the night,
O! London without pity!
    O! ghastly flaring light!

.    .    .    .    .    .

It fell on faces, bloated
    With many hideous crimes,
On some, whose thoughts had floated
    Away to long past times.

It fell on hungry faces,
    Thin lips, despairing frown,
Truly a dismal place is
    That grim, gold-pavéd town.

He goes on to describe a desolate woman walking alone in the streets of the city:

> There is an old, old garden,
>    She cometh to it soon;
> An old, old house is its warden
>    In the sun and in the moon.
>
> And many, many lilies
>    Do in its garden grow,
> Red poppies, and white lilies
>    And lime-trees in a row.
>
> And the house stands very quaintly
>    With roses up its walls,
> And the smell of the limes comes faintly
>    And falls, when the light wind falls.

Then he follows the woman's steps until her inevitable (for any adolescent) death:

> Between the lilies and the limes
>    The woman lay a-dying,
> Her head thrown back as in old times
>    Amid the flowers lying.
>
> I think the leaves will bury her,
> The snowy lilies look on her,
>    They look as if they love her;
> The bee will look as he goes by,
> The sun will look when he is high;
>    No sound will ever move her.

Two characteristic aspects of young William's early thought are apparent in this poem: his natural dislike of city life and of the conventionalized ways of living which killed the inhabitants in body and in mind; and, secondly, a romanticized love of nature and of beauty. One can understand that the kind of beauty which Morris here felt and expressed as a young boy is in harmony with that which he later felt and expressed as a companion of the Pre-Raphaelites. Thus, one may guess that if the very youthful Morris had wanted some paintings to express the spirit of his closing garden scene in the above poem, he would have turned instinctively to an artist such as Edward Burne-Jones.

It is noteworthy that as a child Morris never cared much for mechanical toys or occupations. He lived in his imagination a wild clear dream of great and good and chivalrous activity, and in his mind he constructed a *Utopia* of his own making, blended from art, poetry, religion and romance. And with all this there was blended an insurmountable love of nature in all her varied manifestations.

What he loved most of all was to explore the dark hornbeam thickets of Epping Forest. Fifty years later he wrote:

I was born and bred in its neighbourhood, and when I was a boy and young man I knew every yard of it from Wanstead to the Theydons, and from Hale End to the Fairlop Oak. . . . Nothing could be more interesting and romantic than the effect of the long poles of the hornbeams rising from the trunks and seen against the mass of the wood behind. It has a peculiar charm of its own not to be found in any other forest.

So the small boy went steadily and excitedly about the task of educating himself and developing his powers of imagination, in libraries, fields and forests, among old churches, country houses and ruins of an earlier day—indeed, at all odd hours when he was not trudging back and forth to school in George's Lane.

# CHAPTER IV

## A DREAM WORLD DISAPPEARS

FOR the first five years that William lived at Woodford Hall everything seemed to go nicely with the Morris family. The father's business prospered, and at regular intervals new infants joined the family circle.

In the third year William's father obtained the coveted coat-of-arms. It seemed a miracle to the young boy, for he had long been interested in heraldry and for years afterward he took a special pride in the family's medieval emblem. Indeed, even after his marriage, when he moved into the Red House at Bexley Heath, Upton in Kent, the family arms (I regret to report) appeared in many prominent places, emblazoned and put there by Morris himself, on tile and glass. But that was "a mere boyhood hang-over."

Even better was to follow, for in the fourth year William's father purchased 1024 one-pound shares in the Devon Great Consols Company which was to work a newly discovered copper vein near Tavistock. Within six months these shares increased in value to eighty pounds each; and within a comparatively short time the Morris holdings were valued at more than two hundred thousand pounds. Long after, when they decreased notably in value, the adversity was to have some important bearings upon the future views and activities of William Morris.

Meanwhile, as the years at Woodford passed pleasantly, William was shooting up rapidly into a strong and healthy boy. The parents, doubting their full ability to discipline and restrain the active youngster, began to think more and more of a suitable boarding school. The child had outgrown his pony and his armour, and if he were ever to be converted into a young gentleman, it seemed that the time to do it was at hand.

22

So, in the autumn of 1845 he was sent to Doctor Greg's Boarding School, near by. There he remained for two years, most unhappily secluded and most unhappily interfered with in all his activities. Only in church on Sundays was he allowed to see his family, and even then he was not permitted to speak to them. Here was Victorian rigour at its fullest—an effective if somewhat harsh method of producing a dignified, restrained young gentleman, capable of manifesting gentlemanly control no matter how bad the situation. From experiences such as these, and they lasted until he was well advanced in his fourteenth year, one can understand how William Morris came to develop an almost unnatural craving for fellowship and love. But all that he could do was to rebel silently and hint of his disaffection in letters.

It may have been that in 1847 William's father had some inkling of his own impending death, as well as some awareness of his oldest son's unhappiness. In any event he arranged rather suddenly to send William away once more—this time to Marlborough College, near Swindon on the edge of Savernake—to complete the boy's preparation for his future studies at Oxford University.

Marlborough College was a recently founded High Church school, administered by one Doctor Wilkinson, a rather weak principal who believed in keeping his clientèle happy by allowing the boys (of whom there were then about two hundred) a large degree of individual freedom. Unlike the majority of Church schools, Marlborough had no high traditions, no elaborate social code, no complex machinery designed to secure a typically public-school type of product. In brief, Marlborough discipline was just the opposite of what had existed during William's life at Doctor Greg's Boarding School. Marlborough more nearly resembled the Quaker schools in emphasis upon free and unrestrained student development. It was quite modern.

The snows were deep upon the fields and forests when William, with about one hundred other new boys, descended upon

Marlborough in February, 1848. He then lacked a month of being fourteen years of age, but one might have thought that he was sixteen at least. For by this time his healthy country life had overcome completely any sign of constitutional weakness. He appeared to be a strong, healthy, thick-set boy of high colour. His skin and hair were burnt a slightly golden-reddish hue by wind and sun. In disposition, so a schoolmate wrote, "he was good-natured and kind, most of the time—but with a fearful temper upon occasion!"

The youngster had developed a pretty good opinion of himself by this time, and what he thought of Marlborough College had better be left unsaid. It was plain for any intelligent adolescent eye to perceive, however, that a terrific amount of hypocrisy cloaked the place, from principal to clientèle. The boys were a bunch of "clams and eels" who "lacked the stamina to get into such places as Eton and Harrow." They were "lazy" for the most part, "and uninformed." They seemed to lack the spirit to indulge in any sport except occasional fighting and mock-battles with clubs: a game which they called "single-sticks" and which had evolved, no doubt, from the old Anglo-Saxon customs of the Middle Ages. "Cricket and football simply did not exist," but it must be remembered, of course, that the latter was not yet developed. Consequently, athletics were not "compulsory," and so William, like most of the other students, was left to his own devices when not in classrooms, chapel, or "study hall."

Needless to say, in such circumstances, the boy did not mix well with the majority of his companions. Most of his "play hours" were usually spent in hiking over the surrounding hills and through the forest of Savernake. He was still living in a dream world of his own making, and the prosaic forces which everywhere hemmed him in were not to his liking. And so, as events turned, the boy's life at Marlborough was to prove just as lonely as it had at Doctor Greg's school. Moreover, the death of his father in the autumn of the preceding year had brought tragedy into his life—a tragedy much closer than that which he had felt when examining the graves of long dead monks and knights. Only the yearning memory of past happiness at Woodford Hall now remained to him; but those days seemed to be gone forever, now that his mother and the remainder of the family had removed to The Water House, a large mansion in Walthamstow, after his father's death.

There was one advantage, so far as he could see, in the life at Marlborough. The library was well stocked with books, and in the library the youthful student entered new realms of learning—in history, in archæology, in church music and in church architecture. During the spring months of 1848, when the bright, sunny skies of England brought no hint of the revolutionary movements which were simmering on the Continent, young William Morris undertook his first archæological investigations. And he was in the very midst of a rich, ancient heritage. Near by lay the Neolithic barrows overlooking Pewsey Vale, the round barrow on Silbury Hill, the stone dolmens of Avebury, and the remains of the Roman villas at Kennet. Near Savernake Forest there were also a number of old country houses—and the royal castle of Henry III "seemed almost as real" to the young boy as the seventeenth-century structure which had replaced it.

So the youthful Morris, oblivious to those about him, continued in the process of self-education. In the circumstances, of course, it was not altogether unnatural that his schoolmates considered him "strange, or perhaps a little mad," for in these revolutionary days of 1848 he was constantly pouring forth "endless stories of knights and chivalry"—tale upon tale—to any one who would listen, the narratives sometimes connected and flowing on from day to day and from week to week over an entire term!

The Water House in Walthamstow, to which William returned for his holidays during the years which he spent at Marlborough and later at Oxford, was a massive Georgian mansion of yellow brick. It boasted "a square hall paved with marble flags, from which a broad staircase, floored and wainscoted with Spanish chestnut, led up to a large upper hall, or gallery." In the large lawn behind the house there was an ancient moat, about forty feet in breadth, which gave the house its name. This moat was fringed with hawthorns, chestnuts and hollies, and it contained a little island—"a fairy land for all the Morris children, who almost lived on it."

For years to come William spent most of his holidays at The Water House, swimming in its waters, and boating about the little island in an old rowboat, the while he wrote chivalrous and knightly poetry for the amusement of all his sisters. Once more, it seemed, the days were becoming glorious if not altogether golden. For his mother and aunt had set their hearts upon his entering the Church. Young William loved the Church —its music, its architecture, and its traditions—but the idea of quietly preaching to some "little flock" did not strike him as an idea that was altogether "inspired." To tell the truth he craved excitement and danger.

As for his schooling, it must be admitted that the scholastic standards of Marlborough College could not be called "distinguished." William's letters home reflected his lack of "formal" educational "progress," at least in spelling, and it was soon decided by his mother that he should not return to school after 1851. "Good," wrote William, "at Christmas I am through!"

But he stayed on just long enough to meet with one exciting adventure. For in November of that year a student rebellion against Doctor Wilkinson broke out. Such an event was almost unheard of in the history of English boarding schools. Just what exactly happened is not known for a certainty, but Miss May Morris well remembered "Father telling us of Marlborough and the great rebellion—'the fruition of the insubordination' reigning in obscure corners long after the initial week of uproar. Doctor Wilkinson asked the boys to state their grievances. His must have been a weak rule!"

The educational loss was not so great, however, as might be supposed, for William did not return to Marlborough after the Christmas holidays. He was now approaching his seventeenth birthday, and by this time, thanks to his own efforts, he was extremely well read in archæology and in history. He knew most of what was then to be known about English Gothic, according to Doctor Mackail; and he was at heart a pronounced Anglo-Catholic.

Having returned home, pending his entrance into Exeter College, Oxford, William studied under the Reverend Mr. F. B. Guy of the Forest School in Walthamstow (a man of high character and rich attainment, who was later to be Canon of Saint Alban's). Under Mr. Guy's instruction, William increased his knowledge of art, archæology, history, and the classics. Years afterward he said that the germs of his first famous long poem, *The Life and Death of Jason*, might be traced to his reading of the *Medea* in the original Greek, under the tuition of Mr. Guy.

The tuition at length completed, in June, 1852, William, now eighteen years of age, went up to Oxford University and passed his examinations for matriculation without difficulty. In the examination hall at Exeter College there sat next to him a young man from Birmingham. These two youths did not speak, yet each remembered the other. Edward Burne-Jones, for he it was, noticed that the stout, genial-faced fellow beside him finished his Horace examination "early in the morning, folded it, and wrote upon it the name of William Morris."

When they saw each other again, upon entering Exeter College in January, 1853, each remembered the other—and the acquaintanceship which followed soon developed into the most enduring friendship which either of these two famous men was afterward to know.

In the meantime, having passed his entrance examinations, William returned to Mr. Guy's tuition for another six months in order "to make up everything which he could possibly have missed at Marlborough."

They spent the long vacation in Devonshire and at the opening of the new year, 1853, young Morris went up to Oxford to stay. He was now approaching his nineteenth birthday.

# CHAPTER V

## A PRE-OXFORD SUMMARY

THE twelve years which had elapsed from the time when the Morris family moved to Woodford Hall to the time when Morris entered Oxford University represent strongly formative years in the development and in the education of the boy. He had passed many mental and emotional milestones in the course of that development. They were years of alternating exuberance and depression during which impressions of happiness developed side by side with impressions of beauty and of ugliness. Partly because of some inborn, inherited characteristics, no doubt, the imaginative child was early attracted to the mysterious, the mystical and the unknown. We have seen these qualities in his earliest writings; we have witnessed some small part of the wonderment which he felt in the presence of natural and artistic beauty. The magic of old times grew in him from the days of his *Waverley* reading to the days when he explored old churches and old ruins. The thrill of nature, which has been called the "essence of romance," struck him with the force of an inexplicable and gigantic phenomenon.

His childlike reverence and wonder, the capacity for which he never lost, were closely akin to the spirit of medieval simplicity. It was this which led him to comprehend and to sympathize with the medieval point of view.

Here was no mere imitative tendency which might, as has sometimes been suggested, lead him into the imitation of old writings: here was the very spirit of old writings. Later in his life, Professors Wyatt and Magnússon, with whom he collaborated in *Beowulf* and in the Icelandic *Sagas*, and other critics as well, noted but little the similarity of phrase and the truth of detail in his poetic translations; they marvelled most at the transmutations of spirit. Morris reproduced the moods of the medieval singers of old tales because they had become his own and he could use them at will.

As a youth Morris saw the beauty of the world as some magical quality that could be carved by an artist with many "flowers and histories," as he himself once said. He loved nature and art; he loved history and archæology; he forever felt the individualism and the beauty, wherever they existed, in England's old buildings, decorations, people, and traditions. These tendencies of his spiritual thought were clearly marked by the time he left Marlborough College and started upon his Oxford student days.

It was out of these tendencies and these experiences that he had built for himself a little dream-world of happy thoughts and ideals. Yet there is also evidence in his early life and in his early writings that he began when very young to realize the tragic incidents and conditions of human life. He himself had now known sorrow, tragedy, and loss, as well as loneliness; and it was only natural, perhaps, that as an adolescent boy he saw them and felt them both in his imaginative world of romance and in that contemporary world which stood so far apart from his dreams.

Thus, the death of Malmston's love and of Malmston in his youthful ballad is no mere adolescent vision of glamorous times: already the boy had caught the tragic spirit of the Middle Ages. In his long poem called *Fame* he felt the ache along with the sweetness; he recognized the death and the rebirth of all things—which "die and come again." He wept for "the lonely poor" and for "the love of one" which keeps man from loving all; he wept for the universal love—the sacrifice of the one to the glory of the whole realm of humanity, which "may come again" (!) Indeed, this entire poem may be considered as a boyhood depiction, however unconscious, of the forces which distinguished the *universalism* of the medieval ages from the *individualism* of the modern: on the one side the desire for asceticism, love of God and love of humanity—on the other, the desire for individual love and fame.

Again, he is filled with the tragedy of a ruined church, of the "shivered spire," of the "crow flying over the head of the lover,"—the tragedy of the "stone-carved knight,"

> With his hands clasped together,
> Praying there forever.

Or, turning from the past world to the present, he sees modern urban life in a "ghastly, flaring light." He shrinks mentally and spiritually from "the hideous faces bloated with many hideous crimes," from the hunger and despair which have no rightful place, he thinks, on "London's grim, gold-pavéd streets"—and carrying on the tragedy of that picture, he portrays the death of the woman of whom he writes and paints a beautiful picture of that death. For it is obvious to any poetic instinct that he believes death preferable to life amidst such modern depravity. And as time goes on it will be interesting to note how these early views developed and slowly rounded themselves into a new philosophy of social and political development.

In brief, during all these years, while still a child in years—though perhaps in years only, for poets see and feel the world more clearly than ordinary mortals do—the boy had built his dream *Utopia* out of art, poetry, religion, and romance; and he had seen this little dream-world go crashing down in ruins.

And now, after his years of study and of childhood's disillusionment, he was almost ready to try to build again. He was to keep on building his dreams of happiness for his fellow men, if not for himself, as long as he lived. It was not an idle thought, therefore, when he wrote, even as a child,

> I will go help you, brother men.

And it is hardly an exaggeration, under these circumstances, to say that by the time young William Morris was nearing his nineteenth birthday and entering Oxford, he had already developed a strongly pronounced feeling that all was not well with the contemporary state of art, of beauty, of education, and of society. It is no wonder that before long he and his new friend, Edward Burne-Jones, were heading "a young crusaders' movement" to reform the world!

## CHAPTER VI

OXONIANS ARE CHRISTIANS, SOCIALISTS AND

CHRISTIAN-SOCIALISTS, IT SEEMS

EXETER College even today is not a very lovely place: a square and rather ugly quadrangle of brown stone inclosing a well-trodden court almost devoid of vegetation. In Morris's time it must have been even more unlovely. Though old, it reeked of modernity, for it was filled with the sons of the newly rich. In 1853 it was so overcrowded that for the first two terms Morris and Edward Burne-Jones took lodgings together in the town.

For that matter, life throughout the entire university had little to recommend it in those days. Morris found the place "pitiably disappointing." The head of Morris's college, holding a safe and easy sinecure, never even bothered to go near the place, while the dons, more idle and more ignorant than those of today, exercised no restraint upon their natural tediousness. According to Evelyn Waugh, hunting and whoring marked the chief pleasures of those undergraduates who possessed any spark of life and who were not total bores. Of course, such questionable activities had declined somewhat in popularity since the days of Gibbon and "the university decadence," and it is likely that Morris and his friends, who certainly could not have been termed bores, were able to retain a goodly share of their virginal charm. But there were a few feminine acquaintances in Oxford about whom practically nothing has been written.

Yet it would be a mistake to assume that life in the Oxford of the eighteen-fifties was altogether dead. Victorian customs and prejudices did, of course, exist, but many a student and many a don found some means of escape. Like London, Oxford was slowly taking on an appearance of modernity. The recent growth of the old town, the coming of the railroad, and the effects of nineteenth-century "restoration" were rapidly altering the outward appearance of things. As for mental life, some new ideas for the bettering of human life were being voiced by devoted followers of Keble, Newman, Pusey, and others in the world of religion; Socialism was being argued for the first time in the quarters of the intelligentsia; while Christian Socialism had already made of "social reform" a moral issue. In art, Pre-Raphaelitism, a new movement, was endeavouring to combine the romantic spirit with the natural. In brief, all those changes which had begun to mark the life of the 'forties and 'fifties both in the university and in the nation were rapidly bringing Oxford into contact with modernizing thoughts and activities. A number of the dons and younger fellows were decidedly liberal, if not a little radical, in their social and political thought. So were some of the students, as we shall soon see.

In 1853, however, it can truly be said that for the most part neither teaching nor discipline at Oxford was marked by much intellectual distinction. "As for the lectures," wrote one of Morris's best friends, "I have long since ceased to hope that I would learn anything at them which I did not know before!"

Morris's roommate, Edward Burne-Jones, who seemed but the lanky shadow of a pale and serious æsthete continuously frustrated in the conflict occasioned by a puritanically religious upbringing and an overweening sense of humour, wrote home to the effect that "Gloomy and angry disappointment and disillusion were settling down upon me in this first term's experience of Oxford. It was clear that we had lighted on a distasteful land in our choice of a college. . . ." Exeter was turning out to be a paradise for *parvenus*.

But in Pembroke College the two young men discovered a little colony of kindred spirits. They came from Birmingham, the coal and iron center, but they were doing their best to overcome that handicap. Before long this group formed, with Morris and Burne-Jones, a little set of their own, devoted to art, history, literature, religion, mathematics, and philosophy. With a single unanimous accord they cherished culture and "eschewed materialism." If ideals could conquer, they intended to make the most of them.

All told, there were eight of these boys, and they comprised the original set which joined forces with Vernon Lushington and Wilfred Heeley of Trinity College, Cambridge, in 1855, to form "The Brotherhood" and publish *The Oxford and Cambridge Magazine* which was to flourish throughout the twelve months of 1856.

Of these eight Oxford youths the first was William Morris, a ruddy faced, well-built young fellow of "almost nineteen" who had come up from Marlborough. Then there was his friend and roommate, Edward Burne-Jones, an animated slender wreath of a boy, filled with enthusiasms for everything that was good, noble, true, cultural, and religious. He had come up from King Edward's School in Birmingham. Then there was Richard W. Dixon, likewise from Birmingham, a serious and studious chap, and a church canon in the making. He was one who had his career all cut out in advance and was pleased with the prospect of one day preaching to an admiring flock and turning out an occasional volume of literary and historical essays and poetry. There was also William Fulford, a year ahead of the others. He was a little chap, full of vivacity and words, and was also destined for the ministry (at least he thought so). Fulford was a natural-born critic of everything under the sun, though he was very likable and highly intelligent. Then there was Charles Joseph Faulkner, a tall, handsome, strongly featured individual, a little above the average in age, with a warm personality and an intense devotion to mathematics. Although a mathematical genius, Faulkner was fickle in his love: before long he was to be diverted, along with his sisters, into art. But what better combination existed, said he, than "art and mathematics"? Without knowing it, he was fated to become an Oxford don as well as an artist and a craftsman. Another young fellow who came from Balliol College was added to the set; his name was Godfrey Lushington and he was chiefly famous among them for his good looks and pleasing personality.

Two other boys, who came up from King Edward's School at the beginning of 1854, completed the set. Their names were Cormell Price, who became one of Morris's best friends, and Harry Macdonald, who was an old friend of Edward Burne-Jones's.

Most of the Pembroke group, with the exception of Dixon, had little genuine interest in the religious questions which frequently engrossed Edward Burne-Jones. Poor Edward's conscience smote him. Intended for the ministry, he was already struggling with the desire to become an artist, an æsthete, and a happily married husband of one Georgie Macdonald. It was, for him, a matter of love and art *versus* love and religion. But art was going to win out, as well as love.

Price, Faulkner, Heeley and the rest of the fraternity were far more interested in the social, economic, and scientific problems of the day than they were in matters of religious reform and conformity. Nevertheless, the new emphasis which everywhere in Oxford was then being placed upon religion and Christianity for a while determined some of their chief interests. The influence of Wilberforce and Pusey was then pronounced, and during their first two years at Oxford, Morris and Burne-Jones were filled with Anglo-Catholic, if not indeed with Catholic, admirations. It is difficult to know how much influence was exerted upon Morris by Edward Burne-Jones, and also by Mrs. Morris, who wanted her son to become a rector in the Church. But one thing is certain: the reading of the two youths was virtually identical during their first two years, and their tastes seemed to converge toward a common standard of thought and conduct.

Early in his college career Morris began the habit of reading aloud to his friend—a habit which was to be continued

throughout life. And to Morris, at this time, history, archæology, art and poetry meant education and culture. The academic life proved to be so exceedingly dull, however, that the
two friends soon learned to "feed themselves with the food
that fitted them." So Morris began to ransack the Bodleian
Library at Oxford in search of medieval illuminated manuscripts and old books. He unearthed thousands of them. And
he delved deeply into the study of Gothic architecture in all
its bearings. Years afterward he was to have some very pertinent and up-to-date words to say on the subject of medieval
civilization and of Gothic architecture in particular. In fact, he
evolved much of his entire philosophy of history out of his
Oxford researches.

Between his friends and his studies Morris was able to keep
himself as busy as even he could have desired. For already he
was developing a tremendous capacity for work, a love of work
which was to become one of his chief characteristics in life. And
he was lucky in having for his friend a person such as Edward
Burne-Jones, whose tastes so neatly complemented his own.
Edward had brought to Oxford, among other things, a variety
of literary enthusiasms. So ardent a lover of poetry was he that
for a long time William did not confide in his best friend the
fact that he himself, prior to his Oxford days, had attempted
to write poetry! When, after another year or more, William
did produce some poetry, he allowed the members of his set
to think that it must represent a maiden effort—and ever since
then his critics have assumed that he did not begin to write
until his second year at Oxford.

The whole set did their best to keep up with modern literature. Thorpe's *Northern Mythology* was a revelation to
Morris, and he and Burne-Jones were especially fond of the
writings of Charles Kingsley, Thomas Carlyle and John Ruskin. When the latter's *Stones of Venice* appeared in 1853, it
seized upon the imaginations and the hearts of the two friends.
The sixth chapter, "On the Nature of Gothic," became the
veritable Bible of a new faith to Morris, serving, perhaps, to

co-ordinate his own ideas of the significance of the Gothic spirit with the diverse bits of knowledge gleaned by him while a student at Marlborough. Edward, writing about Ruskin's new *opus* to Harry Macdonald on November 8 of that year, expressed the following view of it: "No one half understands Ruskin; he leaves them all behind. . . . In this last work he transcends himself in diction, more Saxon pure and simple than ever—in prose what Tennyson is in poetry, and what the Pre-Raphaelites are in painting—full of devotion and love for the subject, Insular and Northern in all their affections, giving us the very ideal of Teutonic beauty."[1]

Motivated to some extent by the teachings of the Christian Socialists, Morris and Burne-Jones, especially the latter, played with the idea of founding a "monastic settlement"—a sort of forerunner of the latter-day University Settlements—devoted to conventual revolt against the materialistic tendencies of the age. As early as May, 1853, Edward had written: "I have set my heart on our founding a Brotherhood. . . . I have enlisted one in the project up here, heart and soul."

The "one" referred to Dixon who was much more "religious" than the others.

A little later Burne-Jones wrote of enlisting "yet others in this Crusade and Holy Warfare against the age," and this time he probably referred to Morris and Fulford, both of whose parents intended them for the Church. By the autumn of 1855, however, his dream seemed as remote as ever, although he still asserted: "I know that it will come some day!" We shall see, a little later, why it did not come true.

[1] These "northern ideals" are significant, appearing as they did a year before Kingsley's *Cambridge Lectures*. Incidentally, this letter disproves the assumption made by earlier critics that Morris and Burne-Jones were at this time unacquainted with the Pre-Raphaelites and the Christian Socialists. Regarding Maurice and Kingsley, the leading Christian-Socialists of that day, Burne-Jones went on to say: "You have heard, of course, of the resignation of Maurice at Kings College, London, and the writings which led to it. It is a hard question to decide upon, but I am very sorry—for the Christian Socialists, if Maurice and Kingsley are fair examples, must be glorious fellows." *Memorials of Edward Burne-Jones*, I, 92. Permission Macmillan Company.

To young William Morris these days at Oxford revealed new capacities and new and fervent interests. For the first time in his life he felt himself to be amid congenial spirits of his own age and his own likes and dislikes. He was still far from mature, but his personality was beginning to expand; he felt more at ease with the world, and for the first time he began to assert his strongly growing individuality.

Very early in his college career he succeeded in impressing both his personality and his intellect upon his fellows. Canon Dixon wrote long afterward of Faulkner's often remarking how Morris seemed to "know" things; and Dixon added on his own account: "I observed how decisive he was: how accurate, without effort or formality . . . and how many things he knew that were quite out of our way."

Before the first college year was over Burne-Jones wrote that "Morris is one of the cleverest fellows that I know. . . . His taste and criticism in Art and Æsthetics generally I should any day infinitely prefer to Fulford's, who you know was my old ideal. . . . He is full of enthusiasm for things holy and beautiful and true, and, what is rarest, of the most exquisite perception and judgment."

Charles Faulkner occupied commodious quarters and in his rooms Morris and the rest often met for readings and discussions, and (how childishly!) for the apparent purpose, sometimes, of denouncing and mimicking the hated Oxford dons, whom most of the students detested. Morris by this time was nicknamed "Top" or "Topsy" by his friends and he was learning to indulge publicly in many violently humorous demonstrations. He talked in a low, vehement voice, very emphatically, and Burne-Jones and Dixon frequently wrote about his "fire and impetuosity," his "great bodily strength and high temper." These were sometimes astonishing: "for example, his habit of beating his own head and dealing himself vigorous blows."[2]

---

[2]At this stage in his career he must have resembled Mr. Thomas Wolfe's famous hero!

Meanwhile, this rebelliously inclined group of young students were busily engaged in the pleasant task of introducing some new habits into the staid routine of complacent Oxford. They were in search of "a new and better life" and so they frequently encroached upon Oxonian customs of dress and speech, of physical exercise (or rather the lack of it in those days) and upon Oxford's "general lack of adaptability to life."

William himself, like others of his set, was fond of talking, and when he talked it was "like a husky shout." Also, he was fond of "going down the river" with Faulkner, who, like himself, was a good oarsman. A number of the group used to box, fence, and play at singlesticks (a game which Morris is supposed to have introduced from Marlborough College) at Maclaren's Gymnasium in Oriel Lane.

The amiable proprietor of Maclaren's Gymnasium was a likable, personable man, with two attractive daughters. Often the members of Morris's set managed to get themselves invited to dine with the Maclaren family, who lived near by at Summertown, and for at least one brief period Morris almost lived there. But whether or not he fell slightly in love with one of the Maclaren girls is a dark secret.

In these diverse ways did Morris and his new friends discover new worlds and "learn to live and behave like human beings" instead of like dull and bored young students in search of degrees. Indeed, their activities and some of their accomplishments, as judged by the university standards of the Victorian Age, were remarkable, if not, indeed, unexampled.

# CHAPTER VII

## THE PRE-RAPHAELITES ARE DISCOVERED

THROUGHOUT his Oxford days, the continued influence of Ruskin's writings, together with the companionship of Edward Burne-Jones, who was forever drawing pictures, served to keep alive Morris's natural appreciation of art and architecture. He was a devoted subscriber to *The Builder* and he studied scrupulously examples of medieval design and decoration in the Bodleian manuscripts. He was also taking a new interest in painting; besides drawing numberless architectural designs, he was beginning to decorate all his letters with half-unconscious attempts at "floriated ornament."

During the long vacation of 1853, Morris spent most of his time exploring the old churches of England. In the following year he made his first foreign tour, visiting the cathedrals and other medieval landmarks of Belgium and northern France. This trip seems to have exercised upon his mind a significance hardly less than that of Goethe's first Italian journey upon the great poet of Germany.

It was on his first foreign trip in the summer of 1854 that Morris became acquainted with the paintings of Hans Memling and the Van Eycks. For Morris, Memling was destined to remain "the unapproachable master of all time." In architecture, Morris considered the cathedrals of Rouen, Amiens, Beauvais and Chartres to be among "the noblest monuments of man."

When he came back to Oxford he brought with him photographs of Albrecht Dürer's engravings and some medieval paintings and illuminations from the Musée Cluny and the

Louvre. His taste, by this time, had turned definitely in the direction of "things northern and medieval," as he himself put it. From this long vacation he also brought back "an increased hatred of the classicists" and "for their sake, of the classics."

In the following summer Morris, Burne-Jones, and William Fulford went on a three-weeks walking tour of northern France. Morris, describing the visit in a letter to Cormell Price, dwelt for a long time on "the glory of the churches." He wrote that he had feared he might be disappointed with Rouen (his favourite of all French towns and cathedrals) after his fond recollections of 1854, "but wasn't a bit . . . ! O! what a place it is!"

Then, while walking on the quay at Havre one evening, Morris and Burne-Jones fought out the war between art and religion. They definitely decided to give up their churchly ambitions and become artists. For they had increased their knowledge of Pre-Raphaelite work during the preceding year, and at Chartres they had attended the Beaux Arts Exhibition where no less than seven Pre-Raphaelite works had been on display. At last the Pre-Raphaelites were being recognized, abroad as well as at home! To the two youths it now seemed as if the death of a decadent post-classicism was assured.

Soon after returning to Oxford, Morris began to read for his Final School examinations. But he also entered into negotiations with Mr. G. E. Street, the well-known architect, for a position in his Oxford office. At this time Morris was dreaming of designing a neo-Gothic cathedral.

In September, in the midst of his studies, he wrote to Cormell Price of his new architectural ambitions and of his work in hand: "My life is going to become a burden to me, for I am going to read for six hours a day at Livy, Ethics, etc.,—please pity me." And a little later: "Make your mind easy about my coming back next term; I am certainly coming back, though I should not have done so if it had not been for my mother. . . . I am going, if I can, to be an architect. . . . I am too old already and there is no time to lose . . . not that I regret having gone to Oxford, how could I?"

He wrote and spoke confidently; but he had a battle ahead of him. For his mother and aunt, and the rest of the family, too, had always taken it for granted that William would enter the Church; and at home the young man, now about to begin his fourth and last year at Oxford, only dared to hint vaguely of his new desires and intentions. But his mind was firmly made up, and within a few weeks of his return to Oxford he decided that it would be wise to break the news. He wrote to his mother a full account, therefore, explaining his reasons for desiring to take this unprecedented plunge into the mad life of Bohemia, saying:

My dear Mother:

I am almost afraid you thought me scarcely in earnest when I told you a month or two ago that I did not intend taking Holy Orders. . . . You said then, you remember, and said very truly, that it was an evil thing to be an idle, objectless man; I am fully determined not to incur this reproach; I was so then. . . . I wish now to be an architect, an occupation that I have often had hankerings after. . . . If I were not to follow this occupation, I in truth know not what I should follow with any chance of success or hope of happiness in my work. . . . I shall be master too of a useful trade; one by which I should hope to earn money, not altogether precariously, if other things fail. . . . I will by no means give up things that I have thought of for the bettering of the world, in so far as in me lies.

You see I do not hope to be great at all in anything, but perhaps I may reasonably hope to be happy in my work; and sometimes when I am idle and doing nothing, pleasant visions go past me of the things that may be. . . .

My best love to yourself, and Henrietta, and Aunt, and all of them:

                                        Your affectionate son,
Exeter College, Oxford,                        William.
November 11, 1855.

The lure of Gothic architecture and of Pre-Raphaelite painting could no longer be resisted. The historical investigations of both Morris and Burne-Jones, as well as their travels, confirmed to them once and for all the truth of their beliefs in what they now saw and experienced. By the autumn of 1855 the fate of Burne-Jones had been decided. He would get out and "go to his work!" Perhaps only the fact that Morris lacked the born genius to become a really great painter was all that prevented him, too, from having the course of his future life definitely charted at this time.

Among all the Pre-Raphaelites there was one man, Dante Gabriel Rossetti, then in his twenty-eighth year, who appeared before the eyes of Burne-Jones as spirit incarnate—poet and painter both, and in both pre-eminently a Pre-Raphaelite. An interesting letter describes the effort made by Edward to meet Rossetti during the Christmas holidays of 1855—and of how he visited the Workingmen's College in Great Ormond Street, where Rossetti was then teaching, of how he attended an evening meeting at the college and finally met his new hero a few nights afterward at the Doctors' Commons of the College:

And by-and-bye Rossetti came, and I was taken up to him and had my first fearful talk with him. . . . But before I left that night, Rossetti bade me come to his studio next day. It was at the top of the last house by Blackfriars Bridge . . . and I found him painting at a water-colour. . . . He received me very courteously, and asked much about Morris, one or two of whose poems he knew already. (!) I think that was our principal subject of talk, for he seemed much interested about him. . . . No books were on his shelves. . . .

I stayed long and watched him at work, not knowing until many a day afterward that this was a thing he greatly hated, and when, for shame, I could stay no longer, I went away, having carefully concealed from him the desire I had to be a painter.

At Easter, 1856, Burne-Jones left Oxford to become a painter, without waiting to take his degree. Morris, while still enrolled in the university, went to work in Street's offices on January 21, 1856; and there he became acquainted with a young man named Philip Webb, a famous architect to be, with whom he was to develop a lifelong friendship.

If Morris was not destined to become a painter, the fact remains that he was to be first an architect and afterward a craftsman of the first order. It was while he was in the employ of G. E. Street & Company that he also undertook his first serious efforts in the lesser arts and crafts.

But during all these months and years of soul-searching and career-seeking, Morris never lost his interest in poetry and in literature. These were to remain for him always a constant avocation and source of delight. And inasmuch as his literary efforts at Oxford represent the most interesting aspect of his many-sided Oxford experiences, it is only fitting that we should now turn back the calendar just a little and follow the course of his literary efforts while he was still an undergraduate— determining, if possible, whether these efforts had anything to do with his historical ideas and with his future outlook upon the needs of society.

And in this connection it is interesting to remember that these undergraduate writings still comprise the great majority of Morrisiana which appear in most of our standard anthologies, even today.

# CHAPTER VIII

## "THE OXFORD AND CAMBRIDGE MAGAZINE"
## FLOURISHES AMID CHAOS

SOON after beginning his second year at Oxford, William began to read samples of his poetic efforts to his friends. The first which he read aloud was the manuscript of "The Willow and the Red Cliff," which he afterward destroyed. In the opinion of Burne-Jones, "Topsy" was already "a big poet!"

At this time the Crimean War began and powerful reform agitation was in the air. Christian Socialists and humanitarians made their pleas for social betterment, while critics of military and political inefficiency and intrigue attacked the government. It was probably these forces which turned the attention of Morris and his friends away from religious asceticism in the direction of social and political regeneration. In any event, the Brotherhood's ideas of monastic life suddenly began to dwindle.

In 1855 Morris wrote his first prose romance. Its "Crimean influence" is clearly marked as he begins:

Till late that night I administered to the sick in that hospital; but when I went away, I walked down to the sea, and paced to and fro over the hard sands: and the moon showed bloody in the hot mist.

But Morris himself was not so much interested in the politics of his day as were Fulford, Price, Heeley, and Lushington; and as the war drew to a close his thoughts turned more seriously toward art and poetry.

It is likely that the elements of mysticism, beauty, weirdness, and the rather odd mixture of smoothness and slovenliness of rhyme which characterized much of Morris's poetry at this

45

time resulted from the new influences of Robert and Elizabeth Browning, whose works were now much admired by him. Through the poetry of Mrs. Browning he became acquainted with that of her husband; and him he came to regard in succeeding years as "first or second among the poets of our time." But among the poets of all time, Chaucer seemed to be his favourite. As poetry attracted him more and more, his ideas of art, of literature, and of social brotherhood appeared much brighter than did Burne-Jones's ascetic and monastic concepts.

Early in the summer of 1855 the idea of founding a magazine became a definite plan in the minds of the group. Dixon suggested it; then Heeley at Trinity College, Cambridge, was sounded for ideas of possible collaboration from that quarter. At the end of term, Morris and Burne-Jones visited him at Cambridge to discuss the project, and plans were considered for establishing *The Oxford and Cambridge Magazine* in the following year.

A few days after the return of Morris, Fulford, and Burne-Jones from their walking tour of northern France, the newly organized "Brotherhood" arranged to meet in Birmingham at the home of Cormell Price, in order to complete their plans to launch a magazine. Three weeks were spent in "furious reading and debate." Morris, according to Price's younger sister, "got so excited that he punched his own head and threw his arms about frantically." According to Cormell Price, they discussed architecture, the organization of labour, the nature of critical reviews (for at that time only *Frasers* and *Blackwoods* seemed to be worthy of much attention) and determined "the future policy" of "our magazine."

They decided that there should be no "showing-off," no quips or jests, no sneers or lampoons. Politics were to be "almost eschewed," the body of the publication given up to critiques, social articles, poetry, and tales.

What made possible the financing of the new publication was the fact that in March, 1855, Morris had passed his twenty-first birthday and received an uncontrolled income of about nine hundred pounds per annum. Consequently he could now think more seriously of long contemplated enterprises, and with a certain portion of this income he decided to subsidize what he and Burne-Jones fondly called "The Mag."

Meanwhile, Morris passed the Final Schools at Oxford, and his negotiations with the firm of G. E. Street & Company came to a successful conclusion. The last few weeks of 1855 were therefore spent in arranging the launching of *The Oxford and Cambridge Magazine*. It was decided that Messrs. Bell & Daldy of London should be the publishers, that the periodical should appear monthly, contain about seventy-two pages per issue, and retail at one shilling per copy. In November the diary of Cormell Price records evenings spent with Morris, Dixon, Burne-Jones and Fulford: "to concoct a letter to the publisher . . . to hold a solemn conclave . . . to grind at the prospectus with Top, Fulford joining in and doing the lion's share."

Fulford was in London, having graduated a year in advance of the rest, and since much time and effort would be required in managing the publication, it was arranged that Fulford should take over the task of running it from its London office. Without his efforts it would hardly have continued to appear regularly, for the promised contributions were often slow in appearing. Heeley soon left for the colonies on a Civil Service Commission, and much of the contents of the periodical was weighted by Fulford's own contributions, hastily written at the last moment to fill blank spaces, and by the miscellaneous writings which Morris and Burne-Jones had produced during the preceding year.

Price, Heeley, and Dixon were familiar with the unhealthy conditions of labour in England's "Black Country" (the one great social problem with which "The Mag" was concerned) and a number of their essays betray signs of crusading fervour. Wrote Cormell Price:

In the forties and fifties things were at their worst. There was no protection for the mill-hand or miner—no amusements but prize-fighting, dog-fighting, cock-fighting, and drinking. When a little boy, I saw many prize fights, bestial scenes: at one a combatant was killed. The country was going to hell apace. . . . I remember one Saturday night, walking five miles from Birmingham into the Black Country, and in the last three miles I counted more than thirty people lying dead drunk on the ground, nearly half of them women.

The January issue of *The Oxford and Cambridge Magazine* contained Morris's tale, "The Story of the Unknown Church," and his poem called "Winter Weather," very similar to the one called "Riding Together" (which appeared in the May issue and was included later in *The Defense of Guenevere and Other Poems*). Its verse might well have merited the attention of Rossetti; certainly it struck a discordant note in the chorus of Victorian poetical works.

In "The Story of the Unknown Church," Morris wrote words which characterized and explained his love of Gothic:

And in process of time I raised a marble canopy that reached quite up to the top of the arch, and I painted it too as far as I could, and carved it all about with many flowers and histories.

This, symbolically stated, was what he strove to do in his own life, and it is not hard to believe that in his hero, the monkish mason, he visualized himself and his ideals.

Occasionally other authors, such as Dante Gabriel Rossetti, contributed to the magazine. Ruskin was among those who promised assistance, although he wrote to Burne-Jones that he was "despondent about the success of the venture" because "people don't want honest criticism!" He had "never known an honest journal to get on yet."

One of the outstanding articles which incidentally strayed far from the original intention of the Brotherhood not to engage in quips, sneers or lampooning, was Wilfred Heeley's "Essay on Mr. Macaulay" in the March issue. It shows a hostility to Whig or Liberal politics which cannot be laid to Tory prejudice, but rather to the recognition that Liberal reform did not go to the heart of the reform problem. The whole article is characteristic of Morris's own attitude, twenty years later, concerning "Whiggery."

Can a Whig write history at all? When you call a man a Whig, do you not imply something of this kind—that he is a well-meaning man, with much confidence in commonsense and logic . . . but not seeing far; not seeing that his traditions and Whig principles, true though they may be, are but a one-sided and fractional view of *The Truth*; noticing the *differentiae*, the peculiarities of a thing far more readily than the great general laws which connect it with the rest of creation? . . . Make your Whig also a rhetorician, and you have Mr. Macaulay, the best and the worst of him, in one glance.

The rhetorical power, uncontrolled by reverence, has led Mr. Macaulay into grievous temptations. His shallowness of thought peeps out in every page; and in every page you see some paltry sacrifice of truth at the shrine of fine language, some reputation damaged to preserve an antithesis, some character misjudged for the sake of three superlatives.

It was long ago asserted that rhetoric was one of the basest of all arts . . . for whereas all true art had its foundation deep in the principles of things, and sought as its end the bettering of our nature, these had no foundation but in empirical rules, and no object but the immediate gratification of the senses. . . . Mr. Macaulay's style is at first sight beautiful; there are certain arrangements of neatness and clearness and perfection about it, which fascinate you till you look into it and see what has been sacrificed to gain them.

It would seem that this young critic also was "born out of his due time." His essays on "Kingsley's Sermons" and "Sir Philip Sidney" show a keen critical mind that was sacrificed to the dull routine of the Civil Service. Not until the advent of twentieth-century Marxist and Fascist denunciation has more withering criticism of Liberal authorship been so sharply and keenly levelled. But what its effect upon the public was to be, John Ruskin could have prophesied!

Four of Morris's five poems which appeared in *The Oxford and Cambridge Magazine* were later reprinted in *The Defense of Guenevere* (1858). Dante Gabriel Rossetti contributed two hitherto unpublished poems in addition to a revised copy of

"The Blesséd Damosel." Yet the amateur attempts of young Morris compare favourably with "The Burden of Nineveh" and "The Staff and Scrip" of the older poet. One has but to read "Riding Together," "The Chapel in Lyonness," "Pray But One Prayer for Me," and "Hands" (later reprinted as "The Prince's Song" in *Rapunzel*) to see that Morris was in many respects already "a big poet."[1] No informed person can read the opening lines of Sir Ozana in "The Chapel in Lyonness" without realizing that here was an original spirit in English poetry:

> All day long and every day,
> From Christmas-Eve to Whit-Sunday,
> Within that Chapel-aisle I lay,
> And no man came anear.

> Naked to the waist was I,
> And deep within my breast did lie,
> Though no man any blood could spy,
> The truncheon of a spear.

> Many a time I tried to shout;
> But as in dream or battle-rout,
> My frozen speech would not well out;
> I could not even weep.

Morris's poem "Riding Together" (as indeed his "Winter Weather") may well indicate that he had not been completely carried away by the golden aspect of the medieval scene. Its closing stanza is no rhapsody for My Lady's Bower:

> They bound my blood-stained hands together,
> They bound his corpse to nod by my side;
> Then on we rode in the bright March weather,
> With clash of cymbals did we ride.

In "Lindenberg Pool," a tale based upon part of his reading of Thorpe's *Northern Mythology*, Morris tells of a nineteenth-

---

[1]*Loc. cit.*, V, IX, X, VII, respectively. Rossetti's two originals appear in Nos. XII and VIII, respectively.

century man being thrown back, as in a dream, to the thirteenth
century. The setting of this story is semi-historical. At the
climax:

These outrageous people skirled with intolerable laughter, rising to
shrieks that were fearfuller than any scream of agony I ever heard;
the hundreds of people through all those grand rooms danced and reeled
about me, shrieking, hemming me in with interlaced arms, the women
loosing their long hair and thrusting forward their horribly grinning
unsexed faces toward me till I felt their hot breath. Oh! how I hated
them! almost hated all mankind for their sakes; how I longed to get
right quit of all men; among whom, as it seemed, all sacredest things
were made a mock of. I looked about me fiercely, I sprang forward
and clutched a sword from the gilded belt of one of those who stood
near me; with savage blows that threw the blood about the gilded
walls, and their hangings right over the heads of those—things, I cleared
myself from them.

Morris's earliest "Sigurd influence" dates from his story,
"Gertha's Lovers," published in two parts in the July and
August issues. This story told of a northern people who had
settled in a fair lowland valley, between "the washing of the
purple waves" and "the solemn watchfulness of the purple
mountains."

And they grew and grew, for God favoured them; and those who
dwelt nearest to the "Savage Land," as it used to be called, grew more
and more like the strangers, and their good rule spread. . . .
Judge, therefore, whether the tyrant kings feared these brave, free
men! Judge whether, growing more and more cruel as they grew more
and more fearful, they strained the chain over the miserable millions
of their subjects so that with many it grew intolerable, and was broken
asunder.

It is also noticeable that when the king would "have given
Sigurd presents of money and jewels . . . Sigurd would not
take them."

There are evidences here of Morris's doubts of wealth and

power, and of the need for oppression anywhere, and of his admiration, sometimes, for "the savage land" and for the rudeness, simplicity and virtue of the barbarians of the north. These likes were to come forward again and again in his later writings, and they helped to influence his later view of social and historic development.

There is much blood and thunder in the prose romances of Morris's undergraduate days. For example, when Sebald, one of the characters in "Gertha's Lovers," whose sister had been wronged by the dead king, comes upon the latter's corpse after the battle, "he stooped down and put his hands to the warm blood that flowed from the wounds, and raised them to his lips and drank, and the draught seemed to please him." Throughout the story it is explicit that Gertha's common sense keeps her from wishing to be Queen. She says at the close: "Think now! I am but Gertha, the peasant's daughter. . . . But if I were Queen for long, I should come to be only Gertha again; so I must go."

In "Svend and His Brethren" there are even more indications of a developing Socialist thought. Again Morris tells of a civilized olden people:

All things this people could do; they levelled mountains, that over the smooth roads the wains might go . . . they drained lakes, that the land might yield more and more, as year by year the serfs, driven like cattle, but worse fed, worse housed, died slowly, scarce knowing that they had souls; they builded them huge ships, and said that they were masters of the sea too. . . .

Should not then their king be proud of them? Moreover they could fashion stone and brass into the shapes of men; they could write books; they knew the names of the stars and their number; they knew what moved the passions of men in the hearts of them, and could draw you up cunningly, catalogues of virtues and vices; their wise men could prove to you that any lie was true, and that any truth was false, till your head grew dizzy, and your heart sick, and you almost doubted if there were a God.

Should not then their king be proud of them? Their men were strong in body. . . . Their women's faces were very fair in red and white, their skins fair and half-transparent like the marble of the mountains. . . .

Should not then their king be proud of such a people, who seemed to help so much in carrying on the world to its consummate perfection, which they even hoped their grandchildren would see?

Alas! Alas! they were slaves. . . .

They could do everything but justice, truth and mercy; therefore God's judgment hung over their heads, not fallen yet, but surely soon to fall.

Morris concludes, with more than a touch of youthful prophecy *in this, his first allegory of modern England:* "And I, John, who wrote this history, saw all this [destruction] with mine own eyes."

"The Hollow Land," the most famous and the most artistic of the prose romances which Morris contributed to the magazine, appeared in the September and October issues, preceded by a scrap from the *Niebelungen Lied.* It contains some lyrics which might well have come out of the songs of the Minnesingers:

> Christ keep the Hollow Land
> All the summer-tide,

and "Queen Swanhilda's Christmas Carol":

> Queen Mary's crown was gold,
> King Joseph's crown was red,
> But Jesus's crown was diamond
> That lit up all the bed.
> *Mariæ Virginis.*

> Ships sail through the Heaven
> With red banners dress'd,
> Carrying the planets seven
> To see the white breast.
> *Mariæ Virginis.*

Besides the imaginative qualities displayed in *The Hollow Land,* which include the vision of a life after death and a penetration of the matter of death itself, even to the witnessing of one's own death and resurrection in another world (these matters which Morris has sometimes been accused of fearing to deal with by certain of his critics)—and in addition to the sheer beauty of the writing—there are also evidences of that vague social and political questioning which Morris at this time was experiencing, even when endeavouring to lose himself in literature and in art. Thus, Morris asks (in the person of Florian, the "I" of the story) "How was it, by the way, that no one ever made Hugh [his faithful retainer] a knight?" Again, Florian questions the prevalence of evil and injustice in the world, saying that "God suffers the wicked to go their own ways pretty much," but "we, brave men and brothers, ought to be masters of *simulacra.*" Of the tale-teller himself, the young author says that "it is narrated that men say you hardly believe any doctrine such as other men do, and will only go to Heaven round about, as it were." It must be remembered that this was written at about the time when Morris is said to have stated that he would never graduate from Oxford if he had to subscribe to the Thirty-nine Articles. He was no longer an ardent Anglo-Catholic, or even an ardent Anglican: Oxford's three and a half years had produced in his mind some new concepts.

At the close of the story, when the hero entered his new heaven:

We came to a fair place, cloistered off in the old time, before the city grew golden from the din and hubbub of traffic; those who dwelt there in the old ungolden times had had their own joys, their own sorrows, apart from the sorrows of the multitudes; so, in like manner, was it now cloistered off from the eager leaning of the golden dwellings: so now it had its own gaiety, its own solemnity, apart from theirs, unchanged, unchangeable. . . .

Is it possible that these writings show "the idle singer of an empty day" in embryo—or merely "his long anguish of the fear of death," if one may borrow a phrase from Mr. Alfred Noyes? Or is it not more likely that they merely carried a step farther some natural tendencies which Morris had already developed in his youth, and that these now began to crystallize into the nucleus of a new concept of the meaning of the good life?

Whatever they show, this much is evident: England had produced, if not discovered, a new creative genius who possessed boldness of imagination, as well as talent and independence of mind. And in this new creative genius there had long been simmering ideas that dwelt upon beauty, justice and truth in the spirit—and literary, social, and artistic revolution in the flesh. He was beginning to see, as through a glass darkly, the inspiring image of "that new heaven the new faith tells of"— that same fair image of which he was to write twenty years later in *Sigurd the Volsung*, and of which he was to write again and again during still another twenty years which were yet to come.

## CHAPTER IX

PLUNGING INTO THE CENTER OF LIFE: ART, PAINTING,

POETRY AND DIRT

I T OUGHT to be evident that by this time Morris was not
primarily a religiously inclined youngster, as so many of
his critics have claimed. It is equally evident that he had
developed a reformist tendency which was not derived solely
from his reading of the works of Carlyle, Kingsley and Ruskin.
And for the rest of the Morris set, it would seem that a number of the group were not motivated, even from the first, by
any firm religious conviction. Even Morris and Burne-Jones
easily lost their early adherence to strongly pronounced faith
and dogma, although both boys had come naturally to regard
the Church as a directing and informing agency to a better life.
This does not imply that they were antireligious; it merely
means that they had been evolving an ethical philosophy of
their own. As Professor Walter Phelps Hall has said of Morris,
"although in all his many volumes there is no indication that he
was influenced by the Christian example," yet "few men have
ever loved their fellows more than this great, red-bearded man,
born a gentleman yet by choice a craftsman."[1]

It is probable that Morris's early interest in High Church
religion resulted from two characteristics: first, a natural rebellion against the evangelical attitude of his own family, and
secondly, a realization of the beauty of High Church customs
and usages which had come to him during his Marlborough
days and been nourished upon history, church architecture
and church music. Doubtless adolescent sincerity and idealism

[1]Hall and Albion, *A History of England and the British Empire*, p. 781.

56

had to run their course in him as in most young people; yet of idealism Morris surely had more than a normal share throughout his entire life.

That is why he seems like a young Galahad in the majority of his Oxford writings, even though personally he appeared as a rough-and-ready young gentleman of rather pugnacious proclivities who was not a little abrupt in expressing his opinions of ideas with which he did not agree. The first reliable portrait of him shows a well-dressed, good-looking and rather serious young man. His hair, reddish brown with streaks of gold still visible, was fine in texture, thick and inclined to be wavy and unruly. His eyes were dark gray, almost black at times, and already becoming deep-set. His mouth also was firmer and more serious than one might have expected, to judge from his usual exuberance and careless gaiety. He had lost, for a few years at least, his rather thick-set appearance, although he was strongly built and just a trifle taller than the average young man of his acquaintance. Faulkner and Burne-Jones were considerably taller than he was, but slender in comparison. Compared with Morris, Burne-Jones was like a living wraith, fated to remain thin and frail, at least in appearance, for the remainder of his life.

Although Morris was nominally a student in Oxford University in 1856, his new association with G. E. Street and his activities in connection with *The Oxford and Cambridge Magazine* really mark the end of his period of formal education and the beginning of his professional career. The period of formal education was now to give way to a period of informal education during which he engaged in those activities and studies to which he felt attracted. For some twenty-five more years he was to continue to develop. Certainly the well-rounded man did not emerge full-grown before 1882, and even then his development was far from being at an end. He matured very late in life, if, indeed, he ever reached his full, potential maturity. As late as 1877, when he was forty-three years of age, a craftsman and poet who had achieved world-wide recognition and fame, he was still young in appearance and boyish in manner, despite his carefully cultivated beard. It was in that year, by the way, that he rejected the nomination for the chair of poetry at Oxford.

In addition to his literary efforts on behalf of "The Mag" and his architectural activities for G. E. Street & Company, Morris began, in 1856, to engage in the study and practice of a number of handicrafts: clay modelling, illuminating, and carving in wood and in stone. For at the age of twenty-two, it seemed, he was still as restless and unsettled as he had been when a child. He looked about him, among all his friends, marvelling at the apparent ease with which they settled into their chosen careers, and felt exceedingly uncomfortable. He did not know that his own career was to take shape very slowly, and that often the penalty of genius is much mental turmoil regarding one's activities in life.

During the first quarter of 1856 the majority of The Brotherhood were still in Oxford, although Fulford was already in London, and Heeley and Burne-Jones were about to begin their careers. Many of Morris's evenings were spent with members of the old set; but after Burne-Jones went to London to practise painting under Rossetti, his newly found master, Morris formed the habit of spending week-ends with Edward in the latter's rooms in Chelsea. Frequently the two friends went to Rossetti's studio on the embankment overlooking Blackfriars Bridge, often remaining until three or four o'clock in the morning. During these months Rossetti's influence began to weigh heavily upon the two impressionable young men; both of them came more than ever under the spell of Malory's *Morte d'Arthur,* which Rossetti held to be "the greatest book in the world."

In the late summer of 1856 the firm of G. E. Street & Company moved its headquarters to London, and Morris and Burne-Jones thereupon took rooms together in Upper Gordon Street, in Bloomsbury. In so doing they moved a step further into the gay life of Bohemia. Before long they would become denizens of a newer and more unconventional world than the one which they had known in Oxford.

Street's firm had been engaged in the "restoration" of certain Oxford churches, a type of activity that was distasteful to Morris; and now, under the incentive of Rossetti and Burne-Jones, he decided, at long last, to give up architecture and turn to painting. By this time he had met another Pre-Raphaelite, Holman Hunt, of slightly less disconcerting demeanour than Rossetti and a much more "natural fellow." This may have given Morris some encouragement. But there is evidence that he was still engaged in vigorous soul-searching as to his future career. For a while, however, the enthusiasm of Rossetti and Burne-Jones was to carry him along.

In the autumn of 1856 Morris and Mr. Street made a trip to Holland and Belgium, where a new world of domestic architecture and interior decoration was spread before the enraptured gaze of the young artist-poet. Old Dutch interiors must have made an indelible impression upon his mind, for traces of their influence can be detected in nearly all his future work. New realms were also opened to him in the art of painting; he came back with a permanent enthusiasm for Dutch and Flemish painters—and also with a new personal motto which he derived from the *Als ich kanne* of Johann van Eyck.

From this time onward his interest in architecture lagged. He saw no hope of indulging his own tastes in a worth-while architectural career in England, for native architectural standards seemed to be at their nadir. Indeed, he had been doubting the wisdom of his choice of a career for a long time now, having written, as early as July:

One won't get much enjoyment out of life at this rate. . . . Love and work, these two things only. . . . I can't enter into politico-social subjects, for on the whole I see that things are in a muddle, and I have no power or vocation to set them right. . . . For the present, my work is the embodiment of dreams, in one form or another. . . .

His old, cherished idea of reforming the world, together

with his interest in the original purposes of *The Oxford and Cambridge Magazine*, waned rapidly under the pressure exerted by his new Pre-Raphaelite friends. Conceivably, but for them, he might have become a permanent politico-social reformer in 1856, instead of a miserably discouraged young man who was turning half-heartedly to painting: half-heartedly because he knew in his heart that he could never match the works of the Dutch and Flemish masters. As events turned, however, he was to become first the artist, craftsman and man of letters, and only latterly the reformer. Indeed, even without the circumstantial evidence contained in the paragraphs above, we have, in one of Morris's letters to his friend,[2] Andreas Scheu, his own word for it that art postponed his entry into social-reform works.

It is interesting to note that in the same letter Morris went on to state that after leaving Oxford he had extended his historical readings, as a result of which he "fell in" with some translations of the Old Norse literature and "found them a good corrective for the maundering side of medievalism." (This for those of his hostile critics who declared him to be living ever after in a dream world of golden medievalism.)

His significant interest in Old Norse was not to develop fully, however, for several more years. But his interest in *literary reform* was unabated, and during this year and the next his revolutionary examples of ballads, lyrics, prose romances and romantic dialogues were continued.

[2]Recounting briefly his past career, Morris wrote: "My Father was a business man in the city, and well-to-do; and we lived in the ordinary bourgeois style of comfort; and since we belonged to the evangelical section of the English Church, I was brought up in what I should call rich establishmentarian puritanism; a religion which even as a boy I never took to. . . . I went to Oxford in 1853 . . . fell to very vigorously on history and specially medieval history, all the more perhaps because at this time I fell under the influence of the High Church or Puseyite School; this latter phase however did not last me long, as it was corrected by the books of John Ruskin. . . . I was also a good deal influenced by the books of Charles Kingsley, and got into my head therefrom some socio-political ideas which would have developed probably but for the attractions of art and poetry. . . ."

Meanwhile he turned to art. During the daylight hours he worked in Street's offices, taking only a single holiday to go up to Oxford and receive his degree. In the evenings he and Burne-Jones attended a "life-school" of painting in Newman Street. Slowly he learned to comprehend something of the grime and dirt which had ground itself into London life. Morris sometimes referred to the city as "the center of filth."

But this strenuous life proved too difficult to maintain for a long time, and since he saw no hope of realizing any great architectural accomplishment in connection with the contemporary state of Victorian restoration work, he left Street's employ and turned seriously to the Bloomsbury activities of painting and writing.

From the time that he obtained his bachelor's degree he began to let his hair and beard grow long. He determined to become an artist in appearance as well as in reality.

# II

## FROM OXFORD TO THE
## DEMOCRATIC FEDERATION

*And if, the while ye toiled and sorrowed most*
*The sound of your lamenting seemed all lost,*
*And from my land no answer came again,*
*It was because of that your toil and pain*
*A house was building, and your bitter sighs*
*Came hither, as toil-helping melodies;*
*And in the mortar of our gem-built wall*
*Your tears were mingled mid the rise and fall*
*Of golden trowels tinkling in the hands*
*Of builders gathered wide from all the lands.*

## CHAPTER I

MORRIS AND BURNE-JONES HAVE A STUDIO

IN RED LION SQUARE

TOWARD the end of the year 1856 Morris and Burne-Jones searched for more appropriate artists' quarters and found them on the first floor of the house at 17, Red Lion Square, where Rossetti and Walter Deverell had roomed five years before. Red Lion Square was "dark and dirty"—much more so then than now—but interesting from a Bohemian point of view.

Of their life at Red Lion Square, Burne-Jones soon wrote:

Topsy and I live together in the quaintest room in all London, hung with brasses of old knights and drawings of Albert Dürer. We know Rossetti as a daily friend, and we know Browning too, who is the greatest poet alive, and we know Arthur Hughes, and Woolner, and Madox Brown—Madox Brown is a lark. . . . Topsy will be a painter, he works hard, is prepared to wait twenty years, loves art more and more every day. He has written several poems, exceedingly dramatic—the Brownings, I hear, have spoken very highly of one that was read to them: Rossetti thinks one called "Rapunzel" is equal to Tennyson: he is now illuminating "Guendolen" for Georgie. . . .

The Mag is going to smash—let it go! The world is not converted and never will be. . . . I shall not write for it again, no more will Topsy—we cannot do more than one thing at a time, and our hours are too valuable to spend so.[1]

Every one seemed to agree that the time was not yet ripe for political effort, and so Morris was to have his interest in social and political reform temporarily checked in favour of artistic and literary reform. This was probably a good thing, for he was not yet learned enough in social, political and economic

[1] Burne-Jones to his family, August 20, 1856. "Georgie" refers to the girl (Georgia Macdonald) whom he was later to marry.

matters to evolve any plan or idea worth positing. He was still immature from the philosophic and intellectual points of view; for he was still in a formative and somewhat imitative stage of development.

Even in literature Morris was not yet sure of his originality. In prose the study of medieval French romances and in poetry the influence of Poe, the Brownings, and the Rossettis made themselves felt, that of Robert Browning especially. The young poet was drawn as if by instinct to dramatic dialogues and lyrics. In the matter of rhyming, when he now employed it, he seemed to be torn between the styles employed by Mrs. Browning and by Edgar Allan Poe. Melody was born in him, and it seemed to come out naturally, rhyme or no rhyme. Perhaps it may have been the realization of this gift that inspired, for a while, his attempts at dramatic dialogue.

Toward the close of the year Burne-Jones, who kept up a far more active correspondence than did Morris, wrote to Georgie: "To-day we are to go and see Ruskin," and after the return:

Just come back from being with our hero for four hours—so happy we've been: he is so kind to us, calls us his dear boys and makes us feel like such old friends. To-night he comes down to our rooms to carry off my drawing and show it to lots of people; to-morrow night he comes again, and every Thursday night the same—isn't that like a dream?[2]

After Morris came to live in London, he and Burne-Jones frequently spent week-ends at Oxford, carrying with them "the banner of art and revolt." But their old Brotherhood was

[2] Of the two boys, Burne-Jones was always more intimate with Ruskin, and for him Ruskin remained the great and enviable hero to a somewhat larger extent than he did for Morris. In after years Morris was to see Ruskin but rarely. Yet some of Edward's enthusiasm for the great man must have been transferred to Morris, for both always admired Ruskin greatly and on several occasions Morris was afterward to refer to him as his own master. On other occasions, however, there were references less laudatory, and many years afterward Bernard Shaw told of having heard Morris remark that Ruskin could write the most profound truths imaginable, and five minutes afterward forget about them.

Morris and Burne-Jones have a studio in Red Lion Square

A Drawing by Burne-Jones

rapidly diminishing. Faulkner was now a Fellow of University College, and there, in his new rooms, he received his guests from London; the group usually consisted of William and Edward, Fulford and Vernon Lushington. Dixon came sometimes, and once, having met Rossetti and listened to his views on art, declared that he, too, was going to become a painter!

Meanwhile, as leisure from artistic, literary and social activities permitted, Morris and his friends gave vent to their artistic instincts by refurnishing and redecorating the rooms at 17, Red Lion Square. They wished to have a fairly permanent abode, for here they were to live and work for a long time, they thought.

So they set about constructing a new kind of studio apartment, and what a weird and outlandish place they made of it! The two windows of the large room in front were enlarged from floor to ceiling, to admit more northern light, and all three rooms on the first floor were refurnished and repainted in "an intensely medieval fashion," as Burne-Jones put it. Morris sought out Philip Webb to help select furnishings, but no "suitable and medieval" furniture was to be found anywhere in London. Moreover, they discovered that cabinetmakers, if and when such a brood of men had existed, which Morris doubted, simply did not exist any longer. So Morris drew his own designs for furniture and hired two ordinary carpenters to work out his ideas in wood, brass, and iron. Thus, a huge round table was constructed, "as firm and as heavy as a rock," and tall strong chairs to match it, such as "a Barbarossa might have sat in." Then there appeared an enormous settle, with one long seat below, and with three huge cupboards above: a tremendous object, fit for a cathedral chapter. "We were out," wrote Burne-Jones, "when it reached the house, but when we came in, all the passages and stairways were choked with timber—vast blocks of it—and there was a scene. I think the measurements had perhaps been given a little wrongly." Morris was so angry that he kicked the bedroom door off its hinges to make room for the huge object to be turned around. "But set up it was finally, and our studio was one-third less in size." Rossetti came over to view the results. He laughed, but he approved.

A considerable amount of time was then occupied by Rossetti in the task of covering the new-old furniture with appropriate oil paintings, a task for which Morris must have paid well. The central panels of the cupboard doors were emblazoned with depictions of Dante meeting Beatrice in Florence and later in Paradise; between them a design was executed for "Love Between the Sun and the Moon." The backs of the two larger chairs were then covered by Rossetti's paintings of scenes from two of Morris's recent poems. One of them, a scene for "Rapunzel" showed the princess Guendolen letting down her long golden hair from a witch-tower; the other represented the arming of the knight: a scene from the Christmas mystery, "Sir Galahad."

Early in 1857 a large wardrobe was acquired and Burne-Jones covered it with scenes from "The Prioress's Tale" of Chaucer. This piece of beautified furniture was to remain one of Morris's most prized possessions for the rest of his life; three decades later it occupied the most prominent place in Morris's drawing room at Kelmscott House in London.

During the daylight hours Morris worked hard at painting and illumination and developed a remarkable facility for pattern designing. At painting he did not excel, so that even Rossetti despaired, yet the Pre-Raphaelite was generous enough to admit that "In all illumination and work of that kind, he is quite unrivalled by anything modern that I know."

In the evenings, when the two friends were not engaged with calls and visitors, Morris continued to write poetry. He selected from his Oxford efforts a large amount which appealed to him as being worthy of publication. To this he added a few of the Bloomsbury poems. The rest of his writings he burnt without compunction. He planned to publish a small volume of poetry entitled *The Defense of Guenevere and Other Poems.*

So life at 17, Red Lion Square, continued pleasantly enough. Yet these three years cannot be passed by without some account of the social activities of the two young Bohemians. For as time went on they became more and more Bohemian, Morris especially. That young man was becoming burly of figure, and his burliness was now enhanced by the growth of a short, bristling beard, by his affectation of a short, stubby pipe, and by his insistence upon wearing loose, woolly, informal garments, a blue shirt open at the neck, and no hat. More than one butler was astounded by the appearance of an obvious tramp who demanded admittance to an informal gathering under the name of William Morris. Once admitted, this strange young gentleman would pull out his pipe and light it. He delighted in lighting it upon almost all occasions. Thus, without his realizing it, his fame began to precede him everywhere. More and more people were beginning to admire his poetic efforts. With such advocates as Rossetti, Ruskin and Browning, they could hardly afford not to admit that it was very good poetry, however strange.

But the most unusual character who dwelt within the precincts of 17, Red Lion Square, was "Red Lion Mary." Mary was the maid of the house. She has been described as a plain woman of unflinching character and unfailing good humour. Mary appreciated the newer culture which had been precipitated upon the household. Very obviously she was a woman who intended to make the most of her opportunities. She turned ardently to the reading of poetry in her leisure hours; she helped herself to the books of the "two young gentlemen"; she read their writings with avidity, and also their mail. She cleaned the rooms, cooked meals when they were in, mended their shirts and socks, and allowed the other inmates of the house to wait her pleasure while she stood behind Messrs. Morris and Burne-Jones and watched them paint noble pictures. On more than one occasion she even aspired to become a model, but it is not definitely known whether this high honour was accorded her. Sometimes aspiring young poets would come to visit Morris in the hope of securing financial help or moral encouragement. On such occasions Mary would poke her head through the doorway and shout the following announcement: "Young gentleman out of Byron to see you, Sir!"

## CHAPTER II

JANE BURDEN IS DISCOVERED: "I CANNOT PAINT YOU, BUT I LOVE YOU"

DANTE GABRIEL ROSSETTI had acquired an effective if somewhat insolent technique of gaining acquaintance with women who attracted him. One of his affairs was begun by pulling down the hair of a young country girl in a London restaurant "to see how it looked." For some years past he had been engaged to the sickly, pale and almost deathlike Elizabeth Siddal, whom he was later to marry. There was also another woman who occupied a permanent place in his affections. One day in 1854 he had met her: a beautiful vision from the slums of East London eating nuts and laughingly throwing the shells at innocent passers-by. She was a healthy and voluptuous vision, impatient and saucy, and her hair resembled spun gold. Rossetti lost no time in getting in the way of her showers of nutshells. It turned out to be a case of mutual attraction, of sorts. Artistic-æsthetic eyes looked into naïvely physical eyes. Their possessors smiled, and talked; and Fanny Cornforth (Mrs. Schott) agreed to become his model. She became also a part of his life, encroaching upon it forever after—a veritable disease of Rossetti's mind. She was with him in many of his best paintings; she was with him at his deathbed, attempting, so her enemies said, to persuade him to make a will in her favour. She haunted his poetic efforts throughout his life. When he was old he wrote in *The House of Life* of "The witch he loved before the gift of Eve."

It was Rossetti's genius in the art of becoming acquainted with women which led directly to Morris's meeting with the girl he was destined to marry. This is how it came about.

71

Woodward, the arch-fiend of Oxford's architectural restoration, had designed the new Union Debating Hall at the university. Above the gallery around it there was a bare belt of wall, divided into ten bays, containing only circular windows. This blank space would provide opportunities for murals, so Rossetti informed Mr. Woodward, and the information was accepted at its face value. At that time nothing was known in England of mural painting; but Rossetti was nothing if not confident. The result of Rossetti's high-pressure sales talk was that Mr. Woodward and Doctor Ackland, who supervised the building committee at Oxford, were bullied into the acceptance of Rossetti's offer to provide a mural decoration, based upon scenes from Malory's *Morte d'Arthur*.

Rossetti then endeavoured to persuade Madox Brown to undertake the project with him. When Brown refused, Rossetti decided to assign one bay each to Morris and Burne-Jones, who would do the work under his own supervision. Four other artists were also drawn into the scheme: Val Princep, Hungerford Pollen, Spencer Stanhope, and Arthur Hughes. Without much plan or forethought the seven descended upon the Oxford Union during the long vacation of 1857.

Morris was the first to arrive and no one worked more ambitiously or precipitately than did he. This was his first big commitment; it would decide whether or not he could become a successful painter.

The old friends, joined by Faulkner of University College, spent a grand winter. Feted by the university students, painting with small brushes upon damp mortar covered with whitewash, they faced a hopeless task with optimism if not with competence. Working from tall ladders and hanging from swinging ropes, Morris, who was beginning to get stout again, resembled nothing more nearly than an anthropoid cousin of humanity exploring new domains. So enthusiastic was he that he designed a suit of mail and hired a local blacksmith to put it together. Once again he became a knight in shining armour, to the amusement of artists and students.

Christmas came and Morris went to visit his mother in Walthamstow. She was greatly disappointed, as she had been for a long time, that Edward Burne-Jones, as she put it, had lured him into art.

Morris returned to Oxford feeling a bit gloomier and more morose. At this time art was everything to him. And in such a frame of mind he was susceptible to the idea of a new home of his own and to a new feminine influence that would be more appreciative of art and beauty generally. And as luck turned, it was in this frame of mind that he made the acquaintance of Jane Burden, daughter of Robert Burden, who lived on Holywell Street. Just as it was Rossetti who had brought Morris to Oxford again, so it was Rossetti who now introduced him to "the most beautiful woman in England."

Just before Morris came back, Rossetti and Burne-Jones had followed their day's work at the Union with a visit to the little Oxford theatre. Jane Burden and her sister were sitting just behind them. Rossetti lost no time, it seems, in noticing them. He "remembered" Jane: her unusually artistic face; he had met her before—was it at Doctor Ackland's, perhaps? He and his friend were among the group of artists now painting the murals at the new Union hall. He himself was a portrait painter. Wouldn't she, while they were here in Oxford, sit for him? She would make a strikingly beautiful and æsthetic portrait.

Jane was naturally impressed. Here were university people, artists and graduates of Oxford, too; and Jane was quite willing to fall in love with art and beauty. Under such circumstances it was only natural that she should have been flattered. As many another woman had done before her, this young girl—she was then about twenty—agreed to sit for Rossetti.

Rossetti promptly fell in love with her, as he did with most women; but Jane never usurped the positions in his heart that were held by Elizabeth Siddal and Fanny Schott. Nevertheless, Jane, with her tall, æsthetic figure, her dark coils of massy, burnished hair, her high ascetic face, her so thoroughly un-

English type of beauty, must be made one of the Pre-Raphaelite group. Rossetti would have loved to go on painting her forever.

So he sang her praises loudly and long. Burne-Jones was already engaged to Georgie, or as good as engaged—but Morris!—there was the finger of fate itself. All that was necessary to bring Jane into the magic circle was to have her marry Morris. And Rossetti's opinions were not only laws unto themselves, but also unto Morris at this particular stage of his career. So it turned out that Morris soon came to regard Jane Burden as the apotheosis of what Rossetti called "a stunner." Rossetti envisaged for Morris a new and magnificent home amid new and magnificent surroundings—"The Towers of Topsy," Rossetti called it—dominated by the woman who represented the very ideal of Pre-Raphaelite beauty. And Morris was not twenty-four years old—hardly mature for any man and certainly not for Morris. So he became cheerfully and innocently enamored of Rossetti's golden dream of beauty and his own happy future. But he had not yet proposed to the girl.

Meanwhile, as the sad fate of the murals became more and more apparent to Rossetti's eyes, he began to tire of the new job. He had managed to complete one of his own bays, but the others were more nearly paintings in distemper. Long before the spring of 1858 came on, the paintings had begun to crumble and fade when scarcely half finished. The Pre-Raphaelites were heartily sick of the job and London beckoned; so they packed up and disappeared from Oxford: that is, all of them except Morris. He stayed on, living in the rarefied atmosphere of feminine perfection, and writing a few love poems on the side, such as the *Beata mea Domina*.

The Oxford building committee had to hire Rivière to finish the art work on the Union. A few months afterward Coventry Patmore wrote the official blurb when he announced that the murals were "Sweet, bright, and pure as a cloud in the sunrise . . . so brilliant as to make the walls look like the margin of an illuminated manuscript."

So ended Morris's first commission as a painter, through no fault of his, or lack of personal effort. But he was not discouraged. He himself would now undertake to complete the portrait of Jane which Rossetti had not done justice to.

But Jane's dark beauty, growing more and more inhuman as progress in æsthetics opened new vistas to the lovely girl, eluded Morris as it eluded all other painters, except, perhaps, Rossetti. So Morris went home again to see his mother.

This time he received a cool welcome. Love and art, it seemed, were even worse than art alone, not to mention unfinished business! His mother made it clear that she regarded him as a mere dabbler.

Morris left home and went back to Burne-Jones and the studio in Red Lion Square. He would prepare his finished manuscript of *The Defense of Guenevere*. If painting failed, poetry might suffice.

Long before he had finished preparing the manuscript and completing his arrangements for its publication by Bell and Daldy, Oxford was again beckoning. Back he went, to paint Jane and to make love to her.

Morris at this time was a mixture of shyness, humility, and burly violence. He was neither subtle nor romantic, so far as outward appearances were concerned; yet underlying his external apparition—his soft hat, pipe and bearded countenance— he possessed sincerity, romance and enthusiasm. It is said that he scribbled across the back of one of his attempted portraits of Jane: "I cannot paint you, but I love you." And then, shortly after his first published volume of poetry appeared, in March, 1858, he and "the silent, slender, stately girl with the dark tresses and the strong hands" became engaged.

Burne-Jones now fell seriously ill and for the next few months Morris spent most of his time flitting discontentedly about and not knowing what to do with himself, now that he was faced by the serious reality of marriage. He could be seen sometimes at his mother's new home in Leyton, occasionally at Red Lion Square, where he still retained bachelor quarters, sometimes at Little Holland House, whither Burne-Jones had been sent to be nursed back to health by Mrs. Hughes; but sooner or later, and most of the time, he would be back in Oxford again. When not with Jane he was at the Maclaren home in Summertown, practising at painting in the orchard. But he was beginning to despair of painting.

In August, he and Faulkner and Philip Webb visited northern France and rowed adventurously down the Seine from Paris, carrying with them three carpet-bags and a half dozen bottles of wine. On this trip Morris and Philip Webb discussed plans for building the new house: plans which were to be communicated in detail to Rossetti, and heartily approved by him, upon Morris's return to London. In October, Morris was back in France purchasing old manuscripts, armour, ironwork and enamel, for the decoration of the forthcoming "Towers of Topsy."

The winter of 1858–1859 passed at last, and on April 26, 1859, the most brilliant young poet-artist of the age and the most beautiful young woman in England were married in the little parish church of Saint Michael's in Oxford.

Dixon, now a rector in the Church, came down to perform the ceremony. It was a festive occasion for him and for every one else. But the Reverend Mr. Dixon was so nervous and excited when he pronounced the couple man and wife that he referred to them as "William and Mary."

# CHAPTER III

## "THE DEFENSE OF GUENEVERE"

ALTHOUGH *The Defense of Guenevere and Other Poems* was lauded by Swinburne and by Browning, the slim volume was ill adapted to the demands of a Victorian public. It smote the ear and turned the stomach of the average reader, and such critics as reviewed the book for the press regarded the verses of Morris as curiosities or, worse, as affectations. "A Pre-Raphaelite eccentricity" was the pronouncement of *The Athenæum*, and "a curiosity which shows how far affectation may lead an earnest man toward the fogland of art"—while later Mr. R. H. Stoddard, in *Appleton's Journal*, referred to it as "the strangest collection of poetry not confessedly insane, in the language."

Scarcely two hundred and fifty copies of the edition were sold and given away; other copies remained on the publisher's shelves for fourteen years. Judged solely by form, rather than by the spirit of their content, the poems showed clearly the influence upon the young man of Poe and the Brownings. They also showed, to some extent, the influence of the old ballad forms which had appealed to Morris in his youth. But few critics noted these resemblances of form and method.[1]

[1]Among Morris's admirers must be included George Moore, who, much later, wrote to Miss Nancy Cunard (the daughter of Lady Cunard):

"The poem I sent you is very beautiful, one of the most beautiful things in English poetry. I am sending you to-day the volume from which it was taken, 'The Defense of Guenevere and Other Poems' by William Morris, the most perfect first volume of poems ever published by any man. . . . Morris is our only improvisatore, perhaps the only great improvisatore that ever lived. . . . Read it, Nancy, and admire the perfect craftsmanship of every thing in the volume." (Joseph Hone, *Life of George Moore*. London: Gollancz, 1936, pp. 360–1.)

No one who knew George Moore would have expected such an unrestricted eulogy for any poet or prose writer of his own time.

There is evidence in *The Defense of Guenevere* of the soul-searching and questioning of the newly forming poet and artist. Thus, in *King Arthur's Tomb*, he speaks of

> Skies, earth, men's looks and deeds, all that has part,
>   Not being ourselves, in that half-sleep, half-strife,
>
> Strange sleep, strange strife, that men call living;

and he ends on a note of defeat, when

>                                    Everywhere
> The knights come foiled from the great quest, in vain:
>   In vain they struggle for the vision fair.

And thus the prince of *Rapunzel*, "who rides to dream,"

> I have heard tales of men, who in the night
>   Saw paths of stars let down to earth from heaven,—

but, on awakening, in real life, he saw only "the proofs of a great loneliness that sickened me"—

> Making me feel a doubt that was not fear,
>   Whether my whole life long had been a dream,
> And I should wake up soon in some place, where
>   The piled-up arms of fighting angels gleam;
>
> Not born as yet, but going to be born,
>   No naked baby as I was at first;
> But an arméd Knight, whom fire, hate and scorn
>   Could turn from nothing: my heart almost burst
>
> Beneath the beeches as I lay a-dreaming,
>   I tried so hard to read this riddle through,
> To catch some golden cord that I saw gleaming
>   Like gossamer against the autumn blue.

In these suggestions of unrest, one sees what Morris meant when he wrote "I see that things are in a muddle, and I have no power or vocation to set them right. . . . My work is the embodiment of dreams." Yet in his poetry, at the age of twenty-four, Morris was only hinting vaguely at his own unrest—so vaguely that those critics whose knowledge of the man was based solely upon the slender *Defense of Guenevere*, did not recognize it.

The influence of Robert Browning is most clearly marked, perhaps, in *Sir Peter Harpdon's End*; yet there is also evident a definite grasp of the historic situation with which the English in the Hundred Years War were faced just after the demises of Edward III and the Black Prince. When John Curzon, one of the soldiers in the beleaguered castle in Poictou, says "We can send some villaynes to get stone," Sir Peter replies:

> Alas! John, that we cannot bring them back,
> They would go off to Clisson or Sanxere,
> And tell them we were weak in walls and men,
> Then down we go; for, look you, times are changed,
> And now no longer does the country shake
> At sound of English names; our captains fade
> From off our muster-rolls. At Lusac Bridge
> I dare say you may even yet see the hole
> That Chandos beat in dying; far in Spain
> Pembroke is prisoner; Phelton is prisoner here;
> Manny lies buried in the Charterhouse;
> Oliver Clisson turn'd these years agone;
> The Captal died in prison; and, over all,
> Edward the Prince lies underneath the ground,
> Edward the King is dead, at Westminster
> The carvers smooth the curls of his long beard.
> Everything goes to rack—eh! and we too.

A little later, while bargaining for the surrender of the castle, Sir Peter well expresses that sympathy for the under-dog which marked so clearly Morris's own attitude throughout life. Says he:

> Take note
> How almost all men, reading that sad siege,
> Hold for the Trojans; as I did at least;
> Thought Hector the best knight a long way:

                                                Now
Why should I not do this thing that I think,
For even when I come to count the gains,
I have them on my side: men will talk, you know,
(We talk of Hector, dead so long agone)
When I am dead, of how this Peter clung
To what he thought the right; of how he died,
Perchance, at last, doing some desperate deed
Few men would care do now, and this is gain
To me, as ease and money is to you,
Moreover, I, too, like the straining game
Of striving well to hold up things that fall;
So one becomes great; see you! in good times
All men live well together, and you, too,
Live dull and happy—happy? not so quick,
Suppose sharp thoughts begin to burn you up.
Why then, but just to fight as I do now,
A halter round my neck, would be great bliss.
Oh! I am well off.


At the close of the drama, Sir Peter's fiancée, hearing of his
hanging, echoes his own thought:

Yea, some men sing, what is it then they sing?
Eh, Launcelot, and love, and fate and death;
They ought to sing of him who was as wight
As Launcelot or Wade, and yet availed
Just nothing, but to fail and fail and fail,
And so at last to die and leave me here,
Alone and wretched; yea, perhaps they will,
When many years are past, make songs of us;
God help me, though, truly I never thought
That I should make a story in this way,
A story that his eyes can never see.


Her reflections are interrupted by the sound of a troubadour's
voice from without, stridently singing, not of Sir Peter Harpdon's end, but of Launcelot, and love and fate and death:

Yet he was so glad,
That his son Lord Galahad
That high joyaunce had
All his life-days.

Sing we therefore then
Launcelot's praise again,
For he wan crownés ten,
If he wan not twelve.

And this, as Morris saw it and heard it, was the way of the world, in the fourteenth century as in the nineteenth. But his critics, if they comprehended his meaning, thought him indecorous.

Morris gave another poetic portrayal of the evil aspect of the Middle Ages in his poem *Concerning Geffray Teste Noire:*

Often, God help me! I remember when
I was a simple boy, fifteen years old,
The Jacquerie froze up the blood of men
With their fell deeds, not fit now to be told!

That last line was an echo of the prevailing mood. Tennyson's "mild youth" and chivalrous depictions had spoiled Morris's public; the truth of the matter was that the depictions of medieval life in the entire volume of the young poet grated upon the prevailing romantic views which typified Victorian belief in the Middle Ages. Indeed, Morris's main concept of the Arthurian cycle seems to be based upon a struggle among the forces of beauty and adultery, blood, plunder, lust and death.

But Morris continues:

God help again! we enter'd Beauvais town
Slaying them fast, whereto I help'd, mere boy
As I was then; we gentles cut them down,
These burners and defilers, with great joy.

Reason for that, too, in the great church there
    These fiends had lit a fire, that soon went out,
The church at Beauvais being so great and fair—
    My father, who was by me, gave a shout

Between a beast's howl and a woman's scream,
    Then, panting, chuckled to me: "John, look! look!
Count the dames' skeletons." . . .

And I, being faint with smelling the burnt bones,
    And very hot with fighting down the street,
And sick of such a life, fell down, with groans
    My head went weakly nodding to my feet.

.    .    .    .    .    .    .

How could it be? never before that day,
    However much a soldier I might be,
Could I look on a skeleton and say
    I care not for it, shudder not—

.    .    .    .    .    .    .

In my new castle, down beside the Eure,
    There is a little chapel of squared stone,
Painted inside and out; in green nook pure
    There did I lay them, every wearied bone;

And over it they lay, with stone-white hands
    Clasped fast together, hair made bright with gold,
This, Jacques Picard, known through many lands,
    Wrought cunningly; he's dead now—I am old.

It is worth noting that this Jacques Picard, who "wrought cunningly" for Morris, did so just a year before Claus of Innsbruck "cast in bronze" for Browning's *My Last Duchess*. It is indeed possible, in view of this and in view of what was said above by Burne-Jones, that the "Browning influence" which worked strongly upon Morris during the years 1856–57, was retroactive in effect—that there was also a "Morris influence" that worked upon Browning. Years later, when Morris published *The Earthly Paradise,* Browning wrote to him: "It is a double delight . . . to read such poetry, and know that you of all the world wrote it,—you whose songs I used to sing while galloping by Fiesole in the old days."

Except for *The Gilliflower of Gold* there is scarcely a poem in the entire volume which is not markedly realistic in temper. And even in the Gilliflower, the echoing refrain, *Hah! hah! la belle jaune giroflé,* seems to fling at the reader some echo of the reckless bravado which characterized the medieval tournaments. Yet even this poem contains at the close a hint of the kind of tragedy that marred for his Victorian audience the element of conventional beauty in Morris's first published volume. For the knight, returning victorious from the tournament to his lady, exclaims:

> I almost saw your quiet head
> Bow'd o'er the gilliflower bed,
> The yellow flowers stain'd with red—
> *Hah! hah! la belle jaune giroflé.*

When *The Defense of Guenevere and Other Poems* did not meet with abuse at the hands of critics, it met with worse: the majority of editors simply ignored it. Morris himself had borne the expenses of publication and he felt keenly the lack of appreciation which seemed evidenced everywhere outside his own circle of friends. He developed a repugnance for professional literary criticism which was to remain one of his lasting aversions. His reviewers he regarded as ignorant beggars selling their opinions about other people. But the "beggars" succeeded in quenching his thirst for literary reform.

For seven years he tried to forget poetry. Doubtless his earlier desire to do something with the Arthurian cycle was not encouraged by the success which greeted Tennyson's *Idyls of the King* in 1859. The decorous sobriety and the smooth, imposing brilliance of the Tennysonian version made Morris's five

Arthurian poems (*The Defense of Guenevere; King Arthur's Tomb; Sir Galahad; The Chapel in Lyonness,* and *A Good Knight in Prison*) seem almost barbaric and obscene in comparison.

So Morris laid his poetry aside, as something for which the British public of his day was not yet fitted, and turned to art and to domestic happiness.

## CHAPTER IV

MORRIS & COMPANY: HONEYMOONING, AND

WEEK-ENDING AT RED HOUSE

A FTER having married in April, 1859, Morris and his young bride spent six weeks on a honeymoon in Paris, Flanders and the Rhineland. At Köln and Koblenz the young poet-artist experienced his first encounters with the Köln paintings and with the soft, mild wines of the Rhine and Moselle valleys. Both encounters strongly influenced his tastes thereafter. There it was that he came to the conclusion, afterwards expressed to Bernard Shaw, Bruce Glasier, and others, that "a bottle of wine, an onion and a hunk of bread are enough to make a meal for any man."

In June the couple returned to London to take rooms at 41, Great Ormond Street, preparatory to moving into the Red House, at Bexley Heath, Upton in Kent, a few miles from the city. These were the "Towers of Topsy," which Morris had already commissioned Philip Webb, now an architect in his own right, to build for him. The site selected was in the midst of an orchard section, rich in apple and cherry blossoms, about six miles from London, not far from Watling Street and the railroad station at Abbey Wood.

According to Arthur Clutton-Brock, artist, critic and author, Morris was now about to enter upon the happiest period of his existence: a period of domestic felicity which was to produce happy outlooks and mature changes in the hitherto somewhat disillusioned young man. In years that followed Morris was to achieve renown by "doing what he most desired to do." Under ordinary circumstances that happiness and renown should have lasted all his life; but "like Tolstoy, he was too great to remain content with it, and, like him, he was driven by his own mind beyond happiness to a harder and a lonelier task."

Edward Burne-Jones, or Ned, as he was called by his friends, was busily engaged in paying court to "Georgie," while Madox Brown, the most gifted of the Pre-Raphaelites, lived with the Morrises on Great Ormond Street. Rossetti was on the verge of marrying Elizabeth Siddal, "Lizzie," he called her; but she was at Hastings, desperately ill again. In May, 1860, just after he did marry her, ill as she was, Rossetti wrote to Madox Brown: "If you are still with Top, as Ned told me you were, best love to the Topsies. The Towers of Topsy must darken the air by this."

The need for materials with which to decorate Red House was an important factor in turning Morris into a manufacturing artist. But the idea for the founding of a firm of manufacturing artists—the firm that was later to gain fame under the name of Morris & Company—originated with Rossetti and Madox Brown. The company was to be a sort of co-operative enterprise among friends, Morris supplying most of the financial backing. Webb, who had left G. E. Street & Company to set up an architect's office of his own, was architect for the new firm. Faulkner, who had tired of his Oxford fellowship and his life of academic boredom, was to be accountant and craftsman. Madox Brown and Burne-Jones were to design stained-glass for churches. There was also Peter Marshall, a friend of Madox Brown's. Morris himself was to become the chief designer for the firm and its leading craftsman. Rossetti was to be an associate in design and in administration. Arthur Hughes, the eighth member, withdrew from London and from the undertaking before the firm actually engaged in business.

Morris and his friends faced a difficult task in those days. According to Arthur Clutton-Brock, the arts of today are certainly not flourishing, "but it is difficult to remember or imagine their desperate condition in 1860. In those days nearly all building was subject to a single principle; and that was as wrong as it could be, for it was the principle of disguise. If a house was built of brick it was covered with stucco so that it might look like stone. Every one, of course, knew stucco from stone; but the mere effort at disguise was considered creditable and a sign of gentility. No one, of course, can have thought stucco, so used, a beautiful material; but no one ever considered the question of its beauty or ugliness. It was chosen for its decency and for social, not æsthetic, reasons.

"And there was the same principle of choice in all the applied arts. Towards the close of the Italian Renaissance these arts had been used by the great to express their power, pride and wealth. . . . People had lost the high passion for a celestial glory which expressed itself in the great churches of the Middle Ages and were determined to make for themselves private Heavens here and now; and they did succeed in making them so far as they could be made out of material things. This tradition of Renaissance splendour still dominated all the arts in 1860; but they expressed then a splendour and a pride which no longer existed. There were, of course, rich people, but they did not know, like the Princes of the Renaissance, how to enjoy their riches; and the art which was provided for them was nothing but an advertisement of their wealth. They liked furniture upon which much time and labour had evidently been spent, because it was costly; but they never asked themselves whether the time and labour had been spent in making the furniture ugly, for they did not wish to enjoy the furniture, but only their consciousness that they were able to pay for it. And by those who were not rich, art was employed to give the illusion that they were rich. Machinery had made it possible to produce cheap imitations of costly ornaments, uglier even than the originals. No one can ever have enjoyed these with their natural senses; what they enjoyed, or tried to enjoy, was merely the illusion of riches produced by them. The sense of beauty, in itself quite a simple instinctive thing, had not entirely disappeared, as one might suppose; it had been degraded into a sense of propriety, so that people called those things beautiful which seemed to them proper to their social station. As for art, except in pictures, few persons were conscious of its existence. Most people thought of it as an obsolete activity which modern civilization had outgrown. They could not see that, being thus purposeless and ignored, it still persisted: not consciously expressing anything that was worth expression, but merely betraying all the meannesses and failures and impotent unrest of the industrial age. And even the most intelligent allowed this purposeless tell-tale art to be imposed upon them, just as good men, in evil times, submit to a morality of cowardice and cruel habits."[1]

Red House, which Philip Webb and Morris built, boasted no exquisite or palatial beauties, but a beauty and a homeliness all its own. Unlike other houses of that period, it was built entirely of red brick and roofed with red tiles. The building was L-shaped, two stories in height, standing amidst a veritable forest of apple and cherry trees, so closely to them, in fact, that in after years some of the apples actually fell inside the windows, disturbing many a restless sleeper on hot August nights. There was also a beautifully planned garden, designed as simply as the house itself, and a quadrangle of rose-trellis. In the midst of this, between the two sides of the building, there was a wellhouse of brick and oak, with a round, tiled spiral roof. For Morris, who planned the exterior, gardening was never a "horticultural game," as it so often is, but rather a true domestic "art."

By September, 1860, the newly married couple were installed in Red House, although its interior decoration was then far from complete; and in April, 1861, Morris, Marshall, Faulkner & Company, as the firm was first called, took city premises at 8, Red Lion Square. For the next four years Morris was to commute almost daily between Bexley Heath and London.

The first circular of the new firm was drawn up by Peter Marshall and Rossetti. It was about all that either of these two

[1] Arthur Clutton-Brock, *William Morris: His Work and Influence*, pp. 59–62.

worthies ever contributed to the success of the enterprise. The "imperious accent" and overweening confidence of Rossetti in the fullness of his powers are detectable in the claims which it posited: *viz.*, the ability of Morris, Marshall, Faulkner & Co. to undertake mural decoration, wood carving of all sorts, stained-glass manufacture, fine embroidering and cloth printing, clay modelling, furniture manufacture with figure and pattern painting, and draperies and tapestries.

Morris himself worked at everything; while living at Red Lion Square with Edward he had even mastered the art of

*From a copy in the British Museum Manuscript Collection, by permission of Miss May Morris and The Macmillan Company.*

The "Company" put Morris and Burne-Jones into
stained-glass attitudes

making embroidery on a specially constructed frame. Madox
Brown and Burne-Jones designed stained-glass. One of the
first enterprises of the newly budding firm was to design
stained-glass windows for their new offices at 8, Red Lion
Square, in which Morris and Burne-Jones were put into
"stained-glass attitudes" in comic form. Philip Webb created
new designs for furniture. Various friends, including William
de Morgan, the novelist, and his wife, Simeon Solomon and
Albert Moore also helped from time to time.

But the business of the new firm did not expand by leaps
and bounds. For several years its existence was largely dependent upon Morris's own diminishing resources. That he was able
to carry on at all during the first four or five years of its existence may be attributed to his own persistency, sagacity and
industry. About a dozen men and boys were hired to aid in the
heavier labour of manufacturing. They were drawn mostly from
the Boys' Home in Euston Road and from Camden Town.
Several of them later developed into craftsmen of considerable
ability. Faulkner's two sisters lent a hand in the painting of
pottery and tiles; Morris's wife and sister-in-law worked in
embroidery; Mrs. Burne-Jones (for Edward had finally married Georgie) assisted ably in all these various enterprises; and
Mrs. Campfield, the wife of the foreman of the plant, aided in
the knitting and weaving of fabrics. At the Exhibition of 1862
the new firm was represented by displays in two stalls of furniture, embroideries, church glass and tile. During that same
year the first of Morris's wallpapers and hangings (the rose
trellis, borrowed from the lawn of Red House, and the Daisy
papers, both "inimitable" according to Mr. Clutton-Brock)
were designed and manufactured for the domestic trade.

From what humble beginnings the firm originated may be
gleaned from the following facts: the original capital invest-
ment consisted of one pound from each of the eight original
members and a loan of one hundred pounds from Morris's
mother. In 1862 a levy of nineteen pounds apiece was made,
but Hughes had long since departed and some of the others

were "broke." This capitalization was not increased prior to the dissolution of the original firm, in 1874, and many hundreds of pounds in deficits had to be made up by the Morris fortune, until the business finally attracted enough attention to enable capital to grow out of the profits. By that time Morris himself was the most famous member of the firm.

Meanwhile, during these years, an altogether happy and delightful life was lived at Red House. The young couple kept open house for the multitudes of friends who descended upon them. Every week-end, it seemed, there was a gala picnic or a festive party for some one. Ned and Georgie, the Rossettis, Swinburne, whom Morris had met during his work on the Union Hall at Oxford, Mr. and Mrs. Arthur Hughes, Mr. and Mrs. William De Morgan, Madox Brown and Philip Webb were only a few among the many friends who visited Red House regularly. They played like happy children. Morris himself, who never stood upon dignity, loved to stand upon a chair and descend spread-eagle fashion. Often the guests played at bowls on the lawn, or drove about the surrounding countryside in a leather-curtained carriage which Morris himself had designed. "O the joy of those Saturdays to Mondays at Red House," wrote Mrs. De Morgan, "the getting out at Abbey Wood Station and smelling the sweet air, and then the scrambling, swinging drive of three miles or so to the house; and the beautiful roomy place where we seemed to be coming home. . . . We laughed because we were happy."

On one of these week ends, January 18, 1861, Morris's first child, a girl infant named Jane Alice after Mrs. Morris and Morris's youngest sister, was born, and Morris dashed off the following note to Madox Brown. "Kid having appeared, Mrs. Brown kindly says she will stay till Monday, when you are to come and fetch her, please. . . . Janey and kid (girl) are both very well."

In these blasé words the burly poet and craftsman tried to conceal the very real emotion which he felt.

In the spring of 1862, the day after her father's birthday,

a second daughter was born. She was named Mary (after the Lady of the day) but she was always called May.

Like many of his friends and tens of thousands of compatriots, Morris had joined a volunteer corps during the war scare of 1859 when the French invaded Sardinia. Each spring for the next three years found him in camp practising with a rifle corps. In June, 1861, when he returned from Wimbledon, he brought his family and the Burne-Joneses, who were then living at Red House, news of the great Tooley Street fire. He decided that between the camp and the fire there was not much room for argument. "I always did hate fireworks." Before long, however, Morris began to fear that he was becoming a quiet citizen, or, as he himself later said, "a typical bourgeois." "I grieve to say," wrote Faulkner during the Christmas season of 1863, that "he has only kicked one panel out of a door for this twelve-month past."

Rossetti, who was a frequent visitor, exulted in the satisfaction of knowing that a hollow near Red House was known as "Hog's Hole," and ever after he was fond of calling "The Towers of Topsy" by the new and worthier appellation of "Hog's Hole." But his real opinion was expressed in a letter to a friend in which he declared: "It is a most noble work in every way, and more a poem than a house such as anything else could lead you to conceive, and an admirable place to live in too."

On one of his early visits to Red House, Rossetti found numerous coats-of-arms, complete with the Morris crest, but with open spaces waiting for the Morris motto, "If I can," to be inscribed, and "in his reckless way" he instantly filled them with another motto, "As I can't." When Morris came home that evening, according to Burne-Jones, "it would have puzzled the discriminator of words to know which of those two disputants was most eloquent in the use of violent English."

At this time, wrote Burne-Jones, Morris was slowly making Red House "the beautifulest place on earth!" For a long time, during this period, Ned and Georgie lived in the house with

Topsy and Jane. Morris's hospitality charmed every one. "It was the most beautiful sight in the world," wrote one visitor, "to see Morris coming up from the cellar before dinner, beaming with joy, with his hands full of bottles of wine and others tucked under his arms." For the christening of Jane Alice there were so many guests that "beds were strewn about the drawing-room, and Swinburne slept on a sofa."

Morris, like the rest of them, loved jokes; and many evenings were spent in humorous make-believe and story-telling. Lady Burne-Jones recalled how on one occasion somebody asked, "Who killed his brother Cain?" and Morris, perhaps a trifle muddled from the bibulous exercise of the evening, immediately shouted, "Abel, of course!" amidst general laughter at his expense. A short time afterward Morris attended the wedding of one of his sisters, and amused his own guests on the following morning at breakfast by telling how he had caught the rector unawares. "I asked him," said Morris, " 'Who killed his brother Abel?' and when he answered 'Cain,' I said 'Hah! I knew you'd say that—every one says it!' " while the breakfast party laughed again.[2]

According to Arthur Clutton-Brock,[3] "Morris was one of those men who are chaffed the more they are admired and loved. His friends knew that he was a great man, but did not treat him as one. Indeed, he never gave himself the airs of a great man, and preferred companionship to admiration. No one resented his furies, because he himself laughed at them when they were over, and never used them to enforce his predominance. He was intolerant of certain opinions; but when he flew into a rage it was the opinion that made him angry, not the person who expressed it. It cannot be said that he suffered fools gladly; but he had no cold contempt for them, and grew angry with trying to make them less foolish. One can see from the accounts of his friends that he forgot himself utterly in whatever he was doing at the moment; and it was, perhaps,

[2]*Memorials*, I, 210. Permission Macmillan Company.
[3]*Op. cit.*, n. 1, *supra*, pp. 75–76.

the incongruity between their general idea of him and his appearance when absorbed in some trivial task which made them laugh at him. Morris, coming up from the cellar with his hands and arms full of bottles, was the very picture of a jolly host out of Dickens. No one would have laughed at him if he had been nothing else. But he was the very picture of a hundred different things, great and small, in one day, and always unconsciously. So his friends laughed to see the essential Morris passing through all those changes and venting the same fury upon a door panel as upon a social iniquity. But they laughed because they were at ease in loving him."

## CHAPTER V

THE HOUSE ON QUEEN SQUARE: LIVING THE GOOD LIFE

AND MANUFACTURING ART

DURING the years which had elapsed since Morris left Oxford his power of wide and rapid reading had not diminished. At odd moments he was forever dipping into a book. Froissart, Chaucer, and the Border Ballads still held favoured places in his heart; Tennyson's later poetry he disliked; Browning's later works lost their charm so far as he was concerned; Keats he believed to be the first modern English poet. Carlyle and Ruskin still appealed to him, yet he was no blind follower. Indeed, as early as 1860, when the fifth volume of *Modern Painters* appeared, he was heard to describe it as "mostly gammon." Other authors to whose works he became devoted were George Borrow, F. Surtees, Dickens, and especially William Cobbett, for whom he felt the keenest sort of admiration. It was said that he knew *Rural Rides* almost by heart. We have Morris's own word for it that during this period he was also reading widely in history and in the history of art. He was never the sort of reader who reads for the sake of reading; he always knew when a book appealed to him, and when one did not he simply dropped it. One time he astonished a friend by telling her offhand some obscure recipe, and when asked by her how he came to know it, he replied that he had once spent a night at an inn where the only reading matter was a cookery book. Since he was interested in cooking, and was himself a fair cook, he had proceeded to assimilate its contents during the course of the evening.

It was late in the summer of 1865, nine years after he left Oxford, that a series of changes affected the fortunes of both

Morris and the firm adversely. The output of the copper mine at Tavistock, one of the chief sources of the Morris income, had declined as early as 1862, and the value of the stocks now began to fall off rapidly. The business of manufacturing art was not yet self-sustaining and deficits had to be made up. Then Mrs. Burne-Jones was attacked by scarlet fever and her ill health prevented the Burne-Joneses from coming to Red House. There had been plans for removing the works to Upton; now these had to be changed. Then Morris himself caught a chill on one of his journeys to and from London and this developed into rheumatic fever. Faulkner, discouraged at the slight returns from the business enterprise, had gone back to Oxford during the preceding year, and in view of all these changes in the lives of the intimate friends, the social life at Red House had declined. Moreover, the task of rearing a family was not so easy, now that the Morrises had two small daughters, Jane Alice and May. So at the end of the summer they decided to give up Red House, obtain a larger site for the factory in Bloomsbury, and live there themselves. This site was found at 26, Queen Square, and thither the Morris family and the Morris Company removed in the autumn of 1865.

One of the main factors in the return to London was Morris's affection for his friends. The Burne-Joneses, it seemed, had to live in London, for Edward's income depended upon his daily work, and his health and happiness upon those of his wife. Rossetti, whose beloved "Lizzie" had died, had turned into an unamiable recluse, scarcely ever leaving the city. Faulkner, whose mother and sisters lived on Queen Square, could make frequent trips to the city, while Red House was too much out of the way for his brief week-ends to make possible many visits. And Morris's wife, if the real truth can be hinted at, was not the sort who thrived well in Morris's company alone. She craved a kind of adulation which Morris could express much better in writing than in actual living. Philip Webb also found it necessary to maintain an office in London if his architectural career was to thrive; and it must be admitted that

Morris himself was happier when he could enjoy the good life of fellowship and companionship and forget his financial and domestic worries by losing himself in the work he loved.

Besides manufacturing art there was another incentive which may have prompted the change. The lure of poetry was again in his blood, so much so that for the past year or two he had been planning a cycle of poems dealing with the Trojan War. But the work did not seem to go well at the Red House. Dissatisfied, he threw it aside unfinished. He came to the conclusion that the dramatic method was not for him: that great poetry and great tales always had their basis in narrative, and that, if he wrote again, it would have to be in the form of long continuous narrative poems such as those of Homer, Chaucer, and Dante.

One side of the feeling which Morris felt for Red House and its associations is shown by his attitude in leaving it. He relinquished the life there not without tears; and once his final departure was taken in that autumn, he never set eyes upon it again. The sight of it, he declared long afterward, would have been more than he could bear.

Queen Square today is but a backwater of the old Bloomsbury, yet in the 'sixties it still boasted some of the suburban Queen Anne dignities of its halcyon days. Its more fashionable residents had been moving in the direction of Russell Square, and now an industrial element was working its way in. The old mansion on its East Side, in which Morris and Company and Morris and family were to live for the next seven years, has long since disappeared, but in Morris's day it was still a respectable mansion. The ground floor was turned into an office and showroom. A large ballroom, connected with the dwelling by a gallery through the yard, became the workshop of the firm. Other workshops were built in the small court at the rear, and a storeroom was secured in Ormond Yard, near by.

Soon after Morris arrived in Queen Square there appeared before him a poor gentleman, a former student of Eton who had fallen upon hard times. Mr. George Warrington Taylor was his name, and for lack of a better job he was employed as a check-taker at the Opera in the Haymarket. He wanted work; like Morris he was a lover of art and music; it had been the music of Wagner which had prompted him to accept his unremunerative task at the Opera House. Moreover, he was an enthusiastic follower and admirer of Rossetti and the Pre-Raphaelites. Naturally, Morris took him on, and George Warrington Taylor became business manager of the firm of Morris and Company until his death five years afterward. It was Mr. Taylor's sense for order and commercial efficiency which contributed, as much as anything, to putting the firm's enterprises on a paying basis.

In 1867 the firm obtained its first important commission, aside from some ecclesiastical redecorations. This was the decoration of the Green Dining Room at the South Kensington Museum, and it attracted the attention of many thousands of persons, greatly enhancing the prestige of both Morris and the company.

Morris soon had reason to be glad of the change in his mode of life. Despite the dirt and squalor of the city, which he detested, he felt as if he "could kiss the London pavement." The business of the firm went along more smoothly now; he had three or four extra hours of leisure because he no longer commuted to his place of business every day; and Mr. Taylor's efficiency saved him many hours of office management and bookkeeping—at neither of which tasks, it must be confessed, did he excel.

So it came to pass that he found time to heed again his instinct for story-telling and verse-making. Though he had been long discouraged with his poetic efforts, the new environments and the new activities of the past few years had served to free his mind from the disappointment caused by the cool reception accorded *The Defense of Guenevere*. In any event, by 1867, nine years after the publication of *Guenevere* and nine years in advance of his most famous poem, *Sigurd*, he composed and published *The Life and Death of Jason*. With its publication the period of immaturity seemed to have ended and Morris emerged not only as a contemporary of Rossetti and Swinburne, but also as an equal. The boy had become the man, and the man was now thirty-three years of age.

## CHAPTER VI

## "THE LIFE AND DEATH OF JASON": MORRIS TURNS
## TOWARD A ROMANTIC LITERATURE OF DISCONTENT

IF one examines the basic ideas in Morris's literature one will find that his observations on life, history, and art are in agreement with his philosophy of history (as it slowly developed during the middle years of his life) and with his opinions (expressed during the same period) on the condition of art, of society, and of the individual. The views obtained by his literary pursuits and writings, like those which he gained from his investigations of history and his experiences in the arts and crafts, led him slowly but inexorably toward "the cause of the people." They led him onward toward an ideal of attempting to repurify a decadent modern civilization. Throughout his long literary career certain ideas that pervaded his earlier poetry and prose were not lost sight of, but found a rich and fuller expression in the poetry and prose of his later years.

We are not surprised to find Norse mythology impelling him to write undergraduate prose romances of life in the North, or the inspiration of the *Nibelungen* occasioning those scenes, thoughts, and characters that brighten the pages of *The Hollow Land*. For in all these Northern images, as Miss May Morris has pointed out, he recognized "something familiar." Thus, one is not surprised when the hero of *The Hollow Land* found the "old city" in heaven "cloistered off . . . before the new city grew golden from the din and hubbub of traffic." This older heaven, to Morris, was the "new heaven" that the "new faith" tells of. A dozen years later in *The Earthly Paradise* he dealt with the same imagery, and again twenty years later in his epic *Sigurd the Völsung;* while thirty-four years later, in *The House of the Wolfings,* he damned once more the din and hubbub of the golden city of Rome. These ethical-socialistic views were to continue to develop.

In addition to his interest in Norse mythology and literature, first developed in Oxford but nourished during the years that followed, Morris had been deeply interested in the legends and the literature of ancient Greece, indeed, ever since his reading of the *Medea* under the tuition of Mr. Guy. And now, after long thought, Morris decided to weave a series of Hellenic and Scandinavian legends into narrative poetry. There had been a long tradition of Greek epic poetry in the Middle Ages; scholars of Byzantium had kept it alive from the second century to the fourteenth. And the successful spread of the Hellenic *Anthology* after its final rendition by a Byzantine scholar-ambassador to Venice (in the days of Chaucer and Edward III) gave Morris the idea of blending a series of Teutonic, Celtic, and Scandinavian legends with those of the Hellenes. The preservation of the Greek tongue in many regions during the Middle Ages (*e.g.,* in Russia and in Central Asia, among others) might easily account for a group of Scandinavian wanderers meeting with a group of Hellenic wanderers in the remote islands of the seas and exchanging stories. It was this concept which led him to write *The Earthly Paradise,* and with it, incidentally, *The Life and Death of Jason.*

But when he had completed his first long narrative poem for inclusion in *The Earthly Paradise* group, it was found to be entirely too long—and therefore, in June, 1867, *The Life and Death of Jason* was published as a separate volume by Bell & Daldy at Morris's expense. But in this instance success was immediate. Swinburne's *Atalanta in Calydon* had lately seized upon the imagination of critics who believed that a new poetic school was rising. Critics who had never seen or read *The Defense of Guenevere and Other Poems* now had the sublime "nerve" to *praise* Morris for choosing "again" (of all things!) "a classical subject"! The only adverse comment which the new book received was "a matter of slight moment," the *Pall Mall Gazette* taking umbrage at Morris's "indifference to manners" when he permitted Medea to obtain her first conversation with Jason "by knocking unexpectedly at his chamber door!"

Morris's opinions concerning the critics underwent a slight change for the better. "Naturally I am in good spirits after the puffs," he wrote on June 20, 1867, "I fancy I shall do pretty well; last week I had made up my mind that I shouldn't be able to publish *The Earthly Paradise* and was very low. . . . I am going to set to work hard now."

Here we lack space to consider the quest of the Argonauts for the Golden Fleece, but as one progresses to the later books of *Jason* one finds increasing references to people who may or may not be happy in their condition of life; and there are increasing references to the force of destiny. Thus, in Book XIII, there are the "houseless people" who, "using neither roof nor sheltering wall, dwelt but in tents, and had no wants at all," which in itself is not conclusive of much, except of Morris's own instinctive liking for a life of barbaric simplicity and Spartan endurance. But we are assured, a little later, that "the Gods, wishing the earth to teem with living wills like theirs," have given men forgetfulness so that they may live more happily; and a little later:

> Yea, if we once were free from fear and spell,
> Then, truly, better all things were than well.

The present writer, unlike the majority of critics, cannot regard *Jason* as pure romance, but rather as an example of the Greek tragic spirit interpreted by a man both primitive and modern in his outlook. Jason himself is no mere child of fortune, "led above the eternal tide of tears," but rather a child of destiny—of the type depicted in the dramas of Æschylus and of Euripides. For, in the nine years that had elapsed since the *Guenevere*, Morris had outgrown the more marked of those romantic and dramatic qualities which had first appealed to him in Malory and in Browning. The boy had become the man, and something more! Hence, in *Jason,* though to a lesser degree than in the later *Sigurd,* there is a newly developing epic quality together with a strength and a rapidity of motion that drives the story forward as ineluctably as the forces of nature and as inexorably as destiny.

In Book XIV of *Jason,* when dealing with the contrasting pictures presented by the Sirens and the Thracian minstrel, Orpheus, certain ideas are developed of a dutiful and joyous *life of work* as opposed to the materialistic, sensuous life of well-being as it exists in all ages among the "comfort-seekers." The Sirens lure the Greek adventurers by singing. Orpheus answers them. The Sirens appeal for a life of comfort, free from toil, change, and fear—but it is only a vision of hopeless monotony in the eyes of Orpheus, and, *ipso facto,* in those of Morris. The entire dialogue may be taken for what it really is: *a plea against Utopias.*

First we hear the Sirens remind the Minyæ of the hard toil and the scanty bread of man, and of the weariness that follows toil: but the answer is that the world will, indeed, be born again, when "the sweet year before thee lies"—a time when one's heart may be glad with the thought of coming pain, and then be vexed with memories—again the sense of duty.

The Sirens remind them that they strive with sick and sinking hearts "to cheat themselves that they might live"—a hint of the sordidness of competitive commerce, of which Morris was to have much to say on later occasions. But Orpheus replies: "Toil rather, suffer and be free."

The Sirens offer the joys of peace, of freedom from sickness and desire, and the pleasures of contented forgetfulness "while the kingdoms pass away." Knowledge they offer, and love, godlike, alone with the Sirens, to those who are weary of the world of warring and of gain-seeking strife. But the answer is that to be weary of worldly strife is to exist *as if one had never been:* to feed on pleasures and to have no thought of good or ill in the world is but an idle dream; and these are things to be resisted: in resisting them will lie "our toil and victory."

And so, despite the last appealing cries of those who would turn aside men who have toil and duty ahead of them, the Minyæ sail on, leaving only one Athenian behind them, of whom none heard again! Their "black prow plunges through the sea,"—and they are assured that all their past and coming toil will not be in vain. And it is interesting that Orpheus, in his opposition to the Sirens' song, should have remembered and called attention to the joys of the Maytime and the celebrations of folk singing in their mirth.

Here is a nice problem: one that Morris had begun to face long before, but more or less romantically and idealistically. And it is notable that the one outstanding piece of dramatic dialogue in *The Life and Death of Jason* should have dealt with this problem so realistically and so courageously. Implicit in his answer are *the necessity of love of work, and of struggle in a just cause,* and *unwillingness to seek the easy and materialistic paradise of idle dreamers.* Surely, in view of this, it is an anomaly that Morris, despite his long "introduction" to *The Earthly Paradise,* and despite his own arduous life of toil, should himself have come to be called *an idle dreamer* and a *Utopian.*

Later, in Book XVI, when Jason is made King of the Colchians, Alcestis cries:

> Dost thou think that fate
> Has yet been stopped by any love or hate,
> Or fear of death, or man's far-shouted fame?
> And still doubt not that I, who have to name
> The wise Medea, in such ways as this
> Have long been struggling for a life of bliss
> I shall not gain; and thus do all men do. . . .

These words might almost have come from Euripides' *Alcestis,* for here the strength of fate is inexorable; against it even the Thracian verses of Orpheus are powerless; and against that fate, or destiny, all men may struggle impotently. But the sorcery of Medea gains for Jason a throne and a queen.

At the moment of his coronation Jason stops and declares that the people must first signify *their* wishes; and the people's voices answer: "Most glorious of thy kin! Be thou our king— be thou our king alone, that we may think the age of iron [the age of tyranny] gone, and Saturn come with every peaceful thing."[1]

After ten years Jason and Medea, now in Corinth, find their love ruined by the fair Glauce, daughter of King Creon; and Medea believes then "that to all earthly men, in spite of right or wrong, and love and hate, one day shall come 'the turn of luckless fate' . . . !" "How," she asks, "could I know, unto what cruel folly men will grow?"

And when Jason discovers the manner of Medea's revenge, he knows that "from their heaven, and laughing, the high Gods gaze on foolish men." Yet, despite his adversity, he became King of Corinth.

> And he began again to cast his eyes
> On lovely things, and hope began to rise. . . .
>
> And longings that had long been gathering
> Stirred in his heart, and now he felt the sting
> Of life within him, and at last he said:
> "Why should I move about as move the dead,
> And take no heed of what all men desire? . . .
>
> I won a kingdom, and I cast it by
> For rest and peace, and rest and peace are gone. . . .
>
> For now the world has swerved from truth and right,
> Cumbered with monsters, empty of delight,
> And, 'midst all this, what honour I may win. . . ."

[1] In early Hellenic mythology Saturn was reputed to be the coming king of a coming golden age—and it is indeed noteworthy that Morris should have seized upon this, as well as upon other resemblances between the early Hellenes and the Medieval Teutons and Norsemen, in order to evolve in *Jason* the same general ideas that were later evolved in his *Sigurd*. Thus, Saturn symbolizes in Morris's *Jason* the same idea as that later symbolized by Sigurd in his *Sigurd*. It would indeed seem that Morris recognized the kinship between the early Hellenes and the early Teutons in race, in religion, and in political organization, as early as the eighteen-sixties.

And as he reasons thus with himself he falls asleep beneath the stem of his ship, which, as the winds rise, rolls over and crushes him.

This is not the doom of the gods, nor yet the story which was to be for the people of the coming world what the Tale of Troy was for the ancient Hellenes, but it has its counter-foils. Clearly it displays courage, highmindedness, love of joy in work, a sense of social obligation and of the necessity of the due reward of toil, and also a realization of the injustice that persisted in every age in the workaday worlds of war, of peace, and of competitive commerce. Moreover, it introduces, as later his Old Norse translations and re-creations were to introduce, the sense of Fate, or of Doom, as something which is inescapable!

One might go a little further and state that Morris, having first considered an idyllic materialist's *Utopia* early in *Jason*, later permits his hero to experiment with the kind of "rest and peace" which most Utopians advocate. But when he does so he finds that both "rest and peace are gone"—problems of a different nature having taken the place of the old ones. It was perhaps this feeling in Morris, at the age of thirty-two, when he wrote *Jason*, which still clung to him twenty-two years later when he ridiculed the mechanized and standardized *Utopia* of Mr. Edward Bellamy's *Looking Backward.*

In this latter connection it is also important to note that as long as Morris felt the hopelessness of achieving his ideals amid the world at large, he tried to play no active role. Only in after years, when he saw what he thought to be an opportunity for the world to realize his ideal, did he endeavour to go out to the people with his message. That aspect of his later career connects directly with his active philosophy of *"Practical* Socialism"—just as the earlier *literary* aspects of his work connect indirectly with his passive philosophy of *"Practical* Socialism." And both are related to his view of society and to his philosophy of history.

# CHAPTER VII

THE NORTHERN SAGAS AND "THE EARTHLY PARADISE"

D URING the Long Vacation of 1867 the Burne-Joneses
lived at Oxford, and there, too, went the Morrises
and the Faulkners. They hoped to have a real vacation, Morris running back and forth on the train to London
one or two days each week to attend to business. He hoped, in
addition, to "get a good job of work done" on *The Earthly
Paradise*, now that *Jason* was out of the way. It was his intention
to bring out a beautiful edition, illustrated with five hundred
woodcuts by Edward Burne-Jones and himself. Many an evening he spent in carving blocks of wood. And many a long
portion of *The Earthly Paradise* was written by him while
journeying to and from London and Oxford on the train. Each
time that he returned to the Beaumont Street lodgings, which
they had taken for the summer, he would burst into the house
with a new roll of completed manuscript to read aloud to
family and friends.

Many of the happiest days of their lives were spent during
that summer in exploring the upper tributaries of the Thames
on boating-parties. At least two of these expeditions were recorded in stanzas of *The Earthly Paradise*, and served as a
premonition, perhaps, of his own future home in that region—
where the quiet upper river rises above the marshland and
branches off among the Wytham hills, beyond the "steel-blue
Windrush" at New Bridge, and beyond the meadows of the
Evenlode:

> What better place than this then could we find
> By this sweet stream that knows not of the sea,
> That guesses not the city's misery,
> This little stream whose hamlets scarce have names,
> This far-off, lonely mother of the Thames?

Summer ended, but the poetry-making went on. By the spring of 1868 seventeen of the twenty-four poems were completed and more than a hundred of the woodcuts were ready. But when the Chiswick Press sent back the trial-sheets the artists were discouraged. Type-founders, compositors, printers,

*From a copy in the British Museum Manuscript Collection, by permission of Miss May Morris and Basil Blackwell, Ltd.*

Morris making a wood block for *The Earthly Paradise.*

Sketched by E. Burne-Jones

and wood-engravers all seemed to be unprepared for that sort of work, and Parts I and II had to be published in ordinary book form in 1868. For this publication Morris had arranged with Mr. F. S. Ellis, a bookseller, collector, and publisher with whom Morris had been on terms of friendship for several years. After the second printing of *The Life and Death of Jason,* that work, together with the rights in Morris's other books, past and future, were turned over to Mr. Ellis, who continued to publish Morris's literary works (at no expense to the author) until his retirement from business in 1885.

The autumn holiday of 1868 was spent at Southwold and it was at about this time that Morris met Eiríkr Magnússon, an Icelander who specialized in Danish and Norse literature at

Cambridge. Magnússon was an enthusiast about everything connected with Iceland, and Morris's work on *The Earthly Paradise* had already revived and expanded his own interest in everything pertaining to Old Norse. They struck up a real friendship which was to result in Morris's serious study of Icelandic, under Magnússon's direction, and in their collaboration in translating many of the Sagas.

The new relationship and the new interest were welcomed by Morris, for in November the Burne-Joneses moved to The Grange, in North End Lane, Fulham, where they were to spend the remainder of their lives. Here Morris, and often Philip Webb, came every Sunday to visit them and to discuss various schemes and projects in literature and in art. "This was the beginning of our Sundays," wrote Burne-Jones long afterward. "There were times of discontinuance, at first, for one reason or another. But for all the later years it was Morris's weekly custom that he should come to breakfast and spend the morning . . . and so it continued until the end. The last three Sundays of his life I went to him."

During the winter months of 1868–69 Morris began to master the bulk of "the heroic literature." Hitherto he had merely "dabbled" in the *Sagas*. In April, 1869, the fruits of the new collaboration resulted in the publication of *The Grettis Saga*, the first book of Morris and Magnússon, and in the same year *The Fortnightly Review* printed their translation of "The Saga of Gunnlaug Worm-Tongue," which was later included in the *Northern Love Stories*.

Meanwhile, Morris continued with his *Earthly Paradise*. "Gudrun's Lovers," perhaps the best poem in the entire work, was finished by June, 1869, and work was begun on "The Fostering of Aslaug."

With Rossetti temporarily out of her life, with the Burne-Joneses secluded in the suburbs and the Faulkners in Oxford, Mrs. Morris's ever-delicate health declined. In fact, by this time, she had become something of a neurotic case, and in the late summer of 1869 her doctors recommended that the Morrises spend a couple of months at Bad-Ems in the Rhineland.

It was the second visit to a region which Morris had already learned to love. Here was the land of the *Nibelungen Lied* and the heart of his favourite wine lands. While staying there he continued to work upon *The Earthly Paradise*, and many a scene from the surrounding countryside found its way into his poetry, where " 'Twixt the tree-boles grey" above him did he see "the terraced way,"

> And over that the vine-stocks, row on row,
> Whose dusty leaves, well thinned and yellowing now,
> But little hid the bright-bloomed vine-bunches.

From Bad-Ems Morris wrote several interesting letters. One of them, directed to his friend and publisher, Mr. Ellis, reads in part as follows:

Many thanks for your letter again, and the copy of The Temple Bar, which did not excoriate my thin hide in spite of a tender contempt with which Mr. Austin seemed to regard me. Commercially I suppose I ought to be grateful to him and am so; from the critical point of view, I think there is as much truth as this in his article: that we poets of today have been a good deal made by those of the Byron and Shelley time—however, in another sixty years or so, when it won't matter three skips of a louse to us . . . I suppose we shall quietly fall into our places. . . .

I shall want about a fortnight after I come home before I begin to feed the free burgher of Berwick-upon-Tweed with my immortal manuscript, and after that I hope there will be no hitch. . . . I'm not quite sure now that I shan't be sold to the Prussian government to sweep up horse-dung in Ems streets (they are very particular about it) —My God, what a bargain I should be!

I have not got any good wine at Ems, and perhaps they don't charge for such as they sell you! but the Grünhauser at Cologne and Coblentz was jolly that hot weather.

In late September, shortly before Morris's own return to London, Part III of *The Earthly Paradise* went through the press, and the third and final volume, Part IV, which he brought back from Germany in October, appeared early in 1870. The entire cycle known as *The Earthly Paradise: Spring, Summer, Autumn, and Winter,* was now complete. Sometime thereafter a student from the University of Marburg wrote to Morris asking whether it was true that he had taken Chaucer for his model, and expressing some doubts of his own on this matter. Morris answered that

The resemblance of my work to Chaucer comes of our both using the narrative method: and even then my turn is decidedly more to Romance than was Chaucer's. I admit that I have been a great admirer of Chaucer, and that his work has had, especially in early years, much influence upon me; but I think not much on my style. . . . I by nature turn to Romance rather than to Classicism, and naturally, without effort, shrink from rhetoric. I may say that I am fairly well steeped in medievalism generally; but the Icelandic Sagas, our own Border Ballads, and Froissart (through Berners' translation of about 1520) have had as much influence over me as (or more than) anything else. I have translated a great deal from the Icelandic, a little from the Old French; and of late have translated Beowulf, for which I have a very great admiration.

Meanwhile, publication of the *Saga* translations of Morris and Magnússon went steadily forward. *The Völsunga Saga* appeared before the last sheets of *The Earthly Paradise* left his hands, and on November 25, 1870, Morris exclaimed: "I must try to get something serious to do!" And a little later: "I confess that I am dull now my book is done . . . perhaps something else of importance will turn up soon."

A careful study of the poems in *The Earthly Paradise* shows that as the work had progressed during its five-year period of composition a subtle change had taken place in Morris's development. The romantic and lyrical elements, often called Chaucerian, which had dominated such early poems as *The Life and Death of Jason* and *The Man Born to Be King,* diminished little by little. With *The Lovers of Gudrun* the change had almost been completed, for in it Morris had produced the first epic poem out of modern England.

These poems reflect the cumulative influence of his continued studies of Old Norse after he left Oxford, because he

had already begun his translations of a few of the *Sagas* before
he met Magnússon. Of the Northern (rather than the Hellenic) tales in *The Earthly Paradise,* at least two, "Ogier the
Dane" and "The Land East of the Sun and West of the
Moon," were probably completed before he began to study
with Magnússon. But of them all, *The Lovers of Gudrun*
displays the Northern influence most clearly: a Northern influence that was to be marked in much that Morris wrote and
thought hereafter. This poem was based in part upon Morris's
own adaptation of the *Laxdaela Saga.* Instinct with the forces
of destiny and of doom, it becomes, in his hands, the "November
Tale" of the Northerners:

> Yea, I have looked and seen November there:
> The changeless seal of change it seemed to be,
> Fair death of things that, living once, were fair;
> Bright sign of loneliness too great for me,
> Strange image of the dread eternity,
> In whose void patience, how can these have part,
> These outstretched feverish hands, this restless heart.

*The Lovers of Gudrun* is a tale of what lay behind "the
mask of pensive eyes, world weary,"

> So beguiled
> By ancient folly. . . . What wild
> Strange flickering hopes ineffable might lie,

of people who lived the sort of lives which, "in after years,"
could give

> Some pleasure at the very thought of it . . .
> At least not quite consumed by sordid fear,

and of people who "slowly led the changed and weary days
unto the gateway of the silent place where either rest or utter
change shall be."[1]

The entire poem reads like a sort of dirge to the passing of
the civilization of the old North.

[1]*The Earthly Paradise,* II, 199–200; 315; 381; 382.

## CHAPTER VIII

### DISCOVERING ICELAND AND KELMSCOTT MANOR

DURING the spring months of 1870, just prior to the completion of the *Völsunga Saga,* Morris had been sitting for the well-known portrait by Watts. By May of that year everything seemed to be completed for the time being and Morris was restless for something to do. He dabbled at painting and illumination, presenting Mrs. Burne-Jones with a beautifully illuminated volume of his poems. For a long time thereafter he interested himself, as time permitted, in the illumination of manuscripts.

Watts's famous portrait was an idealization of Morris in the prime of life. The "powerful and beautiful head" was almost Christlike. "The massive head with its thickly clustering dark curls; the vague inexpressive eyes; the sensitive mouth, a little overweighted by the broad, frank brows, are recorded in it with the felicity of genius," according to Doctor J. W. Mackail.

Usually Morris did only what he wanted to do, but at the moment he was not sure of what he wanted and his restlessness consequently increased. He paced the floor, "like a caged lion," so his friends said, and in his superabundant vitality he seemed to display the untamed vehemence of a wild creature. London weighed upon him and he waited impatiently for something of importance to do. But first, it seemed, he must get away for a while.

The "things of importance" which next turned up in Morris's life were the discovery and purchase of Kelmscott Manor and his first Icelandic journey.

Both he and his wife had been thinking rather vaguely of securing another country house in which to spend holidays and summers. Early in 1871 they noted an advertisement for Kelm-scott Manor, near Lechlade in Gloucestershire, about thirty miles above Oxford on the upper Thames. In those days it was approached by a long winding road through the Gloucester-shire hills. It lay in a sleepy, lonely region, woodlands rising to the northwest toward the Cotswolds. The house itself had been built in Stuart times, but in the Elizabethan manner. Morris immediately fell in love with the place, and Rossetti, whose health had been more than usually poor, was anxious that they take it jointly. On May 17, 1871, Morris wrote as follows to Faulkner:

I have been looking about for a house for the wife and kids, and whither do you guess my eye is turned now? Kelmscott, a little village about two miles above Radcott Bridge—a heaven on earth; an old stone Elizabethan house like Water Eaton, and such a garden! close down on the river, a boat house and all things handy. I am going there again on Saturday with Rossetti and my wife: Rossetti because he thinks of sharing it with us if the thing looks likely.

Rossetti and the Morrises moved into the house in July. Rossetti stayed on until a severe illness in the following year forced him to go to Scotland, where he remained with friends until September, 1872.

Meanwhile, a recent acquaintance of Morris's, Mr. W. H. Evans of Forde Abbey in Dorset, had been planning a trip to Iceland, and thither Eiríkr Magnússon was also anxious to go, incidentally to visit his native home and kinsfolk. Faulkner, too, was curious to see Iceland; and Morris's own enthusiasm, of many years duration, had long been stimulated by the Old Norse translations. So to Iceland they went. Morris decided to keep a diary of his journey, with a view to future publication: a project that was faithfully executed but never published.

Early in June the four friends sailed from Granton, and two days later put in at the Faroes. Here Morris noted chiefly the costumes of the natives and the boats that "cannot have changed in the least since the days of the Sagas." He was especially interested in the "odd sort of Phrygian cap" worn by the natives of the islands, by their stockings and knee-breeches, and by their "coats like knights' *just-au-corps.*" Ashore, they hiked across the main island from Thorshaven to Strauney. "We turned," wrote Morris in his diary,

and went along the ridge of the mountain-neck. . . . As we rounded a corner of the stony stepped grey hills, below us lay a deep calm sound, say two miles broad, a hog-backed steep mountain-island form- ing the other side, next to which lay a steeper islet, a mere rock; and then other islands. . . . It was like nothing I had ever seen, but strangely like my old imaginations of places for sea-wanderers to come to. . . . It looked as if you might live for a hundred years before you would ever see a ship sailing into the bay there; as if the old life of the saga-time had gone, and the modern life never reached the place.

Shortly afterward he wrote to his wife:

I have seen nothing out of a dream so strange as our coming out of the last narrow sound into the Atlantic, and the huge wall of rocks astern in the shadowless midnight twilight: nothing I have ever seen has impressed me so much.

Two days after leaving the Faroes they sighted Iceland near Berufirth, where the boat stopped on its way to Reykjavik.

We saw the mainland, a terrible shore indeed: a great mass of dark grey mountains worked into pyramids and shelves, looking as if they had been built and half ruined; they were striped with snow high up, and wreaths of cloud dragged across them here and there. . . . We were far enough presently to look into Berufirth, and to see the great pyramid of Buland's Tindr. . . . On the west side we could see a line of rocks and skerries cut out from the shore, low green slopes behind them, and then the mountain feet; looking up from the firth, which was all sunlighted now, the great peaks lowered till they seemed to run into the same black, green-striped hill-sides as on the east.

On July 14 they reached Reykjavik, where with two guides and twenty horses (later increased to twenty-eight) they pre- pared for a tour of the country, carrying with them 1000 silver dollars in canvas bags. During the two days spent in preparing for their journey they met a number of prominent Icelanders, one of whom was Jón Sigurdson, President of the Althing, "whose editions of Sagas I know very well," wrote Morris in his diary. "He seemed a shy, kind, scholarlike man, and I talked Icelandic all I might to him."

The first night they camped out and Morris was tremendously impressed by the northern night: "It was light enough to see to read; wonderfully clear, but not like daylight, for there were no shadows at all." Thence they proceeded eastward into the region of Njala, by way of Eyrarbakki and Oddi; thence to Bergthorsknoll, the home of Njal, and on to Lithend, the site of Gunnar's Hall, and up the valley of the Markfleet.

Past this the cliffs were much higher, and most unimaginably strange: they overhung in some places . . . they had caves in them just like the hell-mouths in thirteenth century illuminations; or great straight pillars were rent from them with quite flat tops of grass and a sheep or two feeding on it, however the devil they got there: two or three tail-ends of glacier too dribbled over them hereabouts . . . one could see their spiky white waves against the blue sky.

Here the four travellers dismounted and scrambled over one of the cliffs:

Its great blocks cleft into dismal caves . . . and dribbling wretched white streams into the plain below: a cold wind blew over it in the midst of the hot day, and apart from my having nearly broken my neck on it, I was right glad to be in the saddle again.

From Lithend the friends headed northward to the Geysirs. This place, wrote Morris with considerable indignation, "has made Iceland famous to Mangnall's Questions and the rest, who have never heard the names of Sigurd and Brynhild, of Njal, or Gunnar, or Grettir, or Gisli, or Gudrun: not mentioned in any Icelandic writing before the eighteenth century."

On July 29 they started northward again, through "the horrible black mountains of the waste" toward Waterdale and the firths of the North Sea, "including an exploration of the great cave of Surts-hellir." These scenes impressed themselves upon

Morris's imagination unforgettably and were later redescribed by him in such prose romances as *The Well at the World's End,* *The Land of the Glittering Plain,* and *The Wood Beyond the World.*

Pressure of time forced the party to cut short its exploration of the northern region, "where Grettir lived strangely for the last three years of his life and where he died at last in the great fight of the two against the eighteen." Thence they turned westward into Midfirthdale, "where Bjarg, Grettir's birthplace, stands by its castellated rocks." Thence they went on to Thorodstead, and around a long sea inlet into Laxdale, reaching Herdholt on August 6. Here Morris studied the traditions of the region for several days, and then wrote home:

I have seen many marvels and some terrible pieces of country; I slept in the home-field of Njal's house, and Gunnar's, and at Herdholt: I have seen Bjarg, and Bathstead, and the place where Bolli was killed, and am now a half-hour's ride from where Gudrun died. I was there yesterday, and from its door you see a great sea of terrible inky mountains tossing about; there has been a most wonderful sunset this evening that turned them golden.

A week later the party reached Grettir's Lair on the Fairwood-fells; on August 22 they crossed the White-water, whence, after resting for a day at Reykholt, they proceeded to Thingvalla, the last point of their outward journey. Here they spent two days and then rode the remaining distance back to Reykjavik in a rainstorm.

On the evening of the third day their boat came in, and on September 6 it docked at Granton. Here Morris caught the night mail for London. All the way back home he dreamed of "the beautiful and terrible land," and of the many tales that had yet to be told concerning it. These dreams and these tales were to haunt him for the rest of his life. Nothing again could ever quite take the place of the northern light, the northern land, and the northern people.

Soon he was back at Kelmscott Manor, only to discover that

his wife was wrapped up in her dreams of beauty and her wistful yearning for the garden scenes in which Rossetti had endeavoured with blind devotion to exaggerate her beauty on canvas. But Rossetti was now off in Scotland, abject and unwell, his mind a torrent of celestial and horrible imaginings, his soul defeated by the imagined hostility of friends and enemies alike. So life at Kelmscott Manor was not so happy as it might have been.

"I rather miss the mountains," Morris wrote shortly after his return, "which is not what I expected, for I used to consider myself a hater of them." Somehow, the well-loved valley of the upper Thames seemed strangely flat and characterless to him. Strangely enough, he also missed London, for the second time in his life—or perhaps it was merely restlessness—for before the month was out he was writing that he wanted to be in London again. "I feel as if my time were passing with too little done in the country: altogether I fear that I am a London bird; its soot has been rubbed into me, and even these autumn mornings can't wash me clean of loneliness."

## CHAPTER IX

"LOVE IS ENOUGH"—BUT MORRIS IS STILL DISSATISFIED

M ORRIS'S first task after his return from Iceland was the composition of *Love Is Enough*, from which quotations have been taken to introduce the various books of this biography and to end the work. Technically, this poem was the most difficult of all his poetic efforts and one which gave him much trouble. For a long time, he wrote, he "couldn't make it march." But it was completed at length, went to the press in November, 1872, and appeared early in 1873.

*Love Is Enough* summed up what the poet had left unsaid in his lyrical and dramatic verse forms: it was "a dream within a dream," showing the life of the spirit toward which love leads. Pharamond, the hero, sees actuality recede from a late materialistic world which has become strangely unimportant. It is difficult to believe that this poem did not represent, symbolically, a spiritual autobiography of Morris himself. In any event he wrote it for himself and for his wife, and to please only himself. No one else, not even the appreciative Mr. George Bernard Shaw, seemed afterward to be aware of its intended meanings.

The coldness with which this book was received did not disturb the poet: he was used, now, to having unmitigated contempt mixed with uncomprehending praise of his work. He knew also that he had successfully resurrected a poetic form which had been dead for three centuries. What George Meredith or the public at large might say of it did not matter.

Continuing his work of resurrection, both in art and in literature, was to be his chief and almost only joy for several years to follow. These activities were interrupted by only three events of importance: the enlargement of the business at 26,

Queen Square, which necessitated the removal of the Morris family (when it was in London) to a small house on the Turnham Green Road not far from Hammersmith Station, in December, 1872; the Morrises' first Italian tour in the spring of 1873; and Morris's second journey to Iceland in the summer of the same year.

For a while Morris plunged into the arts and crafts with renewed energy: he seemed determined to forget his frustrated soul and his rather empty domestic life in work of the hardest kind. But this could not hold him in his present state of spiritual dissatisfaction: hence his trip to Italy, and his second Icelandic journey.

Italy did not excite him much; he still remained "a northern bird" in his own words. "Do you suppose," he exclaimed, "that I shall see anything in Rome that I cannot see in Whitechapel?" But he was not altogether unappreciative, even though he learned to hate thoroughly Renaissance art and architecture.

In Italy he liked best the late medieval work—which was only natural for a convinced Pre-Raphaelite—and he liked especially the cloisters of the Santa Maria Novella in Florence, all the more since its altar-piece contained the well-loved Van der Goes's "Adoration of Jesus." But from this time onward he lost few opportunities to state his preferences for the art and architecture of the North and for the literature and the ethics of the Old Norse. He returned from Italy so filled with love for Iceland that he decided to revisit immediately that "sad, cold, beautiful" land.

His second journey to Iceland only deepened the adoration which he already felt:

The glorious simplicity of the terrible and tragic, but beautiful land, with its well-remembered stories of brave men. . . . I feel as if a definite space of my life had passed away, now that I have seen Iceland for the last time.

He felt that he dared not return to it again, lest he be tempted to remain forever in solitary happiness.

As I looked up at Charles' Wain tonight, all my travel there seemed to come back on me, made solemn and elevated in one moment, till my heart swelled with the wonder of it.

According to his daughter, Miss May Morris:

It was the northern genius that something deeply rooted in him recognized as *familiar*—the Northman's outlook on life; the keen

From a copy in the British Museum Manuscript Collection, by permission of Miss May Morris and The Macmillan Company.

"Morris has come back from Iceland more enslaved with passion for ice and snow and raw fish than ever."

temper, the logical thought, the directness of action, and, perhaps, above all, the rugged good-humoured acceptance of the world as it is and the absurdities and diversities of mankind. . . . In Gwalia and in the land of Erin the Celtic heroes are nearer akin to our poet; yet their histories, their faults and excellences apart, do not draw him as he is drawn by those of the North Teutonic people.[1]

Morris's prefaces to the *Gretla* and the *Völsunga* Sagas indicate the almost mystical appeal which he felt in these stories: "When the change of the world has made our race nothing more than a name of what has been—a story too—then it should be to those who come after, no less than the Tale of Troy has been to us."

[1]May Morris, I, 447–48.

Edward Burne-Jones, now living in a world of artistic sub-
urbia, wrote to Mr. Fairfax Murray in September of 1873 to
the effect that "Morris has come back from Iceland more enslaved with passion for ice and snow and raw fish than ever
before—I fear I shall never drag him to Italy again,"[2]—and he
decorated his message with one of his inimitable cartoons de-
picting Morris, dressed as an Eskimo, seated on an ice-bound
coast attacking a huge raw fish in approved "watermelon style."

Years afterward, when William Morris was addressing one
of his innumerable Socialist audiences, he so far forgot himself
as to digress on the virtues of the Northmen:

The Northmen considered it disgraceful to brag . . . and still
more to blacken the fame of an enemy—which no doubt his instinct
showed him was the stupidest of slanders, since, if your enemy is an
incompetent coward, the less your glory if you beat him, and the more
your shame if he beats you. . . .

The real religion of these Northern people was the worship of
courage.

Their morality is simple enough: strive to win fair fame, is one
precept. Says Hávamál:

> Waneth wealth and fadeth friend,
> And we ourselves shall die;
> But fair fame dieth nevermore,
> If well ye come thereby.

This, he added, was "not the worship of success," it was just
the opposite.

[2]*Memorials*, II, 45. Permission of The Macmillan Company.

## CHAPTER X

---

SO remarkable and versatile a personality as that of William Morris must have left many impressions, as different as distinct, upon the minds of those who knew him. They recognized in him a brilliant poet, an astute businessman, a natural-born craftsman, a restless traveller and enthusiast of all traditional ways of life, as well as a lovable personality. Walter Crane recalled that he once heard Morris say that of the six different personalities which he recognized within himself at various times, he often wondered which was "the real William Morris." For they who knew him best were well aware that "the idle dreamer of an empty day" could also be an enthusiastic artist and craftsman, a passionate man of action, a shrewd man of business, a keen politician, and a quiet observer of nature and life.

One thing that every one recognized was the fact that Morris practised what he preached and preached what he practised. He was not one of those "arty souls" who believed that æstheticism and romance implied the right to "think, act and love freely." Although Rossetti's attention to his wife must have irritated him exceedingly, he said nothing about it and sought no consolation elsewhere. According to Frank Norris, if we may trust that ubiquitous authority, Morris once declared that ideas of romantic love were nonsense since "all women taste the same," and all were equally unsatisfactory. That may have been his way of justifying his own moral path; in any event, he paid no undue attentions to other women and paid no heed to the personal interests of some of his friends.

His attitude toward the men and boys who worked in his factory was one of faith, justice and personal interest. He asked of no one what he himself was not willing to undertake. Thus, when he began to experiment with the restoration of the art of dyeing, he himself worked at the vats with the other workers. An old friend tells the story of how he called at Morris's "works" one day and, on inquiring for the master, heard a strong, cheery voice call out from some inner den: "I'm dyeing, I'm dyeing, I'm dyeing!" and the well-known, robust figure of the craftsman presently appeared in his blue shirt-sleeves, his hands stained blue from the vat where he had been at work. "He always described himself as an artist working with assistants." He trained others to perform what he himself had learned to accomplish. Mr. Dearle, who became chief of the Merton Abbey Works—whither Morris & Company removed its plant in 1881, after the death of Mr. George Warrington Taylor— became exceedingly skillful. Many other youths owed much of their training and recognition to William Morris's personal interest in their careers.

Meanwhile, his literary resurrections continued, chiefly by means of translations. He worked upon a series of old and new Icelandic tales which were to be published under the somewhat misleading title of *Three Northern Love Stories*, and upon a translation of the *Æneid* of Virgil, done in a spirit more Teutonic than classical. Both works were published in 1875.

But with literary and business successes there came new sordid worries. His associations with wealthy customers, who thought they knew what they wanted by way of rugs, tapestries and wall-papers, frequently sickened him: he told one wealthy customer who craved warm shades of grey and brown that he could find those colours in the road outside, and showed him the door. And now his personal and business associates gave him cause for great personal sadness. There had been a gradually declining friendship with Rossetti since 1871, and in connection with the business of the firm it seems that Rossetti and Marshall, who had contributed less than the others to the success of the enterprise, and Madox Brown, who recognized the "technicalities of the law," were willing to insist upon their legal rights. In other words they demanded a share of the profits instead of seeing present profits go to pay back the past loans from the Morris estate. There resulted a struggle within the company. As the Countess Warwick has said: "In the eyes of the law the partners were equals: in the eyes of common sense Morris was the owner of almost the whole business. Rossetti and Marshall and Madox Brown stood by their legal rights; and when the partnership was dissolved in 1875—leaving the business in Morris's hands alone—the conduct of these three necessarily resulted in the severance of their friendship with the man whose good-nature had not guarded himself against such developments." From that time onward the firm's name was Morris & Company.

It would seem that throughout the 'seventies Morris's mind had been turning ever more in the direction of social inequalities and of what he was later to call the "legalized commercial warfare" of the modern age. His trips to Iceland and his intensive study of the old Norse ways of life could not help but bring before his mind a comparison between medieval and modern standards. For, with its literature, Morris had been drinking in the social and religious ethic of the North. In his mind he saw the dream of the free northern communities—especially the Icelandic Federation—as an ideal which contrasted vigorously with the social, political and economic relationships of his own world. As early as March 26, 1874, he wrote:

Surely, if people lived five hundred years instead of threescore and ten they would find some better way of living than in such a sordid, loathsome place, but now it seems to be nobody's business to try to better things. . . . But look, suppose people lived in little communities among gardens and green fields, so that you could be in the country in five minutes' walk, and had few wants, almost no furniture . . . and no servants, and studied the arts of enjoying life, and finding out what you really wanted: then I think one might hope civilization had really begun. But as it is, the best that one can wish for this country is some great and tragical circumstance, so that if they cannot have pleasant life, which is what one means by civilization, they may at least have a history and something to think of. . . . Sad grumbling, but . . .

Late in the same summer we find him apologizing to Mrs. Howard, after a visit to Naworth, for his part in an argument against the darkness and bleak ideals of contemporary civilization:

I hope you will let me come again some time, and that you will think me less arrogant on the—what shall I say?—Wesleyan-tradesman-unsympathetic-with-art subjects, than you seemed to think me the other day. But I think that to shut one's eyes to ugliness and vulgarity is wrong, even when they show themselves in people not un-human. Do you know, when I see a poor devil drunk and brutal, I always feel a sort of shame, as if I myself had had some hand in it. Neither do I grudge the triumph that the modern mind finds in having made the world quieter and less violent; but I think that this blindness to beauty will draw down a kind of revenge one day: who knows?

So perhaps the gods are preparing troubles and terrors for this world once again, that it may once again become beautiful . . . for I do not believe that they will have it dull and ugly forever.

Perhaps one cause for his grievance was that his imitators in the commercial world were seizing upon his worst past creations. The colours which he had been unable to obtain before he resurrected the art of dyeing did not seem to appeal to the "unionists" of art and industry. Ugly colours which he had foresworn for some time now—the so-called peacock-blue and sage-green, his pet aversions—became obstinately associated with his name through ignorant imitation and careless repetition of gossip as much as by careless or malicious detraction.

In the spring of 1876 Morris resigned his directorship in the Devon Great Consols Company and decided to take another plunge into the fields of literature and scholarship. On this occasion he wrote to his mother:

Dear Mother:—I have just come from the D. G. C. meeting and, I suppose, ended my business there, except for receiving my annual 100 pounds. . . . Afterward, I went down (or up) to Oxford for two days at Whitsuntide, and I am going there about the middle of June again to take my M. A. degree; which is perhaps rather a fad of mine; but I thought I might indulge it for once.

A little later we find his sarcasm against the contemporary scene bursting out in another letter in which he said: *The Athenæum* has been very civil to me about that scrap of poem I published in it the other day, though it was not worth publishing, and has sent me twenty pounds; it seems, such is the world's injustice and stupidity, that it was a success—never mind, I shall pay for it when my new poem [*Sigurd*] comes out."

For upwards of a year he had been seeking distraction from other dissatisfactions by the composition of what he himself said was to be his highest literary achievement: an epic poem, entirely his own, to immortalize the Völsunga Saga. This was his *Sigurd the Volsung*, completed in 1876, which will be treated in our next chapter.

Meanwhile, as his art business had expanded he had come more and more to despise the demands and expectations of what he termed his "bourgeois customers." Art and society, as he had long ago learned from William Cobbett, and later from Carlyle and Ruskin, were becoming "cheap and tawdry." "Cheap and tawdry" was an epithet which Morris himself was soon to employ on an inspired scale to designate the pressing evils of a Victorian society which was, he believed, turning rotten at the core. He had said so at Naworth, and he would say so more frequently as time went on. But in spite of these thoughts he continued to work upon his poetry in almost every leisure moment.

## CHAPTER XI

## "SIGURD THE VOLSUNG" AND A POETRY CHAIR
### AT OXFORD

IN examining the basic ideas of Morris's literary works one finds that his observations regarding life, history and art are in distinct agreement with his views concerning the individual and society under varying historic conditions. One will note, too, that these views led him eventually to the cause of the people—to an attempt to repurify decadent modern civilization—and that the ideas which pervaded his earlier poetry were not lost sight of, but found a richer and fuller expression in the poetry and prose of his later years.

While he was reading and translating the old Norse literature he became much interested in the religion of the Norsemen, and especially in the legend of *ragna rök,* the decline and fall of the gods in their last great battle. This made upon Morris's mind an indelible impression. Henceforth "The Doom of the Gods" and "The Dusk, or Twilight, of the Gods" frequently occur as expressions used by Morris to indicate the "great change" in an old order and the antecedent of a new. As time went on he was to believe more and more firmly in a coming great change, or revolution, within society. In the preceding chapter we have noted that as early as March, 1874, Morris had certainly been thinking of the "revenge of the Gods" against modern civilization.

What Morris did was to fit the ideas of Norse mythology into his own creed. That it helped him to become the Pagan which he afterward claimed to be, there can be little doubt. That Norse ideas and ideals made a more favourable impression upon him than did those of his own time and civilization there can also be but little doubt. As Morris himself once wrote, he found his Icelandic studies a good corrective for "the maundering side of medievalism."

A skeptic might infer that Morris came under the influence of Professor Magnússon, his Cambridge tutor and collaborator, or of Professor John Henry Middleton, whom he had met on his foreign tours, or of the Icelanders themselves, and that consequently his ideas on Northern superiority were not typical of him. As a matter of fact, however, it is in Morris's own writings and not in the ones done in collaboration that such ideas come most forcefully to the front. Even in the earliest of Morris's Oxford poems—a poem of considerable length written in 1853 and entitled *The Dedication of the Temple*—he wrote:

> O, South! O, sky without a cooling cloud;
> · O, sickening yellow sand without a break;
> O, palm with dust a-lying on thy leaves;
> O, scarlet flowers burning in the sun:
> I cannot love thee, South, for all thy sun,
> For all thy scarlet flowers or thy palms;
> But in the North forever dwells my heart.
> The North with all its human sympathies,
> The glorious North, where all amidst the sleet,
> Warm hearts do dwell, warm hearts sing out with joy;
> The North that ever loves the poet well. . . .

This is no isolated instance. Morris's whole life is an exemplification of the fact that Northern and Western ideas and ideals were typical of all that he did and of all that he stood for. Doctor Mackail has said that there seemed to be so much of the Viking spirit in Morris that even his best friend, Edward Burne-Jones, once declared that Morris was really a sort of Viking, set down in these strange times, and making art because there is nothing else, nowadays, for a Viking to do.

In the *Northern Love Stories*, in the translations of the *Grettis Saga* and the *Völsunga Saga*, one sees, presumably, the learning of Magnússon and the literary art of Morris; but one sees also the spirit of the Old Norse heroes implicit in their pages. But one looks in vain for the insertions of typically socialistic Morrisiana, such as distinguish his own writings, or for Northern racial and cultural preferences such as distinguish certain pages of *The Earthly Paradise, Sigurd the Volsung,* and the later prose romances. Of the latter, *The House of the Wolfings* sets forth in no uncertain terms the virtues of the Germanic Goths as contrasted with the decadence of the effete Romans; while in *The Roots of the Mountains* the Germanic tribes of the Alps are the heroes who stand opposed to the Asiatic Huns.

In *Sigurd the Volsung* there are lines referring to

The last of the days of battle, when the host of the Gods is arrayed
And there is an end forever to all who were once afraid;

and to the time,

When the new light yet undreamed of shall shine o'er earth and sea;

and there are the famous lines, after Sigurd kills Regin:

Dead are the foes of God-home that would blend the good and ill;
And the world shall yet be famous, and the Gods shall have their will.
Nor shall I be dead and forgotten, while the earth grows worse and
worse,
With the blind heart blind o'er the people, and binding curse with curse.

As the trials of the Old Norse heroes were done away with in the death of the old gods—the doom of *ragna rök* and the coming new day when peace and happiness will abide in the world—so Morris transferred the situation metaphorically to make it apply to the evils of his own society. There can be no doubt that he hoped for the transformation of mercenary ideals, of competitive commerce, and of all the "old gods" of modern law, of modern morality, of social conventionalities in the Victorian sense, of modern art, and of modern politics and religion. And, if necessary, he wanted them to be destroyed by a revolution in society which would make mankind happy by replacing false and ugly ideals and beliefs with those which Morris felt to be superior. Then man will grow to be an intelligent and artistic animal, experiencing beauty in life and joy in work rather than ugly surroundings and sordid tasks; and this will bring a new fellowship among men.

And thus, although in *Sigurd* Morris was working on the creation of a great epic poem for the race, designed primarily as literature and not as propaganda, and although he was following closely the Old Norse models, he could not help registering his disgust with conditions under the "old gods"—with materialistic concepts—and, by the introduction of his own ideals, hint at the nature of things as they should be.

So it happens that at the very beginning of *Sigurd*, when the people are putting out from shore, we are informed that

> The kings' sons dealt with the sail-sheets, and the earls and dukes of war
> Were the halers of the hawsers and the tuggers at the oar.

Again, at the beginning of the second book, in writing of the birth of Sigurd, the son of Sigmund, Morris says:

> Peace lay on the land of the Helper and the house of Elf his son;
> There merry men went bedward when their tide of toil was done,
> And glad was the dawn's awakening, and the noon-tide fair and glad;
> There no great store had the Franklin, and enough the hireling had. . . .

> 'Twas a country of cunning craftsmen, and many a thing they wrought,
> That the lands of the storm desired, and the homes of warfare sought.

These last lines suggest Morris's hatred of commercial competition and the imperialistic struggles bred by it. Materialistic ambition he detested, and so, in describing the villainous Atli, who wanted to marry Gudrun in order to secure the wealth of the Niblungs, Morris wrote:

> Now there was a king of the Outlands, and Atli was his name,
> The lord of a mighty people, a man of marvellous fame,
> Who craved the utmost increase of all that kings desire;
> Who would reach his hand to the gold as it ran in the ruddy fire,
> Or go down to the ocean-pavements to harry the people beneath,
> Or cast up his sword at the Gods, or bid the friendship of death.

Again and again in *Sigurd* the poet himself seems to look forward to a time when "the new light yet undreamed of shall shine o'er earth and sea," and to a "day of better things," and to "many a hope accomplished, and many an unhoped change."

The conflict in *Sigurd* resolves itself not only around love and greed and envy, but around war and peace as well. When coming war threatens, one feels the poet himself, in keeping with the Norse spirit, rise to higher levels. Thus does Grimhild bid King Giuki's sons good-bye, and thus do they depart:

Be wise and mighty, O kings, and look in mine heart and behold
The craft that prevaileth o'er semblance and the treasured wisdom
    of old;
I hallow you thus for the day, and I hallow you thus for the night,
And I hallow you thus for the dawning with my father's hidden
    might.
Go now, for ye bear my will, while I sit in the hall and spin;
And tonight shall be the weaving, and tomorn the web shall ye win.

So they leap to the saddles aloft, and they ride and speak no word,
But the hills and the dales are awakened by the clink of the sheathéd
    sword:
None looks in the face of the other, but the earth and the heavens gaze,
And behold the kings of battle ride down the ancient ways.

Yet another and more pacific spirit sometimes prevails above the warlike longing, however less spectacular it may be:

And I would that the loving were loved, and I would that the weary
    should sleep,
And that man should harken to man, and that he that soweth should
    reap.

The symbolism of *Sigurd* was excellently summed up by Arthur Clutton-Brock when he wrote that these struggles of which Morris tells do not result from "old, unhappy, far-off things," but rather from the same struggle of forces that produce our own modern conflicts. Morris himself wrote of the original *Völsunga Saga* that "When the change of the world has made our race nothing more than a name of what has been—a story too—then it should be to those who come after us no less than the Tale of Troy has been to us."

But when Morris was completing his poem of *Sigurd the Volsung* he had expressed the foreboding that when it appeared his critics would make him pay for his former unmerited success. He was not to be disappointed. The new volume was "languidly received." It was almost becoming a habit. Yet, as Doctor Mackail has pointed out, "popularity with any large mass of thoughtless opinion was not a thing he very much cared for."

A modicum of success continued, however, to dog him in certain circles. Before the following year was out he was approached by various gentry who informed him that his name had been suggested for the Oxford Chair of Poetry. To these suggestions he at length replied:

I feel that I am not the man to fill the post: I suppose the lectures a Poetry Professor should give ought to be either the result of deep and wide scholarship in the matter, or else pieces of beautiful and ingenious rhetoric. . . . Also may I say without offense that I have a lurking doubt as to whether the Chair of Poetry is more than an ornamental one, and whether the Professor of a wholly incommunicable art is not rather in a false position: nevertheless I would like to see a good man filling it.

As a matter of fact Morris was beginning to rebel against poetry as well as against the unartistic civilization that seemed everywhere to surround him. The current state of politics, with politicians using the new Near Eastern question to conceal their domestic difficulties; the disappointments which he had suffered in his artistic and literary career, and at the hands of at least some of his artistically and poetically minded friends; the ideas which had come to him from the Old Norse literature and ethics; and his own admitted failure (at heart) to resurrect the art and the poetry of the past—all these factors in his discontent were now combining to swing him into the ranks of "the railers against civilization." Meanwhile, his studies in history and archæology continued unabated, and it is likely that they had culminated in his feeling the need of, as well as the desire for, the Oxford degree of Master of Arts.

In brief, he had arrived at a stage in his mental and spiritual development in which positive experiences in his own life, as well as his intellectual investigations, were reawakening the need he had felt twenty years before to do something about the state of the world—if necessary to plunge into the work of reforming it. He was now forty-three years of age and approaching maturity in his mental growth. He was developing a philosophy of life and of historic change which enabled him to glimpse a new image of the things which made for a good civilization. Fortunately for his own peace of mind his business had now grown to a state in which it functioned almost automatically. He had trained many assistants and had become associated with capable artists and business men who were able to look after the affairs of Morris & Company. This meant that he could now afford to indulge a new interest—almost a new hobby—he could begin to do his bit toward mending the ruined fabric of society, or, if that failed, to aid in destroying the old and building the new.

CHAPTER XII

ART, POLITICS AND SOCIETY ARE STILL IN A MUDDLE

IN England during these years there was considerable talk
in favour of the preservation rather than the restoration of
ancient buildings, and in 1877 Morris succeeded in establishing a definite organization—"one closest to his heart"—of
which he became secretary. This was The Society for the Protection of Ancient Buildings, commonly known to the initiated
as "The Anti-Scrape" Society. Through the efforts of Morris
and his friend, William de Morgan (the famous novelist), Mr.
Thomas Carlyle, then an old man, became one of the earliest
members. For years afterward one of Morris's greatest pleasures was lecturing before the members of "Anti-Scrape," and
two of his best lectures were published in book form with an
introduction by Professor John Henry Middleton. But more
of this later.

Twenty years had passed since Morris had left Oxford, and
now, once again, there was trouble in the Near East. Turkish
atrocities occurred in Bosnia and Bulgaria in 1876, Russia in-
tervened, and England, under the leadership of Disraeli (Lord
Beaconsfield) was definitely anti-Tsarist, while Gladstone,
leader of the Liberals, was urging Britons to drive the Turk out
of Europe "bag and baggage." Morris believed that the leaders of both political parties were ready to sacrifice vital domestic
needs to useless foreign adventure. As early as May, 1877, he
addressed a *Manifesto to the Working Men of England*. In
it he said:

Who are they that are leading us into war? Greedy gamblers on the
stock exchange, idle officers of the army and navy, desperate purveyors
of exciting war-news for the comfortable breakfast-tables of those who

have nothing to lose by war; and lastly, in the place of honour, the Tory Rump, that we fools, weary of peace, reason, and justice, chose at the last election. . . .

Working men of England . . . I doubt if you know the bitterness of hatred against freedom and progress that lies at the hearts of a certain part of the richer classes of this country: their newspapers veil it in a kind of decent language; but hear them talking among themselves, as I have often, and I know not whether scorn or anger would prevail in you at their folly and insolence. These men cannot speak of your order, of its aims, of its leaders, without a sneer or an insult: these men, if they had the power (may England perish rather!) would thwart your just aspirations, would silence you, would deliver you bound hand and foot forever to irresponsible capital!

In January, 1878, the question having grown warmer, Morris appeared as a political verse maker with his "Wake, London Lads!" written to the air of "The Hardy Norseman's Home of Yore," of which the last two stanzas were significant:

> Yea, through the fog of unjust war
> What thief on us might steal,
> To rob us of the gifts of yore,
> The hope of England's weal?
> The toilsome years have built and earned,
> Great men in hope have died;
> Shall all the lessons be unlearned,
> The treasure scattered wide?
>
> What! Shall we crouch beneath the load,
> And call the labour sweet,
> And dumb and blind go down the road
> Where shame abides our feet?
> Wake, London Lads! The hour draws nigh,
> The bright sun brings the day;
> Cast off the shame, cast off the lie,
> And cast the Turk away!

Morris's real fear was that Disraeli "has bidden the Turks *not* to make peace, but to draw on the Russians to Constantinople," so that England would have an excuse to intervene against Russia. Hence his words "cast the Turk away" do not mean opposition to the Turk (as Gladstone's words did) but rather the casting away of the idea of fighting for them against Russia. How closely he had been following the situation abroad is shown as early as October 26, 1876, when he wrote to *The Daily News* asking whether he was to be considered a mere sentimentalist for speaking of the responsibilities of civilized governments to their own subjects.

It was his activity in connection with the Eastern Question Association which brought Morris into contact with some of the hitherto almost unnoticed and almost unknown Radical Clubs in London. Before many weeks he was addressing some of them on the subject of Peace *vs.* Imperialism.

Morris's first public address was delivered in 1877, and it was an agony to him. He always suffered somewhat from stage-fright, and often in public he became so angry or so excited that he jumbled his words. It was to require several years before he achieved real distinction as a speaker, and even then he usually wrote each speech beforehand.

In one of his early talks on the Near Eastern Question he said:

It is unfair, perhaps, to lay the blame on the Tory House of Commons. Lord Beaconsfield and his tail rule England at present!—Too true!—But why? Who made the House of Commons a Tory one . . . ? It was ourselves, Sirs, Ourselves!

I do believe that the great crimes of nations, as of individual men, have been caused by stupidity chiefly, rather than by malice. Therefore I say, enlighten the minds of men on war; let them understand all that it means; let them see its worst details uncloaked by conventional words; let them know what they are doing by it!

Several times during 1878 Morris was asked to speak before organizations and groups of various sorts. During 1879 and 1880 his confidence increased; and the time had now definitely come when he parted company with the Liberal Party. But until then there had been no group of men with whom he could associate himself, although his own revolt against the present social and political order had already begun. As yet, the idea of founding an organization of his own does not seem to have occurred to him. But when he suddenly became aware of a new, small body that aimed at the erection of a new state and a new civilization, he was to lose no time in associating himself with it. This group he found, or thought he found, in the Democratic Federation.

It was in 1879, according to Henry Mayers Hyndman, that he first met Morris at a Trade Union parliamentary meeting. Hyndman was there to lecture on the Indian Question, and afterward he was introduced to Morris. This meeting, together with the radical activities upon which Morris had already concentrated his attention for several years, prepared the way for the latter's entry into the Democratic Federation.

At the hall of the Democratic Federation Morris met Andreas Scheu and others with whom he was to become intimate during the remaining sixteen years of his life. Writing of his own past experiences to Scheu, shortly thereafter, Morris said that "Both my historical studies and my practical conflict with the Philistinism of modern society have *forced* on me the conviction that art cannot have a real life and growth under the present system of commercialism and profit-mongering."

It remains to be seen what Morris meant by *art*, and what views he formulated concerning the interaction of art and society, before we proceed to an investigation of his future political activities.

# III

## DAYS OF THOUGHT

*Life worsens here, and ere it reach the worst,*
*Unto the Jove that may be, would I speak,*
*To help my people wandering blind and weak.*

# CHAPTER I

HARD WORDS ON ART, INDUSTRY AND SOCIAL STANDARDS

IT was in 1877, several years before he joined the Democratic Federation, that Morris first began to go down among the people and lecture on his "hopes and fears" regarding the necessity for a restoration of popular art, the art of the people, which is the expression of the life of a society. Five years later, about the time that he decided to become an active member of a Socialist body, but months before he actually took this step, some of his lectures were published under the general title of *Hopes and Fears for Art*. Among them may be found ideas which had long been germinating in Morris's mind: ideas that will illustrate what his philosophy of art and society—and of their interrelationship —meant to him.

This series of lectures was published for the purpose of raising money for the Society for the Protection of Ancient Buildings, and Morris's first important public lecture, "The Lesser Arts," delivered before the Trades Guild of Learning, December 4, 1877, is the first and in some respects the most interesting of the group. In it he tried to drive home the idea that tawdry and imitative manufactured articles were "cheap and nasty," an idea of Cobbett's, Kingsley's, and Carlyle's with which Morris found himself in hearty agreement.

It is only under the involved and intricate system of a highly developed, urbanized, mechanical culture, he says, that the lesser or popular arts "become trivial, mechanical, unintelligent, and incapable of resisting the changes pressed upon them by fashion or dishonesty; while the greater arts, unhelped by the lesser, are sure to lose their dignity and become nothing but the dull adjuncts of unmeaning pomp." Among nations that have contributed to culture "their most vigorous and freest times have been the blossoming times of art." Even among oppressed peoples that contributed to culture, "art, at least, was free. . . . For so strong is the bond between history and decoration, that we cannot, if we would, shake off the influence of past times" any more than those oppressed peoples and their oppressors could rid themselves of a deep artistic tradition.

These lesser arts, he goes on to say, are components of one great system: "they are connected with all history and are clear teachers of it." But the thoughts of men in modern times have become more involved and difficult, and art has become a complex thing to deal with, and its labour, like all labour, has become subject to the evils of division, until today it has become an almost desperate task for those who grapple with it— "their working lives have been one long tragedy of hope and fear, joy and trouble."

For art, in all ages, has had its periods of goodness and fruition for a while, "but like all fruitful growth, it fell into decay."

But how, he asks, can he beg workingmen "passing up and down these hideous streets day by day to care about beauty?" He then paints a picture of the great days of English art and architecture, which flourished in the common walks of life until that time came when, "though art still lived among the cottagers and yeomen, the big houses were being built 'French and fine' . . . for overseas stupid pomp and rigid formalities and rules had extinguished all nature and freedom; and art was become, in France especially, the mere expression of successful and exultant rascality." So England fell into the pit, losing its sense of native values and borrowing from the Continent a glib sophistication of sham-art, coupled with art-profiteering:

Is money to be gathered? Cut down the pleasant trees among the houses, pull down ancient and venerable buildings for the money that a few square yards of London dirt will fetch; blacken rivers, hide the sun, and poison the air! That is all that modern commerce, the count-

ing-house forgetful of the workshop, will do for us.—And Science?—
We have loved her well, and followed her diligently;—What will she
do? I fear she is so much in the pay of the counting-house and the
drill-sergeant, that she is too busy . . . and will do nothing!

Yet he does not totally despair:

I have a sort of hope that men will get wiser. I hope we shall have
leisure from war—war commercial as well as war of the bullet and
the bayonet; leisure from the knowledge that darkens counsel; leisure
above all from the greed of money and the craving for that distinction
which money now brings—I believe that as we have even now partly
achieved LIBERTY, so we shall one day achieve EQUALITY,
which, and which only, means FRATERNITY, and so have leisure
from poverty, with all its gripping, sordid cares.

For leisure, he asserts, will mean time to think about one's
work, to take joy in that work; and from that joy and thought-
fulness will come the return of a worth-while, decorative,
"noble, popular art."

This hope, in brief, was the first public expression of Morris's
"dream of the future," a dream that foreshadowed and determined his future advocacy of a system of political, economic,
and social *Decentralization*—a return to an existence free from
title, pomp and vanity, and a return to *native and traditional
customs in art and in life,* rather than adherence to the enervat-
ing affectations that had been introduced from the Continent.
For in healthy lesser arts he sees the foundation of all great
art and the foundation of a healthy instead of an unhealthy
civilization.

In "The Art of the People," a lecture before the Birmingham Society of Arts and School of Design, February 19, 1879,
he explains again the significant relationships of nature, history, and popular art to the well-being of a society. Arts that
come with the birth of any civilization die only with its death,
he asserts, yet their effects live on and their traditions enhance
the future glory of later civilizations.

Take for example a century of the Byzantine Empire, weary yourselves with reading the names of the pedants, tyrants, and tax-gatherers to whom the terrible chain which long-dead Rome once forged still gave the power of cheating people. . . . Turn then to the lands they governed, and read and forget a long string of what so-called History has left us. . . . How, then, did Europe grow into intelligence and freedom? It seems that there were others than those of whom History (so-called) has left us the names and the deeds. These, the raw material for the treasury and the slave-market, we now call "the people," and we know that they were working all that while . . . for though History (so-called) has forgotten them, yet their work has not been forgotten, but has made another history, the history of Art. . . . From Ispahan to Northumberland there is no building between the seventh and the seventeenth centuries that does not show the influence of the labour of that oppressed and neglected herd of men. . . . Yet how strong their thought was, how long it abided, how far it travelled! . . . History (so-called) has remembered the kings and the warriors, because they destroyed; Art has remembered the people, because they created.

In these passages we do not hear the voice of a mere poetic and artistic genius, drunk with the beauty of life and advocating beauty in life merely because he himself feels it and wants others to do likewise. It would appear that something more realistic and deeper underlay Morris's revolt. At the very outset he makes it clear that he has studied carefully and dwelt thoughtfully upon history and art, and that he has formed conclusions that were, in his days, certainly unconventional and indeed original.

Turning to life in England at the height of the Middle Ages, he asks:

Who was it that designed and ornamented these fine buildings? The great architect, carefully kept for the purpose and guarded from the common troubles of common men? By no means. Sometimes, perhaps, it was the monk, the ploughman's brother; oftenest his own brother, the village carpenter, smith, mason, what not?—a "common fellow" whose everyday labour fashioned works that are to-day the wonder and despair of many a hard-working "cultivated" architect. And did he loathe his work? No, it was impossible! I have seen, as we most of

us have, work done by such men in some out-of-the-way hamlet . . .
work so delicate, so careful, and so inventive, that nothing in its way
could go further. And I will assert, without fear of contradiction, that
no human ingenuity can produce work such as this without pleasure
being a third party to the brain that conceived and to the hand that
fashioned it.

"Look now," he adds, "I admit that civilization does make
certain things well, things which it knows, consciously or unconsciously, are necessary to its present unhealthy condition.
These things, to speak shortly, are chiefly the machines for
carrying on competition in buying and selling, which is falsely
called commerce . . . and machines for war and destruction.
. . . But on the other hand, matters for carrying on that life
of mutual trust, forbearance and help . . . these things the
civilized world makes ill, and *increasingly worse and worse!*"
    If art were anything like what it should be, he believes, brick-
layers and masons would be among the nation's best artists,
doing not only necessary, but also beautiful, artistic, and therefore happy work.
    But the labour which *now* makes things . . . merely as counters for
the commercial war aforesaid . . . needs regulating and reforming.

What is needed is "an art made by the people and for the
people, as a happiness to the maker and the user. *That is the
only real art there is,* the only art which will be instrumental
to the progress of the world! However, I cannot forget that
it is *not possible* to dissociate art from morality, politics, and
religion. Truth in these great matters of principle is one—and
only in formal treatises can it be split up diversely!"
    The one thing that rings most insistently through Morris's
lectures is that "History teaches us" that for a civilization to be
sound at the core, Art must be popular: and that that Art must
include, or rather extend to, all human labour; and that "History teaches us" that these things are possible, even under the
worst sort of oppression. The work of man, he said, is the most
fundamental thing there is. "That is the only real art there is,

the only art which will be an instrument to the progress of the world."

Hence, Morris was to spend the best years of his life—the years when he was at the height of his powers—in revolting against those current conventions which he decried in his lecture upon the Pre-Raphaelites as "weak, poor, and unworthy." If the Victorians, or those who have since echoed their opinions, had said that only the poor can afford to enjoy art, there would be some evidence that they at least understood what Morris meant when he said Art. Yet over and over again he said that it meant the labour of common men. And over and over again his concept has been translated as the creation of something fine, rich and expensive, which only the wealthy could afford! Morris, of course, did not regard an artistic creation as necessarily fine, or rich, or expensive: he regarded it as something beautiful, which would appeal to the creative urge in all men, and hence something that would embrace all other factors in any civilization. That was why he combined art, ethics, politics and religion, as integral factors, in his concept of social development. He believed that free initiative and free creation in the everyday work of the world would bring to humanity a sense of growth and fulfillment—of spiritual, mental, and physical expansion—which would enhance the beauty of life internally as well as externally. That was why he believed that Art was of fundamental importance: Labour properly conceived and executed the great primary cause in the growth and decay of civilization. He had proved his case from the evidence of history, wherein he conceived of all great golden ages as having their origin in "popular art" and their decline in formalism and repression which restricted popular art, or popular expression in labour; and hence he came to the conclusion that any reform is rendered effectual only by its provisions for the art and the customs of a people.

In his address on "The Beauty of Life," delivered before the same Birmingham group on February 19, 1880, Morris set out to prove that men cannot be either educated or civilized without having first been given a share in art. Here again he dwelt upon his favorite aversions: "the so-called Renaissance, when Art took the downward road with terrible swiftness," and the marked decline in both arts and letters which had characterized English life since the time of George II. He paid especial tribute to the Pre-Raphaelites and to Mr. John Ruskin for having been among those few who, during the "century of commerce," had kept alive the "golden chain of thought" that had been dropped three centuries before with the spread of the Renaissance.

"I do not think," he said, "that I undervalue the work of the nineteenth century. It has broken down many a prejudice and taught many a lesson. It has made it possible for many a man to live free. . . . If it has not quite spread peace and justice through the world, it has at least stirred up in many hearts fresh cravings for peace and justice. . . . But recklessness has commonly gone with its energy, blindness too often with its haste, and so the next century, the twentieth, may have to become The Century of Education, not of the select few, but of the many; for once more I say: the remedy lies not in standing still, but in more complete civilization."

Then, after describing the action of artistic-social influences upon successive societies, Morris explains "the terrible significance" of the theory of the *residuum,* stating that the only way in which the modern age can avoid the worst features of the *residuum* of the mercenary defects in its inheritance from Classicism and from the Renaissance is by national, or by universal, education . . . "when all people are educated, not according to the money which they or their parents possess, but according to the capacity of their minds."[1]

He then proceeds to belabour the more hideous aspects of contemporary life: "the posters with which our towns are daubed," and the "gradual disappearance of the natural beauty of the landscape. . . . Do you know what treasures they are?

[1]Popular and compulsory education in England did not come until the Education Act of 1891.

. . . Or what a relief they will be to the hideous dog-holes which (forgive me) you are probably going to build in their places?"

But there are too many people in modern times, he feels, to whom "the attainment of comforts is what makes the difference between civilization and uncivilization"—to all too many, comforts are the very essence of civilization. "If that is what it is, I for my part wish that I were well out of it, and living in a tent on a Persian desert, or in a turf hut on the Iceland hillside. But however it be, I tell you that Art abhors that side of civilization; she cannot breathe in the houses that lie under its stuffy slavery."

On March 10, 1881, Morris delivered a lecture at the London Institution on the "Prospects of Architecture in Civilization." In this lecture he warned his hearers especially against the dangers of social inequality, which have become glaringly apparent under the present system of society with its neglect of the fundamental principles of architecture and of the popular arts. Yet, he adds, "there is no vulgarity which is not shared with perfect fairness between the modern hovels of Bethnal Green and the modern palaces of the West End." But what he chiefly laments is "the reflex of the grinding trouble of those who toil to live that they may live to toil." Art may die, he fears, for she will not continue to live as the "slave of the rich" and as "the token of the enduring slavery of the poor." Labour cannot remain unorganized as it is, forever.

In his famous lecture on "Art and the Beauty of Earth" at Burslem Town Hall, October 13, 1881, Morris again displayed his grasp of the concept of historic evolution as applied to art and to society, especially emphasizing the degree of freedom which distinguished medieval art from "the dead, academical art of ancient Egypt" and from "the standardized, exclusive art of Periclean Greece." The decay of modern art, he said, began with the artists of the Renaissance, who lent their energy to the severance of art from the daily life of common men, leaving art sterile and subsidized by wealthy patrons, leaving life empty.

In Medieval Art, on the other hand, nothing and nobody was wasted; all people east of the Atlantic felt this art; from Bokhara to Galway, from Iceland to Madras, all the world glittered with its brightness and quivered with its vigour. It cast down the partitions of race, and of religion also. Christian and Mussulman were made joyful by it; Celt, Teuton and Latin raised it up together; Persian, Tatar and Arab gave and took its gifts from one another. In the days when Norwegian, Dane and Icelander stalked through the streets of Micklegarth, and hedged with their axes the throne of Kirialax the Greek king, it was alive and vigorous. When blind Dandolo was led from the Venetian galleys onto the conquered wall of Constantinople, it was near to its best and purest days. When Constantine Palæologus came back an old and care-worn man from a peacefuller home in the Morea to his doom in the great city, and the last Cæsar got the muddle of his life solved, not ingloriously, by Turkish swords on the breached and battered walls of that same Constantinople, there were signs of sickness beginning to show in the art that sprang from there to cover east and west alike with its glory.

The men of the Renaissance looked back at the thousand years behind them as a deedless blank, and at all that lay before them as a perpetual triumphal march. The conquered North gained nothing from Italy save an imitation of its worst extravagance, and all that saved the art of England from nothingness was a tradition of the earlier days, still lingering among a people rustic and narrow-minded, but serious, truthful, and of simple habits.

So Morris summed up once more his theory of the degradation which came over modern society, creating an inequality of condition that must be rectified.

"How, then, shall our rebellion begin?" he asks. "I am afraid that whatever answer I may make to that question will disappoint you. . . . I have no infallible nostrum to cure an evil whose growth is centuries old. In those old days of popular art, the world, in spite of all its ills and troubles, was struggling toward civilization and liberty; and it is in that way that we also must struggle. Education on all sides is what we must look to. We may expect, if we do not learn much, to learn this much at least, that we know but little and that knowledge means aspiration, or discontent, call it what you will."

The fostering of discontent—this was to be the object toward which Morris was to devote the rest of his life. Discontent, or aspiration, brought to birth for the turgid mentality of contemporary civilization, to be fostered through the medium of universal education! The core of his Socialism, so called, was the necessity of making people know, of making them think, and of bringing about, by these means, the realization of discernment. It was to be education and discernment based upon the understanding of what history and the popular, or lesser, arts really meant—not the history of the modern economists, who looked no farther back than the history of the Renaissance and the Commercial Revolution; not the art of the modern impressionists and "picture-naturalists" whose "works will hardly be called works of art"—but rather history and art as they should be traced over thousands of years of human activity.

Meanwhile, he hoped that

This great country may yet shake off from her all foreign and colonial entanglements, and turn that mighty force of her respectable people, the greatest power the world has ever seen, to giving the children of these poor folk the pleasures and the hopes of men! Is that really impossible? Is there no hope of it? If so, I can only say that civilization is a delusion and a lie; there is no such thing, and no hope of such a thing!

He closes his lecture on a note of hope, expressing the same optimistic faith in a better time coming that he has expressed in most of his lectures thus far.

I know that cause will conquer in the end. And my very faith leads me to speak according to my knowledge, feeble as it may be and rash as the words may sound; for every man who has a cause at heart is bound to act as if it depended on him alone, however well he may know his own unworthiness; and thus is action brought to birth from mere opinion.

In *The Lesser Arts of Life*, Morris regrets that in modern times "only the higher men" are creating things which satisfy man's spiritual wants. In this connection he adds,

Here, then, we have two kinds of art: one of them would exist if men had no needs but such as are essentially spiritual. . . . The other, called into existence by material needs, is bound no less to recognize the aspirations of the soul and receive the impress of its striving toward perfection.

He then refers to his contemporaries in the *bourgeois* world as living in a Diogenes tub, "lined with padded velvet, lighted by gas, polished and cleaned by vicarious labour, and expecting every morning due visits from the milkman, the butcher, and the fishmonger." For the comfort-seekers, he declares, are the rejectors of the arts and the corrupters of modern civilization:

They do not altogether reject them: they will eat them and drink them and wear them, and use them as lackeys to eke out their grandeur, and as nets to catch money with; but nothing will they learn or care about them. . . . They will reach no helping hand to that which makes labour tolerable; and they themselves are but a part of the crowd that toils without an aim; for they themselves labour with tireless energy to multiply the race of men, and then make the multitude unhappy. . . . Let us pity them, yet resist them. For these things they do unwitting. . . . Well, these men live, the rich and the powerful of the world; they rule civilization at present, and if it were not through ignorance that they err, those who see the fault and lament it would indeed have no choice left but to reject civilization with the ascetic.

After discussing some of the lesser arts of the craftsman he turns back to social problems again and considers clothing, as one of the lesser arts, in connection with styles and fashions:

Rebel as I am, I find it difficult to admit that a chimney-pot hat, or a tail-coat, is the embodiment of wisdom in clothes-philosophy.

And speaking of women's clothes he calls attention to the objects and considerations of the designers of fashionable raiment as follows:

Their chief problem is how to hide and degrade the human body in the most expensive manner. . . . The designer looks upon women as scaffolds on which to hang a bundle of cheap rags, which can be sold dear under the name of a dress. . . . I beg you fervently, do not allow yourselves to be upholstered like so many armchairs!

Lastly, he calls upon women particularly to "resist change for the sake of change," since beautiful things should be loved for their own sakes and not because they are novelties.

In concluding his address he states that he, for one, is willing to accept the conclusion that, if the lesser arts are vain they should not be carried on at all, and that, in such a circumstance, "we should do nothing that we can help doing beyond what is barely necessary to keep ourselves alive." Yet he also regrets that the modern world would reject his scheme of barbarity; for, he says:

I know that the progress of the race from barbarism to civilization has hitherto had a tendency to make our lives more and more complex; to make us more dependent upon one another, and to destroy individuality, which is the breath of life to art. But . . . I know that I cannot be alone in doubting that it has been an unmixed good to us, or in believing that a change will come, perhaps, after some great disaster has chilled us into pausing, and so given us time for reflection. Anyhow, I believe the day is not far distant when the best of men will set to work trying to simplify life on a new basis; when the organization of labour will mean something different from the struggle of the strong to use, each for his own advantage, the necessities and the miseries of the weak!

Of Morris's remaining lectures on art and industry, the majority consist of repetitions of facts and theses above treated, or else are confined to specialized subjects. A few of them introduce nascent aspects of his newly evolving Socialist doctrines, but of them more later. Only one significant exception occurred. That was a lecture read before the Society for the Protection of Ancient Buildings on July 1, 1884. It was entitled "Architecture and History."

The most interesting thing about this lecture was that its ideas were strikingly similar to those expressed later in the volumes on *Socialism: Its Growth and Outcome, Gothic Architecture,* and *The History of Pattern Designing:* three of the most significant of Morris's prose writings. For these reasons, a full treatment of it is needless in the present chapter. There are, however, one or two interesting points which deserve mention. In this essay Morris particularly damns the "clever essayist" whose views of history are determined by historical works regarded as standard only by virtue of the arbitrary criteria of literary critics who know little of history. He damns also the conventional historians of the old school:

At their honestest the writers were compelled to look on life through the spectacles thrust on them by the conventional morality of their own times; at their dishonestest, they were servile flatterers in the pay of the powers that were. . . . The very lies themselves can often be dissolved and precipitated, so to say, into historical substance, into negative evidence of facts. . . . The academical historians were cursed with a fatal, though unconscious, dishonesty.

Such an attitude, perhaps, explains Morris's own reasons for undertaking, years afterward, the composition of his historical outline of history for inclusion in *Socialism: Its Growth and Outcome.*

And thus we see that in Morris's lectures on art and industry, as well as in his historical compositions, the whole thought and life of the man centered upon certain definite and fixed ideas, which sprang from the philosophy of historic development that he had evolved from his interpretation of the nature and significance of art in society, from his view of individual and social life, and from his idea of the interplay between artistic and social forces. All these ideas were strongly interwoven in his mind before he became an active reformer; and they were responsible for his activity in public life.

## CHAPTER II

THIS IS AN AGE OF LITERARY REFORMERS:

CARLYLE, ARNOLD, MORRIS AND RUSKIN

IT was during the decade from 1874 to his entry into the Democratic Federation on January 17, 1883, that Morris began to think about civilization more seriously and pessimistically than ever before. References in his letters to his own reading and to the writings of the great historians from Livy and Tacitus to Carlyle, Freeman and Grosse indicate that he was turning to history with a new interest. On New Year's Day, 1881, he wrote that his mind "is full of the great change" which he thinks is "slowly coming over the world." He hoped that the new year would "do a good turn of work toward the abasement of the rich and the raising up of the poor, which is of all things most to be longed for."

While living at Kelmscott Manor, shortly before his return to London in 1881, Morris wrote:

Last night I took a book and read Carlyle on Mrs. Carlyle. . . . What is one to say of such outrageous blues as this? He is generally very unfair and narrow and whimsical about his likes and dislikes, but 'tis something in these days of hypocrisy that he makes distinctions at all. . . . That is nothing to the ferocity of his gloom; I confess I had no idea of it till I read the book: and yet I find it difficult to say that it ought not to have been printed, and I am sure it ought not to have been garbled. . . . Only should it not have been called The History of a Great Author's Liver? Not to mention symptoms too much, I, in a small way understand something of that: to look upon your own natural work with a sick disgust . . . to be sore and raw with your friends, distrustful of them, antagonistic to them when you are not in their company: to want society and hate it when you've got it—all these things are just as much a part of the disease as physical squeamish-

ness; But you see, poor chap, he was always so bad that he scarcely had
a chance of finding that out. . . . After all, my moral from it is the
excellence of art, its truth, and its power of expression. Set *Sartor
Resartus* by all this, and what a difference!

It has been said that Carlyle was a voice crying in the wilder-
ness of historical transition, railing against the tendencies of an
age which he did not understand. Yet in 1831, three years
before Morris was born, Carlyle had written that the doom
of the old is not only proclaimed but it is even now irrevocable:
indeed, the Old Civilization already is gone forever, "but the
New, alas, has not yet appeared in its stead." Out of the
prophet's own view of chaos he brought forth his *Teufelsdröckh*
to define a New Society and "chase a Socialistic hare."

But Carlyle, although like Morris an admirer of Goethe and
of Cromwell, regarded such men as saviours of society—as beings placed by God above the rank and file—and he called,
therefore, for an industrial Cromwell to be the new dictator—
or for an industrial Frederick the Great—any such genius to be
guided by the wisdom of a Goethe. In this way only, he believed, the New Order of Society might survive its crisis.
Carlyle, evidently, had derived more from the political theories
of Plato and Aristotle than had Morris.

Carlyle's ideas of work and of duty, springing from his doctrines of work, silence and sincerity, are, aside from his desire
for an industrial dictator, about the nearest that he came to an
admonishment of Society's method of grappling with the new
industrial changes that had brought on a revolution. To him,
work was the first and chiefest duty of mankind. The first of all
problems, he said, is that a man find out what kind of work
he is able to do in this universe. For man's work alone is noble
—the grand cure of his maladies and ailments. In his essay on
*Chartism* he wrote that a day will come "when he who has no
work to do . . . will not find it good to show himself in our
quarter of the Solar System."

Unlike Ruskin, Carlyle neglected the fine arts, which he
despised (perhaps with some reason) and carried his religion

of work into the field of the practical crafts, saying that a boundless significance is inherent in work, for therein the humblest craftsman may attain the highest reward. In *Past and Present*, a book that we know Morris admired, Carlyle turned more definitely to economics, stressing the principle of sincerity which represented the ethical need in business and commerce. He carried over the matter of truth from the human aspect of life to the business aspect. To oblivion with all manufactured imitations and adulterations—with all the "cheap and nasty," tainted with the spirit of Mammon. On several occasions Morris expressed the same thought in almost identical words.

Yet here the thought of Carlyle strays away from that of Morris. It hints at the raising up of a class of superior beings in industry; and that is just what Carlyle advocated: "a chivalry of labour"—"a new aristocracy" which would save the new industry from the filth of democratizing processes. Morris, on the other hand, wanted every man to be an aristocrat; he desired equality of condition, with no distinctions or suggestion of distinctions.

It is possible also that the opinions of Morris's best friend, Edward Burne-Jones, may have weighed against Carlyle in Morris's mind. Burne-Jones once remarked to Morris that while *Sartor Resartus* had made him think of the attributed Socratic doctrine of "Know Thyself" with reference to one's work in life, "I soon found that he wanted patching. . . . He says: 'Work at what lies nearest thee, it doesn't matter what, only work at it in earnest, like a nigger,'—or words to that effect. Which is, it may be, sheer atheism. It is neither morality nor religion."

Here, however, we are not concerned with the correctness of the position, we merely face the probabilities. Suffice it to say that for the most part both Morris and Burne-Jones admired some of Carlyle's teachings and writings. These writings may have had some influence upon Morris's ideas, as many scholars have claimed. Personally, I do not think that they had much.

In one of Morris's little-known lectures of the period 1878–

1880, delivered before some London club, he referred to other men who have been urging reform: to "Mr. Ruskin" he referred with "love and respect," and to "Mr. Thomas Carlyle, who still lives to be the glory of England," and who has "warned you off shams and poured his scorn on cant and hypocrisy many a time." Later, he said:

Well, before I cast out my thimbleful of advice . . . I should like to speak to you of another name, that of Mr. Matthew Arnold: all the more because if I had not read his article on Equality in *The Fortnightly Review*, I doubt if I should have had the courage to say a good deal of what I have already said to you. . . . Under his name and example also I will shelter myself against the accusation of impracticability and generalization.

For several years now, Arnold had been admired by Burne-Jones. He had held the chair of poetry at Oxford for which the name of Morris had later been suggested, and his poetry had already inspired Morris and Burne-Jones as early as their first Italian tour. In 1873 Burne-Jones had written:

There was a brilliant and really fine set of essays by Matthew Arnold on the study of Celtic literature, based entirely on guesses, but demonstrably right guesses. He knew absolutely nothing about the subject, but he scented the truth from afar. Besides that poor, thin little volume there is not a line that I know of in English to hint that any one knows or cares for it. Even Morris doesn't, who knows about everything—but he won't leave Iceland or come south of Drontheim.

Here again we have a half-serious admiration of Burne-Jones to take into consideration in determining whether Morris had really been strongly influenced by the works of Matthew Arnold. Yet in a letter to Mr. Wardle, the manager of his plant, in March, 1878, Morris wrote:

Thanks for sending me Arnold's lecture, with the main part of which I heartily agree: the only thing is that if he has any idea of a remedy he durstn't mention it. I think myself that no rose-water will cure us: disaster and misfortune of all kinds, I think, will be the only things which will breed a remedy: in short, nothing can be done till all rich men are made poor by common consent. I suppose he dimly sees this, but is afraid to say it, being, though naturally a courageous man, somewhat infected with the great vice of that cultivated class he was praising so much—cowardice, to wit.

Matthew Arnold, after a lifetime of persistent efforts to rouse the middle class in England to a sense of its shortcomings, had turned to a more revolutionary faith—faith in the working classes. He had formulated his creed in an address delivered to the Ipswich Working Men's College under the title *"Ecce convertimur ad Gentes."* "I have no very ardent interest," Arnold said in that address, "in politics in their present state in this country. What interests me is English civilization. . . . Both the natural reason of the thing and also the proof from practical experience seem to me to show the same thing; that for modern civilization some approach to equality is necessary. . . . Our middle classes know neither man nor the world; they have no light, and can give none." Arnold ended his address by asking the working class to carry forward the needed reforms themselves, since no aid was to be expected from the middle class. "Carry it forward yourselves, and insist on taking the middle classes with you."

Morris's idea, in this connection, was that thus far the middle classes seemed to have been carrying the workers with them, extending their range downward; but that in the future the revolution of society will bring the middle classes into the proletariat. Again, one must consider the greater violence with which Morris made his demands of the day. Thus, in his address on "Art and Socialism," a few months later, we find him saying:

Can the middle classes regenerate themselves? At first glance one would say that a body of people so powerful, who have built up the gigantic edifice of modern Commerce, whose science, invention and energy have subdued the forces of nature . . . could do anything they please. And yet I doubt it: their own creation, the Commerce they are so proud of, has become their master; and we . . . are compelled to admit not that Commerce was made for man, but that man was made for Commerce.

On all sides we are forced to admit it. There are in the English middle class to-day . . . men of the highest aspirations. . . . But both the leaders and the led are incapable of saving so much as half-a-dozen commons from the grasp of inexorable Commerce: they are as helpless in spite of their culture and their genius as if they were so many over-worked shoe-makers. Less happy and less lucky than King Midas, our green fields and clear waters, nay, the very air we breathe, are turned not to gold, but to dirt. . . . Things grow worse year by year, day by day. Let us eat and drink, for to-morrow we die, choked by filth!

There is significance here. While no names are mentioned, Morris points out that the men of "culture and genius" are themselves helpless in the face of conditions which they have created: as helpless as overworked shoemakers. This sentence shows once more some of Morris's innate dislike for the academic mind, for the intellectual critic as opposed to the natural critic. Assuredly, if the man who wrote *Culture and Anarchy* would go so far as to advocate reform from below, Morris would go farther. And so we find him saying in the same address:

These, I say, are the days of combat, when there is no external peace possible to an honest man. . . . If we were in gagged Germany, in gagged Austria, in Russia . . . Ah, my friends, it is a poor tribute to offer on the tombs of the martyrs of liberty—this refusal to take the torch from their dying hands. Is it not told of Goethe that on hearing one say he was going to America to begin life anew, replied "Here is America, or nowhere!"? So for my part I say, "Here is Russia, or nowhere!" To say that the governing classes of England are not afraid of freedom of speech, therefore let us abstain from speaking freely, is a strange paradox. . . . Will any one here tell me that a Russian *moujik* is in a worse state than a sweating-tailor's wage-slave? Do not let us deceive ourselves; the class of victims exists here as in Russia. There are fewer of them?—Maybe; then are they of themselves more helpless, and so have more need of our help.

He closed this address before the Secular Society of Leicester by asking his listeners to "renounce" their bourgeois class and cast in their lot with the "victims." This, of course, is the opposite of Arnold's demand.

About all that remains from these analogies and comparisons, thus far, is the proof that Morris was taking note of what other reformers were doing. It would be going too far, perhaps, to say that Arnold's speeches had any special influence upon Morris's mind, other than to serve as an incentive to his own already precipitated revolt. To complete the picture, however, it is necessary to determine more exactly how the reform theories of Arnold compared with those of Morris.

Matthew Arnold had held the chair of poetry at Oxford from 1857 until 1867, and while so engaged had been instrumental in creating a wave of opposition to the Romantic School in English poetry. He advocated, as an antidote, a return to the Hellenism, or Classicism, of Greek and Latin literature. One of his Parthian shots against Romanticism was his 1859–60 lecture, "On Translating Homer," a lecture which Morris, as a Romantic, naturally detested. Shortly thereafter, Arnold was appointed to a government commission to study Continental trends in education and became a great admirer of the Prussian system. A little later he began a series of lectures and essays which criticized the trends of modern democracy. His final Oxford lecture, "Culture and Its Enemies," was later published as the first chapter of *Culture and Anarchy*, but with its original title changed to "Sweetness and Light."

The volume known as *Culture and Anarchy* appeared in 1869, shortly before the Morrises planned to visit Bad-Ems in Germany. One would like to know whether Morris read the volume at that time. From later references in his speeches it can be judged that he was familiar with Arnold's works—one might even suspect that he had had Arnold in mind when he had refused, with ironic asides, to accept nomination for the chair of poetry a decade after Arnold had surrendered it. There is, however, no available evidence on this point.

In any event, Arnold had turned his powers to the aid of liberalism by recommending culture as "the great help out of our present difficulties." He lamented that the modern idea of progress seemed to "rest on a misconception of what culture truly is, and to be calculated to produce miners, or engineers, or architects, not sweetness and light." Like Morris, he lamented also the "hole-and-corner organization" generated by Puritanism and the tendencies of "our ardent young Liberal friends" who "rush into the arena of politics . . . as if a nation, nourished and reared as ours has been, could give us, just yet, anything but a Philistine Parliament."

In so far as Arnold condemned Puritanism, Liberalism and the inefficacy of parliamentary practices under the present condition of politics and society, Morris was willing to bear him company. In so far as he condemned Romanticism and advocated Classicism, it is evident to any one who knows anything about Morris's opinions that Morris disagreed profoundly. Morris's own philosophy of history and art, as we have already begun to see, precluded any extension of Classical interests to the civilization of Western Europe.

At present, Arnold argues, "our guides" in politics are chosen by the Philistines, the uncultured middle classes, and rule as the Philistines dictate, while they cater to the favour of the populace and tell them that "theirs are the brightest powers of sympathy, and the readiest powers of action," as if that meant anything. He finishes his essay upon "Barbarians, Philistines, Populace," by advocating more *State action* in the spirit of and for the sake of *humanity*. But State action was something of which Morris could never bring himself to approve: he hated any suggestion of despotism, however benevolent.

After Arnold's return from his inspection of the Continental educational systems, he began his agitation for social reform with an essay on "Democracy" which, with the later "Equality," formed an important part of the volume of *Mixed Essays*. In the first of these essays he attacked the attitude of those who regarded State action with jealousy. The completeness of the power and the civilization of France, he pointed out (correctly or incorrectly) was owing to the way in which she had organized her democratic institutions under the "action" of the State. In England, the time has come when the masses are preparing to take a "much more active part than formerly in controlling their destinies." The action to be relied upon for this coming contingency is, he says, "the action of the State." He deplores the abhorrence of the English middle class for State action, because "having never known a beneficent or just State-power, they enlarged their hatred of a cruel and partial State-power." Hence, their "formula of *laissez-faire*, leave us to ourselves!"

What the middle classes of England need, he infers, is culture and dignity; "they want ideas." For character without culture is "raw, blind and dangerous." Therefore he demands more State action in the interests of democracy, of humanity and of culture, regardless of the loss of individual liberty.

Here again there is nothing really decisive except the acknowledgment of a general view, not always supported by the facts. The arguments might be employed for State power of almost any extent, from "democracy" to "totalitarianism."

In "Equality" Matthew Arnold selected Menander's "Choose equality and flee greed," as his text, attacking the sentiments of Froude and others to the effect that equality splits a nation into "a multitude of disconnected units"—that "the masses require leaders whom they can trust"—and that "the natural leaders are the gentry." He laments the fact that feudality died leaving only "a constitution of property full of inequality." He advocates the traditions of governments in "countries where a community has more a will of its own," such as Holland, Switzerland, etc. He extols Switzerland especially: it is "a republic, where the general feeling against inequality is strong," and where "each Swiss canton has its own laws of bequest."

Such countries have been "humanized," he continues, but unfortunately France, at the beginning of the seventeenth century, "entered the prison of Puritanism, and had the key turned upon its spirit for two hundred years." A similar fate befell England: "the claims of intellect and knowledge are not satisfied . . . the middle class will have to acknowledge the hideousness, the immense ennui of the life which this type has created, will have to transform itself thoroughly." Then, after dwelling upon these material defects in the *modern* civilization of England, he comes to the great solution: not of a revolutionary change in the basis of society, but "To remedy our inequality, there must be a change in the law of bequest, as there has been in France." The remedy, he goes on to say, "is not disestablishment . . . it is social equality. . . . To your thoughts I commit it."

One can well imagine a man of Morris's nature adding mentally, "Is that all?" One can almost forgive his exclamation against the bourgeois tameness of Arnold's solution of the difficulty. Here, indeed, was the Philippic of a typical academician: bold words leading forward a single step in a single direction. But in many respects, as Morris admitted, this was "an admirable paper. . . . Still, if he has any idea of a remedy he durstn't mention it. I think myself that no rose-water will cure us."

On the other hand, here was a man, as Morris also admitted freely, and a famous man, who had the courage to point out the decrepitude into which a bourgeois world had fallen, and who felt, with Morris, a repulsion for what Morris himself called "a rich, disestablishmentarian Puritanism." Yet it may be doubted that Arnold's revolt preceded in point of time, or influenced to a great extent, Morris's own views. Two things these "literary reformers" felt in common: resentment against the bourgeoisie, and resentment against Puritanism. But Morris's resentment went back to his childhood days. And Morris probably scoffed inwardly at the idea that medieval civilization was responsible for the kind of social, political and economic inequality which exists today; and at the idea that French civilization was superior to that of England; and that any sound brief could be held for a text derived from the decadent Hellenistic culture of Menander. Morris's idea of Equality was *not* based upon social intercourse and derived from the corruption of good manners; his was an Equality based upon the thought, the spirit, and the workaday labour of all men. It was an Equality of racial and artistic conditions out of which Equality in principles of government and in religion would necessarily emerge.

The third great literary reformer of the age was John Ruskin, who regarded himself primarily as a scholar and an original thinker rather than as the art-critic and man of letters. He was also a sociologist in that he utilized the phenomena of art as a springboard for the elaboration of his ideas upon the economy of life. It has been said that while he showed the influence of Hooker, of Johnson, and of Carlyle, he could outpreach Hooker, overrule Johnson, and outscold Carlyle.

In a letter of 1855 Ruskin had written of his intimacy with the Carlyles; his *Munera Pulveris*, in 1872, was dedicated to Carlyle, and in his later *Crown of Wild Olives* Carlyle is referred to as the "greatest historian since Tacitus," if that means anything. In numerous writings Ruskin referred to Carlyle as his master, just as Morris, on one or two later occasions, referred to Ruskin as his master.

It was in *The Stones of Venice*, completed during Morris's first year at Oxford, that Ruskin expressed those ideas which made the first great impression on the mind of William Morris. In it Ruskin set forth a number of propositions: *viz.*, that art can only be produced by artists; that architecture does not emanate from an architect's office consummated by the rule-of-thumb execution of unintelligent workmen; and that the reign of true art must await the day of workmen-artists, true craftsmen. But more important, to Morris, than any of these things was the fact that Ruskin here set forth in embryo a theory of architecture which not only coincided with the type of mental appreciation already developed by Morris as a boy, but also something that was not far short of a brief interpretation of history. In this theory the most interesting thing is not concerned with the outward form of Gothic but with an inward expression of mentality to be found in Gothic architecture.

First, in this connection, Ruskin considers the "savagery" of Gothic, "in contradistinction to the character of southern and eastern nations." It seemed, says he, "a perpetual reflection of the contrast between the Goth and the Roman in their first encounter. And when that fallen Roman became the model for the imitation of civilized Europe, the word Gothic became a term of unmitigated contempt. . . . For that contempt, by the exertion of the antiquaries and architects of this century, Gothic architecture has been sufficiently vindicated. . . . It is true, greatly and deeply true, that the architecture of the North is rude and wild; but it is not true, for this reason, we are to condemn it. Far otherwise: I believe it is in this very character that it deserves our profoundest reverence."

Ruskin then goes on to speak of its Changefulness, its Naturalism, its Grotesqueness, its Rigidity, and its Redundance, and handles these characteristics in terms of Northern psychology: *i.e.*, in terms of Love of Change, Love of Nature, Disturbed Imagination, Obstinacy, and Generosity.

He then turns to the "servile ornament" of the Greeks, the Ninevites and the Egyptians, and tells how, under Medieval Christianity, this "slavery" was done away with altogether, "Christianity having recognized, in small things as well as great, the individual value of every soul."

Ruskin then dwells at some length upon the implications of the change which has come over modern craftsmanship, or rather industrial labour, as compared with medieval freedom:

It is verily this degradation of the operative into a machine which, more than any other evil of the time, is leading the mass of the nations everywhere into vain, incoherent, destructive struggling for a freedom of which they cannot explain the nature to themselves. . . . It is not that men are pained by the scorn of the upper classes, but they cannot endure their own; for they feel that the kind of labour to which they are condemned is verily a degrading one, and makes them less than men. Never had the upper classes so much sympathy with the lower, or charity for them, as they have at this day, and yet never were they so much hated by them. . . .

It is not, truly speaking, the labour which is divided; but the men:— Divided into mere segments of men—broken into small fragments and crumbs of life. . . . And the great cry that rises from all our manufacturing cities, louder than their furnace blasts, is that we manufacture everything there, except men!

Again reverting to the Gothic spirit, after this socio-economic digression, he finds that it was the Love of Change which enabled it to break through the inviolate laws of order.

After dwelling slightly upon the love of Naturalism and the Disturbed Imagination—the Disquietude—of the Gothic spirit, he considers the "marked distinction" between "the imagination of the Western and Eastern races . . . the Western, or Gothic, delighting most in the representation of facts, and the Eastern in the harmony of colours and forms."

With what Ruskin had to say on the more technical aspects of Gothic, Morris was concerned but slightly; doubtless this was old material to him. But with what Ruskin said on "Gothic History," "Gothic Nature," and "Gothic Rights" he was deeply concerned and reverted to these ideas again and again in his own speeches and writings. We have Morris's own word for it, as well as the words of others, that he was most interested in what Ruskin wrote in his early career. Evidently he did not regard Ruskin's later letters and addresses to the working men of England as being specially significant. It is presumable, therefore, that, as Morris pointed out in his Preface to the Kelmscott edition of *The Nature of Gothic*, it was the "ethical and political" considerations of Ruskin's criticism—it was Ruskin as a teacher of "morals and politics"—which made his work worthy of attention. In any event, it is obvious that Ruskin, by this work, had opened to Morris, while the latter was still an undergraduate, a whole new conception of the unity which underlay art, history, society and human works and accomplishments.

True, Morris afterward repeated many things which Ruskin

had pointed out long before, especially the dangers of mechanization and of the loss of human individualism, and the need for the regeneration of the working classes—all to be accomplished in the Gothic spirit. It is too much, however, to say that Morris's thought was "literally de-moralized derivation from Ruskin":[1] or that here was something which Morris merely echoed. It would be truer to say that here was a kernel of synthesis for Morris's mind while he was still at an impressionable age; and that using these ideas as a foundation, Morris was able, by virtue of his own efforts, to add to them and to round out a philosophy of his own. For Morris carried the "Gothic spirit" in architecture much farther than did Ruskin, and he extended the social and historical implications of Ruskin's theory.

From 1857, when Ruskin published his *Political Economy of Art*, all that he wrote bore heavily upon social and economic considerations. He himself announced, years afterward in the fourth volume of *Fors Clavigera*, that *Modern Painters* taught the claim of all lower nature; that *The Stones of Venice* taught the laws of constructive art and the dependence of human effort upon happy work; that *Unto This Last* taught the laws of life and its dependence upon the "Sun of Justice"; and elaborated the only possible conditions of peace and honour, for high and low, for rich and poor, together. It is noteworthy also that Ruskin claimed to have made "the first contribution to scientific economy, because he alone considered life in its integrity and wholeness, and he alone among economists was acquainted with the value of the products of the highest industrialism, commonly called the fine arts, which had hitherto been ignored by all writers upon economy."

They who have maintained that Morris in practically all respects was a disciple of Ruskin may be able to note two points of departure which preclude him from the picture. First, Morris, himself an artist as opposed to the art-critic that was Ruskin,

[1] Vida D. Scudder, *Social Ideals in English Letters.* Boston, 1922 ed., *passim.* (But see especially pp. 61–62; 289–290.)

was willing to admit a sensuous appeal in art as well as beauty. Secondly, Morris was not a belated romantic of times gone by—for under his own impetus, and in contradistinction to Carlyle, Ruskin and Arnold, all of whom remained merely "intellectual critics" of their age, Morris became a "practical man" and then a "practical Socialist," to use his own words, advocating action and not remaining (to use his own words again) "a mere railer against progress."

In certain other of Ruskin's writings one meets with ideas which may have had some repercussions among Morris's own thoughts regarding history, ethics and economics. In *A Crown of Wild Olives*, published a decade after Morris left Oxford, Ruskin announced that the *later* builders of the great Gothic cathedrals corrupted the spirit of the people and the spirit of Gothic because of their forgetfulness of the people and because of their too great devotion to priestly and æsthetic needs, so that, losing its vitality, Gothic architecture declined in expressiveness and ultimately ceased to be.

Again, in *The Two Paths*, Ruskin stated that "the great lesson of history" is this: "that all the fine arts hitherto, having been supported by the selfish power of the noblesse, and never having extended their range to the comfort or the relief of the mass of the people—the arts, I say, thus practised, and thus matured, have only accelerated the ruin of the states they adorned; and at the moment when, in any kingdom, you point to the triumph of its greatest artists, you point also to the determined hour of the kingdom's decline. The names of the great painters are like passing bells: in the name of Velasquez you hear sounded the fall of Spain; in the name of Leonardo that of Milan; in the name of Raphael that of Rome."

Each of the propositions contained here may have had its effect upon Morris: first, opposition to "priestly" or formal influences in art, and secondly, the idea that good art and good society must be perpetuated by universality and lowliness in art—which meant, in the mind of Morris, the restoration of "popular art."

As Ruskin felt that true art must find its birth in the spirit of a whole people and not in that of a select few, so he believed that a modern and decadent people must be rejuvenated and ennobled through association with art, and that this art could be achieved by participation in the right sort of labour. His enterprises in schools and in the Working Men's College, as well as in society at large, point to his desire for manual labour, to the needed development of character and of idealism in workers, and to his hope of social reform through education. Yet these activities were but a putting into practice of the ideas contained in many of his writings, *e.g.*, the twenty-fifth aphorism of *The Seven Lamps of Architecture*, to the effect that all good work must be hand work, and his ideas on physical education as expressed in *Time and Tide*.

Like Carlyle, Ruskin became a hater of democracy and of Liberalism in its commonly accepted sense; and this hate can be noted also in his attitude toward the United States of America, whose standards he regarded with a chilling distaste.[2] And it is indeed probable that what social activity was actually engaged in by Ruskin found its earliest incentive in Carlyle. It has been claimed that Ruskin's reading of Carlyle's *Heroes and Hero Worship* provided the first point of contact. The two men became personally acquainted about the middle of the century—"grew toward each other in those things which are controlled by temperament," and together declined from a state of optimism to one of pessimism, each, in his mood, calling for rule by the divine sanction of an *aristoi* of gifted persons.

Here again there is marked a distinct line of cleavage between the thought of Morris on the one hand and that of Carlyle and Ruskin on the other. Morris would not decline to pessimism, although there were moments in his career when he approached it. On the whole, he had faith in common man. At no time did he place his faith in either an intellectual or an aristocratic *élite*—and in this one respect he differed fundamentally, both in his philosophy and in his character, from all the

[2] *Cf. Fors Clavigera*, Letter X.

other Victorian "Critics of Democracy." Not only did Morris accept the principle of democratic equality but he even went far beyond it, advocating, before many years had passed, not only equality of political condition, but also equality of social and economic condition among free citizens of free communities. There came also a time when he was willing to fight for these ideals. To this extent he did not remain a mere railer against progress and civilization.

On certain economic principles Morris would have agreed with Ruskin: *e.g.*, when Ruskin said: "So far as I know, there is not in history record of anything so disgraceful to the human intellect as the modern idea that the commercial text, 'Buy in the cheapest market and sell in the dearest' represents, or under any circumstances could represent, an available principle of national economy." Morris would doubtless have agreed that "anarchy and competition, eternally and in all things, are the laws of death," and that the political economy of co-operation is as like that of commercial competition as jewels are like slime. Yet he would not have agreed with Ruskin that a worker must possess the right to have an accumulated sum of wealth, or wages in proportion to what he has justly earned, guaranteed by law, or that "he should keep who has the right to keep, through having justly earned." Morris would have recognized in this not only the principle used to justify competitive commerce, but also the factor of privately accumulated wealth making for decadence both in society and in art.

In his later article on "How I Became a Socialist," Morris stated that he was looking for a society in which there would be neither masters nor masters' men; that his view of Socialism was what he began with—he had no transitional period; and he goes on to say that it was his *ideal* that forced him to become a Practical Socialist. But what was it, he asked, that forced him to conceive of an ideal? The answer to this question, aside from prejudice against the prevailing Whig or Liberal frame of mind, he says, came from the fact that "there were others who had a vague sentiment of repulsion to the triumph of civilization, but

were coerced into silence by the measureless power of Whiggery—a few, say two, Carlyle and Ruskin. The latter, *before
my days of practical Socialism*, [*italics* mine] was my master
toward the ideal aforesaid. . . . It was through him that I
learned to give form to my own discontent, which I must say
was not by any means vague. . . . This was a bad outlook
indeed. . . . Was it all to end in a counting-house on the top
of a cinder-heap, with Podsnap's drawing-room in the offing,
and a Whig committee dealing out champagne to the rich and
margarine to the poor in such convenient proportions as would
make all men contented together, though the pleasure of the
eyes was gone from the world, and the place of Homer was
taken by Huxley?"

Morris went on to say that he "was then in for a pessimistic
view of life, if it had not somehow dawned" on him that
"amidst all this filth, the seeds of a great change were beginning to germinate."

To sum up, then, the study of history and the love and practice of
art forced me into a hatred of civilization which, if things were to
stop as they were, would turn history into inconsequent nonsense, and
make art a collection of curiosities of the past. . . . But the consciousness of revolution stirring amidst our hateful modern society prevented
me, luckier than many others of artistic perceptions, from crystallizing
into a mere railer against "progress" on the one hand, and on the other
from wasting time and energy in any of the numerous schemes by
which the quasi-artistic of the middle classes hope to make art grow
when it has no longer any root, and thus I became a practical Socialist.

Morris wanted no classes, industrial or social, in his society.
His view of Socialism, he states, "is what I began with; I had
no transition period"—his critics to the contrary notwithstanding.

Could Morris have foreseen the signs of a coming great
change without having some view of history and some interpretation of historic progress which he could call his own? If
he were merely a follower in the footsteps of Ruskin, why did
he not think with Ruskin during the 'fifties that "the founda-

tions of society were never shaken as they are at this day?" But while Morris agreed that "politics are in a muddle," he did not seem to think, then, that the future of art and of society was endangered. And later, as we have seen, he disagreed with many of Ruskin's theories and practices, calling them "mostly gammon." Again, on July 24, 1884, Morris wrote to Mr. Thomson: "You must understand first that though I have a great respect for Ruskin and his works (besides personal friendship) he is not a Socialist, that is, not a *practical* one." Again, Morris could not concur with Ruskin's view that the upper classes have never had "so much sympathy with the lower, or charity for them, as they have at this day." Again, Morris could not have agreed that the fine arts have always been "supported by the selfish power of the *noblesse*" and have never "extended their range to the comfort or the relief of the mass of the people." This view of Ruskin's is more in accord with that of Arnold; and Morris, as we have seen, not only thought otherwise but also did not blame the *noblesse* of either feudal or modern times, but rather the modern *bourgeoisie* for the ailments of modern art, politics and society.

Again, although Ruskin hinted that it was a "diseased love of change" which destroyed Gothic art, Ruskin is not at all clear or consistent in that, first, he finds no cause for the disease, and obviously does not know what it is, and, secondly, according to his own theory, it was the possibility of "infinite change and variety" which first made possible the development of Gothic. He might rather have said, with Morris, that it was a diseased love of rigidity, of academic rules of art, which destroyed Gothic. Indeed, Ruskin made no effort at any time to discover the real cause of the disease which attacked modern art, and he remained a lover of great Renaissance art to the end. It is noteworthy that Morris was aware of this, and that the only notable occasion on which Morris made any wholehearted complimentary statement about Renaissance art was in the presence of, and presumably in deference to, John Ruskin.

Lastly, although at first glance Ruskin's references to the

servile ornament of the Greeks, the Ninevites and the Egyptians might be said to agree exactly with the views expressed by Morris on the archaic art of the ancient nations, Ruskin goes on to claim that this "slavery" was done away with altogether because "Christianity . . . recognized, in small things as well as great, the individual value of every soul." In observing this theory closely one sees that it is ambiguous, for the abolition of political slavery need not affect artistic slavery. It was Morris who developed a complete theory of these interactions between art, religion and society; and Morris's view of Christianity does not coincide at all with that of Ruskin. For Morris believed that the early Church had operated as a force which encouraged, indirectly, slavish customs and exclusiveness, even in art.

In conclusion, therefore, while admitting, as Morris himself frankly admitted, that Morris owed much to the thought of John Ruskin, one can also affirm, as did he, that Morris made his own investigations and evolved his own theories, agreeing with Ruskin on certain points, and disagreeing on many others. We may be justified, therefore, in accepting his own word that he gained his own new light mainly through the media of art, history and life. Certainly he did not take over, unquestioningly, the views of other men.

But it was an age of literary reformers just the same, and they spoke their pieces honestly and forcefully.

## CHAPTER III

MORRIS FORMULATES AN ARTISTIC-SOCIAL PHILOSOPHY
—BUT THE WORLD IS NOT DISTURBED

THERE was unity in the spirit, the life and the works of William Morris, so that all his variegated private and public activities are related entities. And so it happens that any distinction or division between the social thinker, the poet, the artist and the socialist is practically impossible. Each aspect of his career turns out to be but one of several approaches toward one conscious and increasing purpose: the regeneration of the thoughts and the habits of society.

Simply stated, the fundamental observations and views upon which Morris built his philosophy of historic development during the two decades that followed his graduation from Oxford amount to this:

History, considered in terms of the quality of culture, is divided into two major divisions: *ancient,* which slowly died during the fourth, fifth and sixth centuries of the Christian era; and *modern,* which came to birth during that dying time.

Both followed to some extent parallel lines of development, and both witnessed the rise of a number of civilized societies, each of which affected the civilization of its entire epoch, or division, in certain marked ways.

It is possible to judge these individual societies in terms of the conditions of their people and of their art. But most of our knowledge that is reliable and dependable has come down to us only through their art: *i.e.,* by the daily works of the people.

For art expresses the old and the new currents of the times in advance of other manifestations. Thus, when man first begins to express himself in "art," it is a sign that man has first begun

174

to think, and as art grows, the mental evolution of man grows.[1]

The art of a society does not, of course, confine itself to the "fine arts"; it is, on the other hand, concerned with every expression of the mental, the spiritual, and the imaginative or creative measures of men. Thus, dish pans as well as vases; houses as well as cathedrals; baskets and carpets as well as tiles and mosaics; fables and folklore as well as epics and lyrics; music as well as prayers; chairs and tables as well as jewel caskets and temples—all these and many other expressions of spiritual and imaginative activity must be considered as examples of the *Art* of a society.

The art of a society mirrors the conditions under which its members live, and enables us to judge, therefore, the permanence and the utility of that society in the historic epoch of which it forms a part. It is through the artistic expression of a group of related people, a society, that the growth and permanency of the thought and imagination of that people may be traced—and it is through modifications and adaptations within its artistic framework and manifestations, as time goes on, that there are always presaged those changes and modifications within society itself: changes of so-called cause and effect which subsequently work themselves out in the fields of politics, social relations, economics, religion and ethics.[2]

In brief, therefore, Morris believed that all historic progress and decay can be interpreted in terms of the interplay between art and society, artistic causes and effects taking precedence over all others.

It is this philosophy of historic change which caused Morris to disagree at heart with the "economics" and "historical materialism" of Karl Marx's *Das Kapital* (just as a similar philosophy caused Benedetto Croce to disagree many years later) and to write to the members of the Marxian Social Democratic Federation that any one who believes that "knife and fork" economics

[1]*Cf. The Lesser Arts; The Art of the People; The History of Pattern Designing; Gothic Architecture; Architecture and History,* and *Socialism: Its Growth and Outcome.*

[2]*Ibid.; cf.* also, *The Art of the People,* and *Art and the Beauty of Earth.*

takes precedence over "art and cultivation . . . does not understand what art means."[3] For art, to Morris, included economics, in so far as conditions governing the life and labour of a people were concerned.[4]

Morris also, like Croce's friend, Pareto, although on a much simpler basis, had a *residual theory* which could be applied to small units of a civilization or to historic epochs themselves. He saw the birth and decay of cultures as caused by an interplay of constructive and destructive forces within the framework of their art, and, consequently, of their society. Whatever was good in an old art or in an old society *might* be perpetuated in the new. But whatever was destructive, decadent, or evil would also carry over as a *residuum* of the old. Even if a society, or a culture, fell before an influx of *barbarians*, as did those of Egypt, the Hittite Empire, Persia, Greece and Rome, and the barbarians were capable of adopting enough of the art of the conquered to bring about a new blossoming or a new springtime of their own culture, they also received, willy nilly, in the resultant mixed or eclectic traditions of art a *residuum:* a residue of vice which was for them the very antithesis of their true art. In short, they inherited from the dead art and from the dead society those residual remains, or influences, which made for decay—so that sooner or later the new art and the new society grew ill, became poisoned, so to say, and died—after which there would come opportunity for a new birth, or a refashioning of the civilization and culture of that society along new lines (a kind of renaissance), thus leading ultimately either to a new progress or to a new decadence and death.

Thus, he thinks, ancient civilization, chained to slavery and to a "principle of exclusiveness," failed; and the barbarian civilization which replaced it and grew into modern Western

[3]*Justice,* June 16, 1894.

[4]Benedetto Croce, *Æsthetics; La Storia ridotta sotto il concetto generale dell' Arte;* and *Historical Materialism and the Economics of Karl Marx.*

It is interesting to note that the events in Croce's life, as related in his *Autobiography,* show almost a parallel development with the formative events in the life of Morris. *Loc. cit.,* pp. 13; 17; 26; 27; 28; 30–31; 31–32.

civilization has had the same choice to make. But modern civilization decreed for civil and political liberty, instead of for economic and artistic liberty, and has, on the other hand, declared for economic and artistic slavery. This decision came about, he thinks, with the Renaissance and the Commercial Revolution which accompanied it. Both ancient and modern civilization have, in their own ways, therefore, declared for *social slavery in fixed strata,* although recognized in modern times only under new names and materialistic principles of determination. He believed that the economic and artistic slaves of the modern world were worse off than the civil and political slaves of the ancient.

Only in the Middle Ages, he declared—only in the period between the death of the ancient and the full development of the modern—was there something approaching an equality of condition among European men; hence his admiration for the medieval, Gothic spirit. Of course, he admits that a Church and a Feudal hierarchy, both partly residual from ancient times, prevented complete equality of condition—yet workers often could attain happiness in their own work.

What was it, he asks, that caused the decline of medieval idealism and the rise of modern economic slavery? Chiefly this: the new civilization had carried with it, as a *residuum* of the old, the poisons that had come in part from the social and economic standards of "Roman landlordism" and in part from the imitative qualities of Roman thought (tendencies which welcomed eclectic philosophies, laws, principles and ethics). These poisons, the *residuum* of the Classical heritage, were to break down the new and fruitful aspects of medievalism; and they will, he adds, eventually destroy this civilization which we call modern and replace it with a new growth, bringing in a new blossoming time of art and a new social life—and resulting in a civilization as different from ours as the so-called modern is different from the so-called ancient.[5]

[5]Morris, *Collected Works,* XXII, pp. 6 *et seq.;* 32 *et seq.;* 63 *et seq.* Cf. also his *History of Pattern Designing.*

In this idea of birth and death, of the health of a civilization, literally considered, of poison and sickness affecting a civilization, Morris foreshadowed the later historical interpretations of Egon Friedel, of Eugen Georg, of Theodor Lessing, and of scientists such as Georg Groddeck and his disciples. Thus Friedel, like Morris long before, came to believe that the mental sickness of the modern age sprang from the Black Death and from the economic and artistic consequences of it upon Western society. He traces the subsequent "degeneration" in terms of the degeneration of architecture: Gothic yielding to baroque, baroque to rococo, etc. Such terms and others like them were frequently utilized in recent times by Spengler, Georg, and their imitators.[6]

Morris, returning to the evils which have accompanied the modern reversal of the ancient status of liberty and slavery, thinks such a change no change at all.

If it [civilization] does not aim at getting rid of this misery and giving some share in the happiness and dignity of life to *all* the people that it has created, and which it spends such unwearying energy in creating, it is simply an organized injustice, a mere instrument for oppression, so much the worse than that which has gone before as its pretensions are higher, its slavery subtler, its mastery harder to overthrow, because supported by such a dense mass of commonplace well-being and comfort.

Surely, he adds, this condition cannot long remain, for "if the *residuum* still clogs all the efforts of modern civilization to rise above mere population-breeding and money-making, the difficulty of dealing with it is the legacy, first, of the ages of violence and almost unconscious brutal injustice, and next of the ages of thoughtlessness, of hurry and blindness."[7] It was this dual legacy that Morris wished to rid society of, and, if that measure

[6]Eugen Georg, *The Adventure of Mankind*, pp. 242 *et seq.*; 264 *et seq.*; 273 *et seq.* Egon Friedel, *A Cultural History of the Modern Age*, Vol. I, Chaps. I and II, *passim.* Oswald Spengler, *The Decline of the West, passim.* Georg Groddeck, *The World of Man*, etc.

[7]Morris, *Collected Works*, XXII, p. 65.

failed, to bring about the destruction of modern civilization in order that a new and, he hoped, a better civilization might have a chance to grow.

The essay in which Morris's whole philosophy appears most clearly is the one upon *The History of Pattern Designing*. Here he divides ancient history into two distinct types: first, archaic (monumental, symbolic and priestly) and individual (progressive and perfectionist). These divisions are of style and not of date, since both types may be found among different societies at different times.

Since archaic forms are priestly and symbolic, they lack definite and rational expression of ideas and facts. Consequently, an archaic art form is mystical, sometimes incomplete, often grotesque. A perfectionist, or progressive, art form may be symbolic or grotesque only incidentally: it has attained the power of expressing thought rather than of registering mere emotional effect. The two types are best illustrated, he tells us, in the art and culture of ancient Egypt and of ancient Greece, respectively. Yet in both lands room for individual expression was denied after the general art forms and methodologies had once been standardized and formalized by rules and laws of art. The arts then became academical and static, rather than progressive.

Morris found in Greek art none of the inferior influence of Egyptian art. Heretofore, it had been usual for historians, antiquaries and archæologists, looking at Greek and Egyptian art, to assume, with the layman's view, that since Egyptian civilization was older, and since there seemed to be vague, external similarities in designs, vases, columns, etc., that the Greeks borrowed their art from Egypt. Morris, examining both arts with one of the most observant and artistic pairs of eyes in the nineteenth century, had no hesitation in saying that there was no real point of resemblance or of similarity. Egyptian art, he asserted, was not only Eastern, or Oriental, but also African. He believed that Negroid elements from Upper Egypt had given to Egyptian art some of its initial impulse. "Take as an indication," he says, "their love of stripes and chequers, that look as if they were borrowed from the mat-maker's craft, and compare them with the work of the African tribes and peoples." But Egyptian love of colour, and boldness in using it, represent a late Eastern, rather than a Southern or Western influence. Nevertheless, he adds, whatever shortcomings clung to Egyptian art, this much must be said: fourteen hundred years before Christ the Egyptians had perfected the arts of figure-weaving and dyeing; they were skilled workers in glass, and in pottery that was "glazed with an opaque glaze variously coloured and figured; and lastly they were as skillful joiners and cabinet-makers as their successors in modern Egypt, who are so clever in making the most of the little scraps of wood which an un-timbered country affords them."

To Morris, the boldness, massiveness and symbolism of Egyptian art exercised no perceptible influence upon the art of Europe. Greek art he regarded as something decidedly European or Western in origin, and especially so wherever its most individual contributions were most clearly marked. He regarded it as fundamentally Aryan in nature (using the word Aryan to apply to all those peoples who spoke an Indo-Germanic or Aryan tongue)—like that of Persia and of India, even though much of the latter, as he admitted, must have been borrowed, and even though all three arts were destined eventually to come under the "formal and repressive" influence of the East.

He did not believe that the columnar Greek temple had been derived from a knowledge of Egyptian columnar buildings; for, as he said, the scale on which the pillars of Egypt were designed was a *residual* remain of the times when their pillars were masses left to support the huge weight of the hillsides and cliffs of their prehistoric temple-caves: whereas, on the other hand, the Greek column was obviously derived from the wooden post, "its lintel a timber beam, and the whole building a holy memory of the earlier days of the race and the little wooden hall that housed the great men and gods of the tribe."

But for certain nobler aspects of architecture and for the accompanying *perfectionist* developments in pattern-designing, Morris regarded Persia as a "holy land." For *there*, he states, "in the process of time, *our art was perfected* (*italics* mine) and thence above all places it spread to cover for a while the world, east and west." Although much of its sculpture was taken from the Assyrians, Persia gave greater architectural dignity to its buildings than did any of the Near Eastern peoples; and "this is accounted for," in his opinion, "by the Aryan stock of the Persians." This superiority was shown still more in "the leap the Persians took in architecture proper."

For the rest, though this is the work of an Aryan race, that race had to go far and suffer much before it could attain to the measured, grave, and orderly beauty which they alone of all races have learned to create. . . .

Morris considered Grecian sculpture to be the most perfect of all time and noted especially its superiority to that of the Eastern nations, "seeming, as it did, to cut off, as if by means of an impassable gulf," all that had gone before. He thought it no matter for wonder that many critics have said "There is nothing to do but imitate," yet differed from them, saying that "unless we are to be forever the barbarians which the Athenians of the time of Pericles would certainly, and not so wrongly, have called us," we must see that even this art had its limitations, for the freedom of their people was a narrow freedom; their society was founded on mental as well as bodily slavery; their artists were soon compelled to follow prescribed forms; and therefore "the iron exclusiveness which first bound their society, after no long while unsettled it, and at last destroyed it."

Passing on to Roman history he sees little that is characteristic of Roman art or of Roman life that is not imitative and eclectic. Yet the Romans consolidated the architectural forms of the past and handed them on to modern civilization, just as they handed on their laws and their ideas regarding social distinctions as a *residuum*. Only when the strength of Rome was waning, its dominions fallen to the status of mere tax-gathering machinery, did the Romans begin to shake off the tyranny of Greece over their imaginative life. Then, in its closing years, the Roman state began to develop scroll-work and mosaics, signs of the coming wave of Persian influence that would turn late-Roman art into Byzantine—the last of the ancient art, the first of the modern.

The first change that marked the coming of a new art and a new society, says Morris, may be seen in Diocletian's palace at Spalato, built "but a few years before the Roman tyranny was rent in twain." For now "unheard of peoples" were thrusting themselves into the Classical World, "nation mingling with nation and blood with blood; the old classical exclusiveness is gone forever:

Dacians, Armenians, Arabs, Goths: from these came the captains of the Roman name; and when the Roman army goes afield . . . it well may be that no Italian goes in its ranks to meet the enemies of Rome. . . . A new art was slowly and unobtrusively getting ready to meet the new thoughts and aspirations of mankind. . . . Modern art was near its birth.

With the change in Europe there came also new changes in the East. After the Græco-Oriental empires of Alexander broke into various knots of anarchical states—the so-called Hellenistic kingdoms—Persia fell under the Parthian sway of Turanian highlanders. But these Tatar nomads, says Morris, did not mingle noticeably with the Persians: like modern Ottomans they rather camped among their conquered enemies. Having no art, the Parthians soon declined, presumably falling victims to the unaccustomed luxuries of civilized life. Thus "Artabanus, the last of the Parthian kings, turned from the victorious field of Nisibis, where he had overcome the men of the Roman name, to meet the rising of his Persian subjects, who, in three days of bloody battle, swept away his life and the dominion of his race. A curious lesson to warring tyrannies. . . ."

Hitherto, says Morris, only the columnar architecture of the Achæmenian Persians had betrayed their Aryan origin, and for three hundred and fifty years these people had been cut off from contact with other branches of their race by the Parthian conquest. But now the restored national or racial pride of the new Aryan Sassanian Empire of Persia, which arose on the ruins of the Parthian power, was expressed anew. Rock-sculptured monuments began to appear, the first commemorating the victory of the Persian Emperor, Sapor the Great, over the Roman army of Valerian, *c.* 260 A.D. This was built less than forty years after the native Persians, under Artaxerxes, had overthrown and slain the last of the Asiatic Parthians on the field of Hormuz.

The next important development in the new artistic birth of Persia, following the expulsion of the Parthian Tatars, is to be traced in the remains of Sassanian buildings, with the egg-shaped domes, their great cavernous porches with small doorways pierced into the sides of the walls, and with the capitals of their columns "curiously like that of fully developed Byzantine architecture." Their architectural carving at the palace of Mashita not only bears strong resemblance to elaborate Byzantine art at its best, but might easily be compared with the work of the Commenian Greeks at Venice and Milan. Moreover, Morris adds, it is very much like the designs on carpets and tiles which were completed nearly a thousand years after the battle of Cadesia in the time of Shah Abbas the Great. But among these greater activities, it should not be forgotten that the Sassanian Empire "preserved and handed down to later ages some forms of ornament which must above all be considered as parts of pattern-designing."

It is plainly evident that Morris felt strongly that a marked racial background underlay the artistic and social expressions of nations and cultures. He laid no claim, however, to ethnological learning, as he modestly pointed out, but he "has noted" the significance of the symbols of the tree of life and of the altar-flame supported by two living creatures, common throughout the early Near East, common in Byzantine art, and common in Medieval. He ventured the opinion that the monsters supporting the tree and the creatures supporting the altar represent "the opposing powers of good and evil"—that the fire and the tree themselves may represent symbols of life and of creation, and that perhaps "they form the leading idea of the dualism that fixed itself to the ancient Zoroastrian creed, the creed in which the Light and the Fire had become the recognized symbol of deity by the time of the Sassanian monarchs." In any event: "It is to the Sassanian Persians that we owe their influence in modern art."

The new Persian influence came to birth with the decay of classical civilization and with the death of classical art. Just as the Germanic influence replaced the classical influence of Rome (in large measure) throughout Medieval Europe, so, we may deduce, the new art of their Aryan-speaking Indo-Germanic cousins in Persia marked a new birth for Medieval civilization in the East—and hence, presumably, the Persian influence must be regarded as an early but integral part of that civilization which is called Medieval and of that architecture which is called Gothic.

The new and elemental development of the newly dawning civilization, says Morris, was freedom, the freedom of the many, at least in the realm of art. In ancient times the workman had to "grind through his work regardless, stick tightly to his gage lest he be beaten or starved, and then go; but now he was rising under the load of contempt which formerly had crushed him." That condition, in Byzantium at least, was not to last for long, yet it produced one great good in those earlier days:

An architecture which was pure in its principles, reasonable in its practice, and beautiful to the eyes of all men—a thing which can never exist in any state of society under which men are divided into intellectual castes.

It was this idea—that castes, even intellectual castes, prohibit the development of a pure art—which enables one to understand why Morris carried his theory of art into his active principles of "practical Socialism." It explains why he was opposed to various forms of State Socialism and even to a Carlylean "aristocracy of talent."

Finally, he concludes,

> When the Roman tyranny grew sick . . . men began to long for the freedom of art; and that, even amidst the confusion and rudeness of a time when one civilization was breaking up that another might be born of it, the mighty impulse which this longing gave to the expression of thought, created speedily a glorious art, full of growth and hope, in the only form which in such a time art could take, architecture to wit; which, of all the forms of art, is that which springs direct from popular impulse, from the partnership of men, great and little, in worthy and exalting aspirations.
>
> So was modern or Gothic art created; and never, till the time of that death or cataleptic sleep of the so-called Renaissance, did it forget its origin, or fail altogether in fulfilling its mission of turning the ancient curse of labour into something more like a blessing. . . .
>
> I love art, and I love history; but it is living art and living history that I love. If we have no hope for the future, I do not see how we can look back on the past with pleasure. If we are to be less than men in time to come, let us forget that we have ever been men. . . . Don't let us vex ourselves over the antepenultimate blunders of the world, but fall to on our own blunders. . . . If the day ever comes [when we have developed an art and an architecture of our own] we shall at last know what beauty, romance and history mean.

Nearly all the speeches and essays from which we have been citing Morris's judgments and opinions on art, industry, history and human indifference, in order to show that he had a profound philosophy and on what he based it, were delivered during a period of from one year to six years before he joined the Democratic Federation of Henry Mayers Hyndman. In themselves, these opinions and judgments would seem to dispose forever of the idea that much of what Morris later wrote and spoke regarding history, the state of society and social control could have been based upon the knowledge of other men such as Arnold, Carlyle, Ruskin, Fourier, Marx, Kropotkin,

Hyndman and Bax. Moreover, they prove conclusively that Morris had formulated views regarding historic evolution and conditions of society long before he delighted naïve minds in British labouring circles with his romantic tales of a golden medieval life and of a golden future *Utopia* which might "almost" be comparable with it.

For such knowledge and views as Morris expressed in these papers alone are not the sort of thing which could be mastered over night. Neither, it can reasonably be assumed, was his dissatisfaction with the existing state of society the result of any sudden conclusion on his part. Indeed, it has been possible to show that not only during the period of his later speeches, articles, books, pamphlets and letters, but also during the middle period of his development, as well as in the earlier period, he had been developing steadily the views expressed in these recent chapters. Finally, it should not be forgotten that these views of history and of the condition of a society in its relation to its people and to its art, had germinated before 1883: *i.e.*, before Morris ever heard of Karl Marx, and therefore before he made his first plunge into the intricacies of *Das Kapital*.

Only a few things remain to complete the picture of Morris's views on art, industry and history. He saw in architecture the creator and originator of all art; and he saw in art the chief essence of every work of man that was built with history behind it. He believed that a true society should develop its own thought and its own traditions, out of which there would emerge a native art, and he believed that this individual art would be expressed in the imaginative works—the literature, the music, the folk dances, the engineering, the manual labour—in brief, by the individual labour and by the social labour of a people; and that it would necessarily follow that these works would express and reveal the social life of the people, together with their thoughts and aspirations.

He did not wish any art to be rigidly exclusive; rather he believed that it was possible to practise "a wise eclecticism" in the adaptation of what was fundamentally useful. But he held that any attempt to exercise an indiscriminate eclecticism would

result in the destruction of the ideas and the ideals of a society
—expressed in its art and in its accompanying literature, and,
consequently, in its ethical, political and economic development. He felt that a society grew from within, and that the
greatest happiness and the finest idealism might be found within
its own peculiar circle of influence—peculiar to its own people
and native to its own conditions and traditions. He did not look
with disapproval upon societies which he felt to be foreign to
those of which he himself most highly approved; but he was
not by any means a cosmopolitan, a citizen of the world, nor
was he a real internationalist in any social or political sense.
Above all, he was an Englishman, and as individualistic a lover
of freedom as any.

He believed that within one society the fullest expression
of individual imagination and initiative should not only be
allowed, but even encouraged, in order to insure growth and
the recruitment of strength from below. His idea of progress
was a positive one, granted that once a native path of development—the true display of a society's own potentialities—had
been determined. He felt that without the freedom to develop
a native art, and therefore an artistic social order, a society must
necessarily be doomed to decay and then to destruction. He felt
very strongly that England was headed toward destruction—
indeed he had hinted of it in his undergraduate writings, and
now he talked repeatedly of the "coming great change" and of
a "coming great disaster" to any one who would listen. He
believed that the arts and the customs of societies of late-
modern times, particularly those which have evolved since the
time of George II in England and Louis XIV in France, have
represented a steadily increasing conglomerate of decadence—
in spite of apparent and superficial commercial and political
gains—and that *unless the people of England* could be persuaded
to turn back to their native line of development, as initiated
during the Gothic period, but altered and debased during the
"cataleptic sleep of the Renaissance," the best thing to do would
be to bring about hastily the destruction of modern civilization
and culture (which of its own accord was bound to fail anyhow,

unless rapidly and radically reformed) in order to facilitate the rise of a new civilization and a new culture.

How different these views are from those expressed by other literary and political "critics of Victorian democracy" can be appreciated only when their total significance is realized.

It was very simple, of course, for people who completely misunderstood Morris, or who felt no personal inclination to make the sacrifices which he suggested in order to "rejuvenate and regenerate" society—in short, for any one who was more wrapped up in his own concerns than in those of Morris—to say easily and hastily that Morris was a visionary. That much was, perhaps, true. Many a prophet is a visionary. And from such a position it was easy enough to point out that he was not in accord with the "progressive" and "forward-looking" tendencies of modern "progress"—that, unfortunately, he wished to plunge society back into the static society of the Middle Ages.

Or, on the other hand, these self-satisfied critics who glanced idly at one or two of his "literary offerings" could merely say that he was "a child of the Gothic Revival," or an "impractical poet and artist who envisioned a fairyland of romantic Utopianism that practical people would never care for," and that the things which he said about the past and the future had "no bearing upon the life of the present." Their historical and philosophical knowledge must have been more than enough to make Morris kick and tear the sheets of his bed in his sleep, while he was still alive, or turn in his grave at Kelmscott Manor after his death. Morris himself would have been the first to point out, as he did, that if civilization could progress without thinking of the past or of the future then there is no such thing as civilization: its very name "is a delusion and a lie" and there is no hope for it.

But now to get back to the story of Morris's life at the time when he had just about decided that the only real solution lay in a social revolution. He was getting along in life, approaching his fifties—although he had never seemed to realize it, thus far—and he was growing angrier every day.

# IV

## THE S. D. F.—AND REVOLUTION

*Have faith, and crave and suffer, and all ye*
*The many mansions of my house shall see*
*In all content: cast shame and pride away,*
*Let honour gild the world's eventless day;*
*Shrink not from change, and shudder not at*
    *crime,*
*Leave lies to rattle in the sieve of time!*

## CHAPTER I

PERHAPS THE SOLUTION LIES IN SOCIAL REVOLUTION

ALTHOUGH the optimistic confidence in middle-class progress and liberal politics that had flourished during the middle years of the Victorian epoch had suffered some severe attacks at the hands of prominent critics and writers, the fundamental complacency of the Victorian public was not noticeably shaken until a demand for social reform spread seriously among the native British proletariat. The re-creation of a native British proletariat along Socialist lines took place during the last two decades of the nineteenth century. In this re-creation there can be no reasonable doubt that William Morris's ideas and activities played a large part—perhaps a more significant part than did those of any other man.

We have seen that for years prior to his entry into the Democratic Federation Morris had been detecting signs of "a great change" at work in the minds of men. This new attitude seemed to be an augury of a coming golden age in the history of humanity: a time when art and true social progress looking toward equality would move forward hand in hand. Long before the 'eighties he believed that the benefits of the coming society would be achieved only after the blessings of life would no longer be exclusive and restricted possessions of a few fortunate individuals. He had come to the conclusion, however, as his private letters testify, that the privileged classes might submit to *political* change, if enough pressure could be brought to bear upon them. But no such change could destroy their *economic* power, which was what he most wanted. Thus, he had come to lose faith in Liberalism and in "party action" directed only along political lines.

It was his loss of faith in Liberalism between 1874 and 1877 which plunged Morris into an active public career. But throughout all the years that followed, his aversion to direct political action and to party methods was to continue as strongly as ever. Almost before this phase of his career was well begun he came to regard radical political clubs and reform societies that aimed to secure changes and reforms through parliamentary legislation as *impractical*. To Morris, these organizations represented merely so much more political machinery, which continued to multiply and which carried into political life an ultramodern complexity of technique that is all too comparable with those multiplications of industrial machinery which complicate economic life and hinder artistic and social development.[1] Thus, he regarded the new political and parliamentary activities of radical organizations as merely a step farther in the direction of that new "constitutional system" of State Socialism which he so heartily despised. He believed that Political Radicalism would have to be replaced by a Revolutionary Socialism which would effect a change in economic power.

It should be noted that only for a while did he play with the idea that a revolution in economic power *might* be effected by means of violence—because the privileged classes would not yield of their own volition. From this standpoint he later receded. Also it will be worth noting that the fine distinction which he made between Radicalism and his own variety of Practical Socialism, or of Revolutionary Socialism, led to a parting of the ways for Morris and every new Socialist group with which he became affiliated; and that the schisms in every instance were caused primarily by Morris's steadfast opposition to direct political action and to arbitrary establishments of

[1]According to Bernard Shaw, Morris was unalterably opposed to intellectual dialectics, since they tended to divide common groups into cliques. Morris disliked the Fabians, says Mr. Shaw, not because they were intellectual superiors, but because they represented one more separate "species" of Socialism. Like Dickens, Morris saw Parliamentarism as the way of failure and was constitutionally opposed to Parliamentary bickerings and obstructionist tactics.— *William Morris as I Knew Him*, pp. 1–7.

power along political lines. On each successive occasion he eschewed both politics and violence and turned to other means.

Morris's means, unlike those advocated or employed by Karl Marx and the advocates of *Scientific Socialism*, were not evolved as the result of economic formulæ, nor were they, as Doctor Mackail has pointed out, the result of economic reasoning. Briefly, Morris had faith in the intrinsic ability of British workingmen to think through the rights and wrongs of things. For he believed that public opinion, when genuinely aroused, could bring about any desirable change. To bring into being his own Practical Socialism, therefore, it was first necessary to educate public opinion, and then to agitate for its organization into a practical program. "Our business," he said again and again throughout his Socialist career, "is to make Socialists." His own contribution was to make his own idea of Socialism seem desirable to the public largely by convincing them of the difference between things as they are and things as they might be. He hoped to create anew the idealism of a native British proletarian spirit which, he thought, had lain dormant during the many years that had elapsed since the Middle Ages. To these ends, the re-creation of the ideal and the true portrayal of the ideal—the depiction of things as they might be—he was to devote most of his energies during the closing years of his life. It was this ideal which, from about 1876, he kept constantly before him. And it was this ideal which impelled him to join forces with all people who appeared to be concerned with the *practical* regeneration of society.

For more than five years before he actually became a member of the Democratic Federation, Morris had been endeavouring to point out to audiences of reputed wealth and culture (as well as to groups of poor labourers) his theories concerning art and society, and the degradation suffered by both under the present political and economic régime. But no wave of understanding greeted his views, and no white heat of passion swayed the bourgeois mentality of his audiences. With Morris it therefore became a matter of proved fact that only they who suffered most would most likely heed his message. His resentment against the vapid stolidity of bourgeois Whiggery, combined with his growing conviction that the toilers and the needy would comprehend his message, turned him to the Radical Clubs. Here, as we have seen, he made the acquaintance of Henry Mayers Hyndman, and, a little later, of Ernest Belfort Bax, the historian. It was Hyndman who founded the Democratic Federation. It was Bax who was chiefly responsible for bringing Morris into it.

## CHAPTER II

HENRY MAYERS HYNDMAN AND THE DEMOCRATIC

FEDERATION

HENRY MAYERS HYNDMAN, the son of a well-to-do family, had been educated at Cambridge. He was a shrewd man, ripe in experience gained by travel round the world, and although reared in the same sort of middle-class, evangelical atmosphere as Morris, Hyndman had caught the spirit of political liberty from early associations with Garibaldi and Mazzini. At Cambridge he had been a student of sociology, especially interesting himself in the communal manifestations of primitive peoples. Later he read the French translation of Marx's *Das Kapital*. In 1880 he made the acquaintance of Karl Marx, who was spending the closing years of his life in England; and in 1881 the beginning of a definitely revolutionary campaign on Hyndman's part was presaged by his publication of an article on "The Dawn of a Revolutionary Epoch."

A few weeks afterward Hyndman gathered about himself and his wife a small band of social reformers and anarchistic philosophers. This ill-defined group, nameless and nebulous, marked the earliest origin of what was to be known in after years as the Democratic Federation, although hardly any one was aware of it in the summer of 1881. The group did not hold together very well, however, for during the first year or more its ideologies and membership changed frequently. But the ideas of its founder did not change; more than any other individual, he was to be the prophet in England of Marxian Communism. Before Marx's doctrines could be popularized, however, support was needed for Hyndman's new enterprise.

At the opening meeting of the Democratic Federation, Hyndman distributed copies of his newly published booklet, *England for All*. Obviously it was the intellectual offspring of his conversations with Marx. Yet remembrance of Marx's Red International and of the bloody days of the Paris Commune of 1871 was still so keen in the minds of people everywhere that Hyndman in his Preface made no mention of the real originator of his views, merely stating that "For the ideas and much of the matter contained in Chapters II and III, I am indebted to the work of a great thinker and original writer, which will, I trust, shortly be made accessible to the majority of my countrymen."

There is no evidence to support the contention that the Democratic Federation was avowedly Socialist from its inception. It is true, of course, that several of its members, including the Hyndmans, Miss Helen Taylor (stepdaughter of John Stuart Mill), Mr. Herbert Burrows, Doctor G. B. Clark, and one or two others were socialistic in their sympathies.

At this time Henry George's *Progress and Poverty* was making a deep impression on English thought, and it is not surprising, therefore, that the foremost Socialist tenet of the new Democratic Federation was the Nationalization of the Land. Such a point could be reconciled easily enough with Marxian Socialism, and therefore Hyndman's earliest agitation was based upon democratic franchise and land nationalization.[1]

Hyndman's *England for All* was followed within the next eighteen months by two Socialist pamphlets: *The Coming Revolution in England* (1882) and *The Social Reconstruction of England* (1883)—and these, in turn, by a large octavo volume, *The Historical Basis of Socialism in England* (1883). The pamphlets were designed mainly to popularize the Marxian method of scientific political economy, and in them the author did not hesitate to acknowledge his indebtedness to Marx. In

---

[1]May Morris, *William Morris*, II, 73. Bruce Glasier, *William Morris and the Early Days of the Socialist Movement*, p. 12. See also Frederick J. Gould's *Hyndman: Prophet of Socialism*; Hyndman's *Record of an Adventurous Life*, esp. 347 *et seq.*; and *More Reminiscences*, *passim*. Hyndman's article named above appeared in *The Nineteenth Century*, January, 1881.

the former Hyndman tried to explain that Marx had discovered his "law of surplus value" from "the iron law of wages"! In the latter he asserted that one must study "Karl Marx's masterly work on 'Capital,' " in order to form any sound judgment on the problem of our existing civilization. Again, in *The Historical Basis of Socialism in England*, Hyndman expressed his indebtedness to Karl Marx, saying: "My indebtedness to the famous German school of political economy headed by Karl Marx, with Friedrich Engels and Rodbertus immediately following, I have fully acknowledged throughout. . . . My references to 'Capital' are to the French edition, for the reason that French is unfortunately much more commonly known in England than German. An authorized English translation will, I am told, certainly appear within the next few months, together with a translation of the unpublished second part."

Although Hyndman thus honoured Marx,[2] and acknowledged his indebtedness[3] to him, he had less to say regarding

[2] Hyndman, *The Historical Basis of Socialism in England*. In explanation of the foregoing statements it may be pointed out that only the first volume of *Das Kapital* had appeared in the French edition of 1873. The same volume was translated and published in England in 1886, by which time Marx's name and works were fairly well known among English Socialists. William Morris, Hyndman, Shaw and others read Marx first in the French edition, according to their own testimony. *Cf. William Morris as I Knew Him*, by Bernard Shaw, p. 3; May Morris, II, 606 n. In *The Record of an Adventurous Life*, pp. 209–10, Hyndman describes his first reading of *Capital* on the occasion of his American journey, especially at Salt Lake City, and his frequent talks with Karl Marx during the winter of 1880–81 in London (p. 273).

[3] Marxian economists reject the "iron law of wages" as unscientific. Ferdinand La Salle, who in 1862 introduced Scientific Socialism into Germany, was responsible for the formula, under which, he held, high wages increase the number of workers, resulting in an overstocked labour market. This, in turn, results in low wages, bringing about a shortage of available workers, causing high wages again, and so forth *ad libitum*. Most modern Marxists hold that the supply of labour always exceeds the demand because the "system" of capitalism has brought to birth an "industrial reserve army" which can be, and is, drawn upon at pleasure by the capitalists. Morris, although on one occasion (in his article in *The Commonweal* on what factories are like) referring to the "iron law of wages," usually evinced a clearer perception of Marxist historical interpretation.

Rodbertus, it might be pointed out, was not a follower of Marx, but rather

Engels's work. There can be little doubt, however, that in many instances Hyndman borrowed freely from Engels.[4]

Meanwhile, Hyndman's acquaintance with Marx during the early months of 1881 brought the two families into close contact for a while. The Hyndmans were friendly not only with Karl Marx, but also with Mrs. Marx and her soon-to-become-famous daughter, Eleanor, who made a common-law marriage with Doctor Edward Aveling. "Marx and Eleanor dined with us more than once in Devonshire Street," Hyndman writes, "but Mrs. Marx was already too ill to leave the house."[5]

Hyndman was not personally an ambitious man, but he craved distinction and recognition; he wanted to be great. Although giving his cohesion almost entirely to Marx, after some disputes about his failure to mention Marx's work in *England for All*, he practically ignored Engels, just as on future occasions he practically ignored contributions to his own writings made by Morris. For example, Bernard Shaw, who attended the meetings at which the "Joint Manifesto of the Socialists of Great Britain" was drawn up years afterward, has testified that the composition itself was entirely Morris's, although Hyndman soon convinced himself that it was both an important contribution and his own.

---

of Karl Marlo (Professor Winkelbach). These two, with La Salle, represent the real formation of the Scientific Socialist school of thought that stemmed from the Hegelian philosophy of the State. According to Professor F. J. C. Hearnshaw, all three of these streams of Socialist thought "met and mingled in the communism of Karl Marx—whose proper Hebrew name was Mordechia." (*The Development of Political Ideas*, 1928, pp. 60–61.)

[4]A statement such as the following needs little more than a glance to discover its origin: "Then follows a partial recognition of the social character of production by the capitalists themselves; the great engines of production and the great highways of the country are taken possession of, first by companies with many shareholders, then by the State." (*The Social Reconstruction of England*, p. 128.) This is little better than a free translation of Engels's: "*Teilweise Anerkennung des gesellschaftlichen Charakters der Produktivkräfte, den Kapitalisten selbst aufgenötigt. Aneignung der grossen Produktions—und Verkehrsorganismen, erst durch Aktiengesellschaften, später durch Trusts, sodann durch den Staat.*" (*Die Entwicklung des Sozialismus von der Utopie zur Wissenschaft.* Berlin [7 Aufl.] p. 53.)

[5]Hyndman, *The Record of an Adventurous Life*, 276.

Hyndman's narration of how he met Morris, together with other remarks concerning him, seems to reflect at its worst that "Tory tradition" which always clung to him. He was a Tory in looks, habits and often in mannerisms, but a radical at heart. And yet, as Miss Morris admits, "he was no self-seeker, and the greater part of his life was given up to work for the cause he had at heart. But with all the vigorous proclamation of the Socialist ideal, his temperament was difficult and made working with him almost impossible." According to Mr. G. B. Shaw, whose wit Hyndman detested, he craved leadership in every Socialist enterprise. At heart, however, he was not unamiable, and the admiration which he aroused among many devoted followers, together with the constant devotion of both his first wife and his second (for he remarried late in life, after having been a widower), indicate that he possessed a number of admirable qualities. Like Doctor Aveling, he was always fashionably attired, something of a dandy, and highly supercilious. He was compared, by some critics, with Sir Charles Dilke and with George Meredith.

On the other hand, Hyndman was not above working with the humblest proletarian in the humblest capacity. In that respect he resembled Morris. One thing was certain: "He was out to tell the world the truth as he saw it—that nothing but a change from 'production for profit' to a system of 'creation for use' would solve the problems by which society was faced." It would be difficult, writes Mr. George Bateman, an early member of Mr. Hyndman's party, to condemn his attitude unless you knew the man. "I have seen Hyndman and his wife —a dear, motherly woman, yet very self-reliant—selling *Justice* in the streets. And later in the day he was writing a leader in the *Justice* office, taking relaxation in the working of a royal size printing press. Compositors who had been at work all day would come along and do overtime without pay."[6]

Hyndman was, admittedly, a doctrinaire. "You must read Marx," he said again and again, "or you can't argue." Mr.

[6]Letter of George Bateman to the author, March 16, 1936.

Henry Wood Nevinson, who joined Hyndman's organization in the middle 'eighties, found the atmosphere too abstract and too opinionated for his liking. Years afterward he wrote: "Resolute and persistent as he was, I thought Hyndman was always a difficult man to work with and to follow. That invariable tall hat, that long frock coat, that wild eye always seeming to look out for the revolution coming round a corner, did not inspire my confidence."[7] Friedrich Engels, perhaps with reasons somewhat similar to those which inspired Bernard Shaw's dislike, wrote of Hyndman and of his organization that they were a group of political self-seekers—"office-seekers who spoil everything"—although Morris was exempted as a *Gemütssozialist*, and his friend Bax as a *philosophischer Paradoxenjäger*.[8]

Hyndman's own portrait of himself, as presented in his *Memoirs*, is not at all unfavorable. But it is impossible to form an accurate or a just characterization of the man on the basis of the many conflicting accounts. With the above portraits we must, therefore, be content, assuring ourselves that Morris's first partner in Socialism was a man of magnetic personality but of little originality. He was avowedly sincere, ardently ambitious for himself and for his friends; and he was ever ready to fight for his convictions. He was successful in drawing many personalities into his Socialist orbit, and although he lost many friends, he kept many.

During the early months of 1881 Hyndman succeeded in

[7] Henry W. Nevinson in *The Clarion*, March 24, 1934, "William Morris: Craftsman and Rebel." *Cf.* also Mr. Nevinson's *Fire of Life*, p. 34. His *Essays on Freedom* contains an excellent estimate of William Morris.

[8] Engels an Sorge, London, April 29, 1886. *Briefe und Auszüge . . . an F. A. Sorge, u.a.*, Stuttgart, 1906, pp. 220–21.

It is a bit difficult to translate *Gemütssozialist* as a "humanitarian socialist" in view of Morris's well-known opinion of "philanthropic humanitarianism." In typically crude German slang, Marx and Engels looked upon Morris—or upon what little they knew of him—as a kind of "butter and egg man" who acted as "angel" for the radicals. Bax, a scholar without money, and primarily a student of philosophy and of history, they regarded as a philosophically inclined hunter of paradoxes and a shallow phrase-maker, perhaps because he wrote both German and English perfectly, in marked contrast to some other Socialists.

attracting several "advanced thinkers" to his group: the Anglicized German student, Ernest Belfort Bax; the Austrian, Andreas Scheu; Henry Quelch, the future editor of the future periodical *Justice;* Jack Williams; J. L. Joynes; James Macdonald, and a number of others. But it was a small group and the outlook was not bright. Morris did not join until January 17, 1883, and such people as Walter Crane, H. H. Champion, Eleanor Marx-Aveling, and Doctor Edward Aveling did not enroll until the beginning of 1884. According to May Morris the men and women who attended the first few meetings of the Democratic Federation had no intention, for the most part, of forming a definitely Socialist body. Even Hyndman, in his early programs, advocated little more than the pushing forward of land, tax, and electoral reforms.

Among future distinguished persons who took an active interest in the Democratic Federation (or rather the Social Democratic Federation, for it soon changed its name) were Professor Beesly, the Positivist, who had acted as chairman of the first public meeting of the First International in 1864; Annie Besant; Justin McCarthy; Joseph Cowen, member for Newcastle; and Edward Carpenter.[9]

Edward Carpenter, after distinguishing himself as a scholar and a poet, had given up a Fellowship at Trinity Hall, Cambridge (1874), and turned to a simple country life near Sheffield, where he devoted himself to writing, to gardening and to handicrafts. His magnificent books, *Towards Democracy,* hailed as the outstanding prose writing of the early 'eighties,[10] *England's Ideal and Civilization,* reminiscent in many ways of

[9] It might be pointed out in passing that while some of these famous personages attended a number of the early meetings of the Democratic Federation, and thereby lent the authority of their names to the enterprise, most of them, for one reason or another, sometimes because of opposition to Hyndman and his policies (as in the case of Miss Helen Taylor), did not remain associated with the Federation for very long. Carpenter went his own road; Annie Besant joined the Fabians, and later gave up her political socialism for the religious socialism of Theosophy. Of those named above, only Cowen remained faithful to Hyndman, as we shall have occasion to observe.

[10] *Oxford History of England,* Vol. XIV, by Ensor, pp. 101; 161.

Clive Bell's famous essay on "Civilization" a half century later, and *England, Awake!* comparable with Lord Godfrey Elton's *England, Arise!* were to make his name famous among poets, artists and social reformers from 1883 onward. Edward Carpenter began his agitation for social reform in the same year that Morris became a Socialist, and in 1886 he founded a Sheffield Branch of Morris's Socialist League.

It was largely owing to Carpenter's initial contribution and to Morris's subsidy that the periodical *Justice: The Organ of the Social Democracy* was founded in January, 1884, and kept running until it could pay its way.[11] Its first editor was an Irish ex-war correspondent named Fitzgerald, but he was soon succeeded by Hyndman. A little later the job of editing was passed on to Harry Quelch, a former Trade Union Secretary who joined the Federation and remained the editor of *Justice* for many years. Quelch, according to the reminiscences of Belfort Bax, was a man of fine intellect, one of the most successful examples of a self-educated person that Bax ever met: "At once a clear thinker and an able and logical exponent of the views he expressed."[12] Harry Quelch was succeeded by Mr. H. W. Lee, who was also the Secretary of the Federation for thirty years, dying only recently.[13]

J. L. Joynes and Henry S. Salt had formerly been masters at Eton, resigning their positions, respectively, because of "indulgement in" and "the desire to indulge in" the new Socialist movement. They became great admirers of Morris, and contributed, with him, both to *Justice* and to Morris's later periodical, *The Commonweal*. These two young men were early friends of Bernard Shaw in the days when he first attended Federation meetings.

Messrs. Will Thorne (at the time of the present writing he

[11]Mackail, II; May Morris, II, 89–90.
[12]Bax, *Reminiscences*, pp. 111–12.
[13]The present author is indebted to Mr. George Bateman, a friend of the late Mr. H. W. Lee, and a prominent London journalist, for his kindness in procuring excerpts from the Minutes of the Federation for use in this book.

is still an "Old Parliamentarian") and John Burns, the famous
ex-Cabinet Minister, were others of the body who were later
to distinguish themselves in political life, although they
joined sometime after Morris and his more immediate friends.
Tom Mann and Jack Williams, two of the workers who fought
repeatedly for less poverty and more free speech, also deserve
mention. These four men, by the way, with Harry Quelch and
Herbert Burrows, were among the more prominent agitators
at the time of the Free Speech campaigns in 1886–1887 and the
great Dock Strike in 1889.

On the whole, the membership of the Democratic Federation, however insignificant it may have appeared to the London
of 1881–1884, was soon to prove itself not unworthy of attention.[14]

Prince Peter Kropotkin, in his *Memoirs of a Revolutionary*,
set forth an interesting picture of that small handful of British,
Russian, German, and Jewish radicals who seemed to be the
"only group in England" in 1881–1882 who were "aware of
either Socialist or Anarchist" thought and activity. In July,
1881, Kropotkin attended "a small anarchist congress" in London, after which he stayed on for a few weeks, writing a series
of articles—the first, he claimed, that were written from a radical standpoint—on the Russian affairs. The English press at that
time, he claimed, was "an echo" of the conservative views of
Madame Novikóff, "and I was most happy when Mr. Joseph
Cowen agreed to give me the hospitality of his paper" (*The
Newcastle Chronicle*). Having been expelled from Switzerland
shortly after his return, both Mr. and "Mrs." Kropotkin removed from Thonon to London in the autumn of the year 1881.

The year that I then passed in London was a year of real exile. For
one who held advanced opinions there was no atmosphere to breathe in.

[14]The author must apologize for the omission of a complete list of names
of all the early members of the S. D. F.— Indeed, it is very improbable that
a complete and accurate list could be treated adequately, even if space permitted. Miss May Morris has given a good account of many in *William
Morris*, II, pp. 86–105.

There was no sign of that animated Socialist movement which I found so largely developed on my return in 1886. Burns, Champion, Hardie and the other Labour leaders were not yet heard of; the Fabians did not exist; Morris had not yet declared himself a Socialist; and the trade unions, limited in London to a few privileged trades only, were hostile to Socialism. The only active and outspoken representatives of the Socialist movement were Mr. and Mrs. Hyndman, with a very few workers grouped around them. They had held in 1881 a small congress, and we used to say jokingly—but it was very nearly true—that Mrs. Hyndman had received the whole congress in her house. . . .

Mr. Hyndman had just published his excellent exposition of Marxist Socialism under the title *England For All;* and I remember, one day in the autumn of 1882, earnestly advising him to start a Socialist paper. I told him what small means we had when we started *Le Révolté,* and predicted a certain success if he would make the attempt. But so unpromising was its general outlook that even he thought the undertaking would be absolutely hopeless unless he had the means to defray all its expenses. Perhaps he was right, but when, less than three years later, he started *Justice,* it found a hearty support among the workers, and early in 1886 there were three small Socialist papers, and the Social Democratic Federation (the later name of the Democratic Federation) was an influential body. . . .

My wife and I felt so lonely in London, and our efforts to awaken a Socialist movement in England seemed so hopeless, that in the autumn of 1882 we decided to remove again to France. We were sure that in France I should soon be arrested; but we often said to each other, "Better a French prison than this grave."[15]

Thus it would seem that as late as November, 1882, the cause of Socialism seemed hopeless in England, even to so optimistic a worker as Prince Kropotkin. Also it seemed to Mr. Hyndman that a Socialist paper might not endure without having its expenses defrayed. But by 1886 all this had changed. When the Kropotkins returned to England in the latter year,

[15]Peter Kropotkin, *op. cit., The Atlantic Monthly,* September, 1899. Reprinted by Houghton, Mifflin Company, Boston, 1900, pp. 436–42. Morris declared himself a Socialist a few weeks after the departure of the Kropotkins. *Justice* first appeared on January 19, 1884, about 14 months after their departure.

not only did *Justice* seem to be in a thriving condition, but two other socialist periodicals had also been founded.

There can be every reason for supposing that William Morris played an important part in the great change which took place between the autumn of 1882 and the spring of 1886, especially as by the later date most of the other important labour leaders and Socialists of future fame had either not yet appeared, or if so, had not yet made noteworthy reputations for themselves or progress for the movement. It remains to be determined, therefore, just what influence William Morris may have had in putting the movement known as British Socialism on its feet.

---

## CHAPTER III

### THE S. D. F.—ENGLAND'S FIRST MARXIST ORGANIZATION

MORRIS was well aware of the sacrifices which others were making in order to pursue their work for the Socialist cause, and he decided that he, too, would have to make sacrifices. After thinking the matter over very carefully he decided that the most significant sacrifice which he could make at the time was to sell some of his treasured books. So in October, 1882, he parted company with a number of them, including his copy of *De Claris Mulieribus*, which had been his earliest bibliographical find, "in order to secure funds" for the cause of Socialism. It was a significant gesture.

During the autumn months of 1882 he prepared his mind still further for the plunge into Socialism by reading and re-reading more and more Socialist literature, especially that which dealt with the theme of British proletarian ideals. Butler's *Erewhon* (a cryptographic title for "Nowhere" or Utopia, first published in 1872) was new to him but none the less admired. He reread Sir Thomas More's *Utopia*, Bacon's *New Atlantis* and began a serious study of Wallace's *Land Nationalization* and Marx's *Capital*, among others.[1] On New Year's Day, 1883, he wrote to a friend: "Do you see the Pope is going to canonize Sir Thomas More? The Socialists ought to look up, if this is to be their late reward!" Thirteen days later he was made an Honorary Fellow of Exeter College, Oxford. And just four days after that, on January 17, 1883, he was inducted into the Democratic Federation.

The step into an active, rather than nominal, Socialist career

[1]Marx's *Capital*, in the French translation of 1873, and Fitzgerald's translation of *Omar Khayam* were greatly admired by Morris during the winter of 1882–83, according to Miss May Morris, (II, 76, ff.).

cost Morris much more than the price of a well-stocked library. It meant a cleavage with various friends who could not possibly understand how so respected a person as William Morris could espouse the cause of the working classes. It meant also a literary sacrifice of no mean importance—the definite surrender of his plan to write a new heroic cycle of Persia, a series of epical romances that should take their place beside his poems and legends of Greece and Scandinavia to complete his heroic depiction of early Aryan civilization. Yet even after his entry into the Federation he continued for a while with his Persian studies. During the early months of 1883 he even began a personal version of the *Shah Nameh*. But now his public activities began to encroach too much upon his time—even his private business interests could demand but little of his attention—and he turned heart and soul to his long-pondered cause, which would, he hoped, have a chance to succeed "now that Henry George's book has been received in this country and in America as a New Gospel."[2]

Within a few days of Morris's entry into the Democratic Federation a friend of Burne-Jones wrote in his diary of how Morris came into the latter's home one Sunday morning, fresh from a Socialist address before some Clerkenwell Radical Club, "bubbling over with Karl Marx" whom he had recently read in the French. "All Socialists are agreed as to education," declared Morris, but he had already found that "while working men are eager to learn, they are also woefully ignorant." Through Burne-Jones's eyes one can see Morris at this time: "Unchanged—little grey tips appearing on his curly mass of hair, no more—not quite so stout nowadays; not one hair less on his head; buttons off more than ever, never any necktie; more eager if anything than ever, but just about the same things as before." His friends were not pleased with his new political manœuvres, at least for the time being. "It was the one time when I failed Morris," wrote Burne-Jones years afterward. "I thought when he went into it," he related to a friend toward

[2]Morris to C. E. Maurice, June 22, 1883.

the turn of the century, "that he would have subdued the ignorant, conceited, mistaken rancour of it all—that he would teach them some humility—with his splendid bird's-eye view of all that has ever happened in the world, and with his genius for history in the abstract. . . . But never a bit—he did them absolutely no good. . . . All the nice men that went into it were never listened to, only the noisy, rancorous ones ever got the ear of the movement."

While to his old friends Morris was still called "Top," to his new ones in the Democratic Federation he appeared as an established luminary and a famous sage. None except Hyndman approached him in age, and Hyndman himself was still relatively young. The support of a man of international renown, such as Morris, would therefore count heavily, and only one or two of the members may have had fleeting fears that Morris's influence might outweigh their own. On the other hand, Morris for the first time in his life seemed to lose his old feeling of being a younger member of a mature set. Long afterward he stated that he now first realized that he was "an elderly duffer."

But with an enthusiasm far more youthful than elderly and far more revolutionary than at other periods of his career, Morris set to work with a will to "make Socialists." Unfortunately, not many of his early speeches for Socialism are now available, but his address before the Radical Working Men's Club of Clerkenwell, and his speeches at Oxford and at the Royal Institution in Manchester, all delivered in 1883, shortly after he joined the Democratic Federation, suffice to point the direction of his new crusade. From them we learn a number of things, but nothing really new.

In *Art and the People: A Socialist's Protest Against the Capitalist Brutality, Addressed to the Working Classes,* he declared that Art is no mere dream of sequential æsthetics, but rather the vanguard of all apparent progress, and that the historians of the grey future will find no beauty or ease in the dim records of the nineteenth century, but rather the chaotic

and lying accounts of statesmen and diplomats—"and thereafter a blank space," a time of anarchy signifying their own
overthrow, no doubt! In this sentiment one can see, once more,
that Morris's revolt was based upon the interaction between
living, progressive art and a growing, vital society. It need
hardly be doubted that the obtuse listeners who watched him
"jumble art with Socialism" had no least apprehension of what
he was talking about.

From Art, Morris turned to Manufacturing and to the place
of the worker in modern industry, stating that people today
were no more than "cog-wheels and cranks" in a profit-making
system that destroyed art and beauty, and therefore humanity.
How, under this system, he asked, can a head of an industry
heed whether what he produces is good or bad, so long as it
sells at a profit? The only solution, he declares, is the death
of profiteering, or the spiritual and mental death of mankind!

Meanwhile, he believes, the masses are hoodwinked by the
two hypocritical pillars of England's greatness: *supply* and
*demand*—words used to cloak the native hideousness of their
true meaning, for both are artificially created illusions. His is
no dream, but a cause; men and women have died for it; they
lie in prison for it and are ruined for it; but the dreams at
last will come true and the "Constructive Revolution" be triumphant.

On February 6, 1883, speaking at The Royal Institution on
the subject of "Art, Wealth and Riches," he pointed out first
the difference between the meanings of Wealth and of Riches,
denounced Competitive Commerce, and then compared the
condition of modern labour with the despised medieval caste-
system:

We do not seem to have quite cast off even the mere superstition
founded, I take it, on the exclusiveness of Roman landlordism (for
our Gothic forefathers were quite free from the twaddle) that handi-
work is degrading. . . . Why in the name of patience should a carpenter be a worse gentleman than a lawyer? His craft is a more useful
one, much harder to master, and at the very worst, even in these days,

much pleasanter; and yet, you see, we gentlemen and ladies durst not set our sons to it unless we have found them to be enthusiasts or philosophers who can accept all the consequences of their "rash acts" and despise the opinion of the world . . . and lie under the ban of that terrible adjective, *eccentric.* . . .

And now I want to get back before I finish to my first three words, Art, Wealth and Riches. I can conceive that many people would like to say to me: You declare yourself in rebellion against the system which creates wealth for the world. It is just that which I deny; it is the destruction of wealth of which I accuse competitive commerce. I say that wealth, or the material means for living a decent life, is created in spite of that system, not because of it. To my mind real wealth is of two kinds . . . things good and necessary for the body, and things good and necessary for the mind. . . . Meanwhile, the first of these two kinds of real wealth competitive commerce largely wastes, the second she largely destroys.

After this denunciation of the treatment of the Victorian poor, he states his counter-demands in quick succession: *viz.,*

1. All persons to be educated according to their capacity.
2. Manners and "breeding" for all, instead of for "gentlemen only."
3. A common tongue for a common people.
4. Wages only for work actually done.
5. Abundant wages for difficult, or disagreeable, work.
6. Science and technology diverted to the paths of the avoidance of human misery.
7. Freedom to refuse to manufacture "cheap and nasty" wares for competitive commerce.
8. Division of labour restricted within reasonable limits, and individual initiative and originality encouraged by all means.
9. Restriction of "the wasteful system of middlemen."
10. Contacts between workers and the public, in order that the public may better evaluate, appreciate, and understand the work done by workers.
11. Workmen to be guaranteed their due share in all profits, just as they now are forced to take more than their due share of "bad fortune" in business.

12. Entrepreneurs and executives to be paid no more than due wages for work actually done in organizing and operating a business.

13. Jobs to be dependent upon skill, merit, and intelligence, rather than upon gifts and personal influence among "the sons of money-bags."

14. Standards of beauty and utility to be applied to all the works of men's hands, in order to regenerate the souls of men.

What duty can be more pressing, today, he urges, than to carry out all our modern rubbish, and burn it piecemeal, "lest some-day there be no easy way of getting rid of it but by burning it up inside with the goods and house and all!" With this parting shot, Morris left the Conversazione of Manchester Societies to its own devices.

For the present Morris was merely looking ahead, endeavouring to arouse as many persons as possible to an awareness of the difficulties under which they existed and would continue to exist unless change were accepted. And he hoped for greater education and superior organization in the future, after his agitation had begun to take effect.

Meanwhile the Democratic Federation was progressing. Soon a periodical would be launched and a more definite policy be announced.

# CHAPTER IV

## THE BRITISH ROYAL COMMISSION AND TESTIMONY
## AT OXFORD

TWO incidents during the years 1882 and 1883 reflect the opposite poles at which the value of Morris's thought was being recognized. One was his report for The British Royal Commission on Technical Instruction, March 17, 1882, and the other his address at Oxford University.

Professor Bernard Samuelson, M.P., F.R.S., was chairman of the Commission when Morris was summoned before the body because of his importance in connection with "the various branches of manufacturing in which designing is an important element."

"The business that I carry on," said Morris, "comprises weaving, dyeing, cotton printing, carpet weaving, glass painting, and cabinet making." In effect, his report warned of the dangers of reckless imitation of Continental designs, and urged the necessity of teaching English youth to think for themselves and to design articles for interior adornment which were based upon native standards and native patterns. He believed that "literary instruction" was absolutely necessary in view of the fact that he himself had often experienced difficulty in dealing with the workmen whom he employed in London, "because of their general ignorance." He pointed out that there was then no "school of professional designers" operating in London, such as those which then existed in Paris. In London, he said, there were too many "half professional designers," and too few who understood anything connected with the basic principles of the art. He affirmed strongly the need of educational facilities in all works connected with the handicrafts.

Through the influence of Faulkner, who now held a Fellowship at University College, Oxford, Morris lectured at University College on November 14, 1883. His subject was "Art Under Democracy," a title which was subsequently changed to "Art Under Plutocracy": a significant substitution of ideas as well as words.

John Ruskin introduced Morris on that occasion, calling him "a great conceiver, a great workman: at once a poet and an artist."

Morris began his address by asking the students to regard art as representative of all the human adaptations of man, and to extend it to all the externals of life. He then went on to develop his historic theory that "civilization dies if art is doomed." This led naturally to a consideration of the lesser arts and the state of the workers. He contrasted medieval concepts with those of a full-blown *laissez faire*, which could create only anarchy through class antagonisms. For art, and hence civilization, to flourish, art must be "man's expression of his joy in labour." But, under plutocratic democracy and *laissez faire* economics, no hope of these can survive—and without them there can be no hope of permanent progress.

It was art, he declared, and not commerce, that caused the Renaissance. It was the creative instinct of European men, which had been allowed to blossom for five centuries before "the glory of the Renaissance" came upon Europe, by virtue of medieval "popular art," which was responsible for that strange period of noble creation.

But with the triumph of the commercial spirit, the soul and the romance were gone from art. A great sickness fell upon the arts, now grown exclusively to be the property of the initiated, and a great sickness consequently fell upon the civilization of Europe.

What has caused the sickness? Machine labour, will you say? . . . Yet look around the world and you must agree with John Stuart Mill in doubting whether all the machinery of modern times has lightened the daily work of one labourer. . . . The phrase labour-saving machinery is elliptical, and means machinery which saves the cost of labour, not the labour itself, which will be expended when saved upon other machines.

It is the superstition of commerce being an end in itself—of man made for commerce, not commerce for man, which has sickened art. This servile acceptance of an uncouth ideal has resulted in the establishment of a plutocratic comfort civilization which, to Morris at least, represents all that the "middle-class liberal ideal of a reformed society" has to offer:

All the world turned *bourgeois*, big and little; peace under the rule of competitive commerce, ease of mind and a good conscience to all and several, under the rule of the devil take the hindmost. . . .

How much nearer are we to the ideal of the bourgeois commonwealth than they were at the time of the Reform Bill, or the time of the Repeal of the Corn Laws? Well, thus much nearer to a great change, perhaps, that there is a chink in the armour of self-satisfaction . . . but as to approaching the ideal of that system reformed into humanity and decency, they are about so much nearer to it as a man is nearer to the moon when he stands on a hayrick!

But don't let's talk of averages, he continues, for while the better-class workingmen live today in a sort of "swinish comfort," they are miserable in other respects. That class is the class of victims, for the Liberal ideal is nothing but an implacable war. "I tell you the very essence of competitive commerce is waste; the waste that comes of the anarchy of war."

Possibly it may be true, he suspected, that the masses of England were without hope and without ambition, yet such an idea, at best, he declares, "is a dastard's point of view."

"I say," he shouted at the top of his voice, "that any such view belongs to slave-holders and to the hangers-on of slave-holders!" For who among us, he demanded, would be content to try to live and support a family "on ten shillings a week"?

Do you doubt that if we had any time, amidst our struggle to live, that we should not look into the titles of those who kept us there, themselves rich and comfortable, under the pretext that it was necessary to society? I tell you there is plenty of discontent—and I call on all those who think there is something better than making money to help in educating that discontent into hope! I am representing reconstructive socialism before you—but there are other people who call themselves Socialists whose aim is not reconstruction, but destruction; people who think that the present state of things is horrible and unbearable (as in very truth it is) and that there is nothing for it but to shake society by constant blows given at any sacrifice, so that it may at last totter and fall. May it not be worth while, think you, to combat such a doctrine by supplying discontent with hope of change that involves reconstruction? Meanwhile, be sure that though the day of change may be long delayed, it will come at last. The middle classes will one day become conscious . . . and cast in their lot with the working men. . . .

There are, he said, only two choices left open: to fight against change at the cost of a violence that none can foresee—or to advance it: "to strive single-heartedly that truth may prevail; and what need you fear? At any rate not your own victory—not your own tyranny!"

We have but one weapon against that terrible organization of selfishness which we attack, and that weapon is Union . . . organized brotherhood to break the spell of anarchical Plutocracy. One man with an idea in his head is in danger of being considered a madman; two men with the same idea may be foolish, but can hardly be mad; ten men sharing an idea begin to act; a hundred draw attention as fanatics; a thousand and society begins to tremble; a hundred thousand and there is war abroad, and the cause has victories tangible and real; and why only a hundred thousand? Why not a hundred million and peace upon earth? You and I who agree together, it is we who have to answer this question.

The Master of University College was afterward quoted in *The London Times* as saying that if he had known Mr. Morris would announce himself a member of a Socialist society and ask for membership and support, the use of the college hall would have been refused. But Mr. Morris had stated, in writing to his friend, Faulkner, that he had no intention of allowing any of the *old* buildings at Oxford to be blown up by Hyndman or by other Socialists.[1]

This lecture was one of Morris's most famous; and in it one notes a number of pronouncements which indicate that Morris was keenly conscious of Ruskin's presence upon the platform and took pains to cater to his opinions upon certain subjects, such as Renaissance art and division of labour.

Some of Morris's other lectures were also having their repercussions. *The Manchester Examiner* saw fit to inquire whether Mr. Morris's lecture on "Art, Wealth and Riches" had not raised another question than one of mere art. To this attack Morris replied: "It was the purpose of my lecture to raise another question than one of mere art. . . . Popular art has no chance of a healthy life, or, indeed, of a life at all, till we are on the way to fill up this terrible gulf between riches and poverty."[2]

These lectures, together with numerous explanations in his correspondence at this period, indicate that Morris was a Socialist with certain qualifications that kept him apart from other Socialists of his time. He was opposed to violent and destructive methods. It is clear that his social revolution was one which began with a pointing of the way for the England of the future, that he believed that the change must come gradually and without destructive influence or violence, and that the signs of change must be accepted by the *bourgeoisie* as well as by the proletariat. Furthermore, it is clear that he believed that "reconstructive Socialism" had to be undertaken before "destructive Socialism" ruined the nation—and that is an odd and significant point worthy of attention.

[1] This letter is printed in part in May Morris, II, 86. *Cf.* Mackail, II.
[2] *The Manchester Examiner*, March 14, 1883. *Cf.* Vallance and Mackail.

# CHAPTER V

## A PERIODICAL KNOWN AS "JUSTICE"

THUS far in its short-lived history the Democratic Federation had been Hyndman's property. For about a year it had been he who paid the rent for the offices and the salary of the secretary. It was he who stood at the head of the body, a seeming cross between a fanatical English Puritan and a Hebrew prophet, come alive out of an earlier day. One fixed idea had rooted itself in his mind: Marx was his God and he, Hyndman, his prophet. Not only did he intend to re-shape England's social and economic life, he also meant to control the destinies of his new subjects. Swearing and drinking he would not tolerate. The mildest indulgence in lewd comment he rebuked. Atheism, however, he would tolerate. And many of the members who now belonged to the Federation were unbelievers. But this was to mean no chaotic freedom, no acceptance of rash or ribald activity. Discipline must be established before the seeds of political organization could be safely sown.

Morris, on the other hand, was easygoing and liberal in his views: indeed, almost a freethinker. To the formalism of Hyndman he represented the "un-discipline" of overripe adolescence. To the scathingly grammatical damnation of capitalism and of society at large, which Hyndman proffered his audiences, Morris offered small encouragement. He fraternized with the "comradeship" in a perfectly amiable manner. "Art, indeed," he would say, "where the hell is it? Where the hell are the people who know or care a damn about it?"

So, as time went on, Morris tended to relax for a while in his preachments regarding art. He attempted to espouse the difficult science of economics. Together with Belfort Bax he studied

217

Marx with great labour, difficulty and lack of sympathy. Again, he lacked sympathy for the abstainers and teetotalers among the fraternity. "I should have liked you to have a drink with me," he would say, half hopefully, only to realize more and more that such a drink turned out usually to be something no stronger than lemonade. For a successful dinner, according to Bernard Shaw, a bottle of wine was an absolute necessity.

In such circumstances it was easily apparent that sooner or later a schism would occur. It would be only natural for the more fanatical, puritanical and ascetic among the Federation to rally around Hyndman—while the easier going members, including most of the German and Austrian "comrades," would rally around Morris. Thus, personal and psychic differences would tend eventually to promote the formation of two cliques, one centering around Morris and Belfort Bax, the other around Hyndman and his most trusted disciple, Harry Quelch.[1]

The real Socialism of the Democratic Federation was not yet in strong evidence and during 1884 efforts were made to strengthen the Scientific basis of its avowed principles. Hyndman and the writers who followed him wrote more and more in the shadow of Marxian formulæ. Evidently Bax, too, accepted the Marxian interpretations of historic and economic growth; and Morris, for a while, came under the influence of them, although his writings do not suggest many Marxian ideas. Nevertheless, he does refer occasionally to "that great thinker."

Then, to emphasize the Marxian trend, at a conclave of the Federation, on August 4, 1884, the name of the body was changed to The Social Democratic Federation.[2] Yet how weak, in reality, the body was is shown by its own computation, for at

---

[1] Henry (Harry) Quelch, besides editing the organ *Justice*, wrote for it under the name of "The Tatler." A letter from an early feminine member of the group states that "H. Q. was a dirty specimen who Kowtowed to Morris in his company, but abused him behind his back." If such remarks were made, it must be pointed out that Quelch followed Hyndman implicitly. Any abuse of Morris he later atoned for in the Memorial Number of *Justice*, which appeared at Morris's death, October 10, 1896.

[2] S. D. F. Minutes, August 4, 1884. Signed, H. H. Champion, Secretary.

the Annual Conference of that year it was estimated that the real activities of the Social Democratic Federation were actually furthered by "less than a dozen men." Most of the others merely attended meetings.

The old program: universal suffrage; equal electoral districts; payment of members of Parliament; triennial meetings of Parliament; abolition of the House of Lords; penal punishment for corruption and bribery; Home Rule for Ireland; self-government for the colonies and dependencies; and Nationalization of the land, could hardly have been called Socialist, though tending in that direction. The first three demands were very old indeed. They were carry-overs from the days of Chartism and, for that matter, went back to the pre-revolutionary demands of Charles James Fox and his adherents in the committee of Westminster electors. The remainder were scarcely different in any form from the demands of political radicals elsewhere. Henry George himself, then receiving much publicity in England, although responsible for the idea of Land Nationalization, had denounced Socialism; and the idea of Land Monopoly in the S. D. F. did not seem to disturb Liberals overmuch so long as capital in the form of money and vested interests in commerce and industry were not interfered with. Indeed, many Liberals advocated steps in the direction of Land Nationalization. It would be a further blow against the landed Tory interests in Britain.

Now, however, the Social Democratic Federation had declared itself for Marxian Socialism, which would "always be fearlessly championed." Indeed, the same conclave of Federation members declared that "from the first the Democratic Federation was a definite Socialist body." This may have been so, in a way; but it was not printed officially until January 19, 1884, in the first issue of *Justice*.

It is true, on the other hand, that steps forward had been taken from time to time. Thus, the first issue of *Justice* also set forth a new program for the Federation, as follows: Adult suffrage; annual Parliaments; proportional representation; payment of members and of the official expenses of elections out of rates (taxes); bribery, treating and corrupt practices at elections to be made acts of felony; abolition of the House of Lords and of all hereditary authorities; legislative independence for Ireland; National and Federal Parliaments, including representation of colonies and dependencies; Nationalization of the land; free justice; disestablishment and disendowment of all State Churches; power of war and treaty-making to be vested in the direct representatives of the people.[3]

This first issue of *Justice* contained a "political fiction" by Morris, entitled "An Old Fable Retold." In this, Morris compared public agitation over politics with the kind of agitation which might exist among a flock of chickens, among which one coxcomb, more independent than the rest, cries out, "I don't want to be eaten." At this a storm of disapprobation breaks loose among the multitude, with cries of "practical politics," "county franchise," "Great Liberal Party," and much useless cackling. These palliatives produce a quieting effect upon the assemblage, and all members withdraw after presenting a new resolution to the government—in this case the farmer's wife and the head poulterer. Presumably the author did not want the public to remain a group of chicken-hearted simpletons.

An editorial by Hyndman on "The Principle of Justice" stated that it would be the purpose of the paper to "stir up discontent," to expose wretched conditions of poverty, and to present the "definite, scientific, historical and economical basis" of Socialism.

The second issue of *Justice* contained an article by Morris on "Cotton and Clay," which dealt with the report of a government commission on sanitary conditions in the weaving sheds and "the decline of the ancient staple," which the Commission "regretted." Morris wrote scathingly of the latest type of textile production—"this cursed heap of filth" which without competitive commerce would "never be made at all."

In *Justice*, February 9, in an article on "Order and Anarchy," Morris attacked plutocratic society as anarchic and irresponsible.

[3] *Justice*, Saturday, January 19, 1884. No. 1.

"Slaves," he declared, "are a necessity to the capitalist organization. Let the governing classes of capitalists feel that they are ruling discontented slaves!" Hyndman's editorial leader in this same issue declared that "no other journal in Great Britain dare put the case of the workers against the confiscating classes as *Justice* will put it," and ended by requesting all members to see to it that the paper shall "be on sale in your neighbourhood." On page 4 of this same issue there was a joint article by Morris and Hyndman entitled "The Bondholders' Battue," in which they stated that "our entire action in Egypt has been shaped by a gang of international loan-mongers from the first outbreak of the soldiery under Arabi until now." Let not Englishmen, by a cry for vengeance or an appeal to spurious patriotism, be deluded, they demand, "whatever may have been the fate of noble General Gordon." For "the workers have many accounts to settle at home, without allowing a Liberal government to promote reaction under the pretext of putting down slave-dealing, or to annex Egypt for the benefit of the upper and middle classes."

The editor, in this same issue, calls attention to the first issue of a new Socialist magazine, *To-Day*, containing "Mr. William Morris's beautifully written essay on 'Art Under Plutocracy,' delivered at Oxford University," as well as Miss Eleanor Marx's able notes on the International Movement. "Altogether," Hyndman concluded, "*To-Day* does credit to English Socialists."

During the spring months Morris began the writing of his Socialist Chants. Between April 5 and June 7, 1884, there appeared "The Day Is Coming"; "The Voice of Toil"; "All for the Cause," and "No Master." Occasionally other poetry appeared; indeed, it now seemed that a well-defined attempt was made to add poetic inspiration to the enthusiasm of the membership. "All for the Cause" received a full page in the issue of April 19, and on May 3, Elizabeth Barrett Browning's "The Cry of the Children" was featured.

Most of Morris's chants, as he called them, were really ballads written to old, familiar tunes. In the first of them he begins with "the wonderful days a-coming when all shall be better than well" and concludes with his vision of the fellowship of the future:

O strange, new wonderful justice! But for whom shall we gather the
    gain?
For ourselves and for each of our fellows, and no hand shall labour
    in vain.

Then all Mine and all Thine shall be Ours, and no more shall any
    man crave
For riches that serve for nothing but to fetter a friend for a slave.

In "The Voice of Toil" he decries the spirit of pessimism among those who believe that evolution must come slowly:

I've heard men saying, Leave hope and praying,
    All days shall be as all have been;
To-day and to-morrow bring fear and sorrow,
    And never-ending toil between.

Then, passing on to the coming age of steam, steel, and electricity:

Where fast and faster our iron master,
    The thing we made, forever drives,
Bids us grind treasure, and fashion pleasure
    For other hopes and other lives.

Where home is a hovel, and dull we grovel,
    Forgetting that the world is fair;
Where no babe we cherish, lest its very soul perish,
    Where our mirth is crime, our love a snare,—

He then goes on to ask "if we shall lie forever in the hell our hands have won":

Let dead hearts tarry, and trade and marry,
    And trembling, nurse their dreams of mirth,
While we, the living, our lives are giving
    To bring the bright new world to birth.[4]

[4]The best treatment of *Chants for Socialists* appears in *Socialism in Song*, by Bruce Glasier. Manchester: National Labour Press, Ltd., (c. 1919.)

In "No Master," he repeats the same question, this time to the tune of "The Hardy Norsemen":

> And we—shall we, too, crouch and quail,
> Ashamed, afraid of strife,
> And lest our lives untimely fail,
> Embrace the Death in Life?
> Nay, cry aloud, and have no fear,
> We few against the world:
> Awake! Arise! The hope we bear
> Against the Curse is hurled.

The twelfth number of *Justice*, April 5, announced that in the three months of its existence the periodical had tripled its circulation. But as yet no circulation statistics were ventured. There can be but little doubt that it was still almost unknown.

Meanwhile, Morris continued with the remainder of his articles on Factory Life, begun April 12 with "Why Not?" On May 17 "A Factory as It Might Be" appeared, and on June 28, "Work in a Factory as It Might Be."

In the issue of June 21, there was a significant statement from William Morris, who was now the Treasurer of the Federation, concerning the expenses of the periodical and publishing the names of "a list of friends who had engaged to subscribe definite weekly sums" toward the support of *Justice*, as follows:

|                      | £ | s. | d. |
|----------------------|---|----|----|
| E. Belfort Bax       |   | 1  | 0  |
| W. H. Campbell       |   | 1  | 0  |
| C. J. Faulkner       |   | 1  | 0  |
| E. F.                |   | 1  | 0  |
| F.                   |   | 1  | 0  |
| H. M. Hyndman        |   | 1  | 0  |
| M. [May?] Morris     |   | 1  | 0  |
| J. L. Joynes         |   | 1  | 0  |
| A. Scheu             |   | 1  | 0  |
| E. Walker            |   | 1  | 0  |
| W. J. Clarke         |   | 1  | 0  |
| C. F.                |   |    | 6  |

|                                         | £ | s. | d.               |
|-----------------------------------------|---|----|------------------|
| R. P. B. Frost                          |   | 1  | 0                |
| A. Howard                               |   | 1  | 0                |
| M. H.                                   |   | 1  | 0                |
| W. Morris                               |   | 5  | 0                |
| A. C. S.                                |   | 1  | 0                |
| P. Webb                                 |   | 1  | 0                |
| A gift from a "Scotch Socialist"        | 1 | 0  | 0                |
| W. Serle                                |   | 1  | 0 (monthly)      |
| "Socrates"                              |   | 2  | 6 (occasionally) |

By July 5 of that year this list was augmented by the addition of the following names:

|                          | £ | s. | d. |
|--------------------------|---|----|----|
| F. Wardle                |   | 1  | 0  |
| M. G.                    |   | 1  | 0  |
| E. M. Geldart            |   |    | 6  |
| F. Keddel                |   | 1  | 0  |
| T. A. Morris             |   | 1  | 0  |
| H. H. Champion           |   | 1  | 0  |
| B. J.                    |   | 1  | 0  |
| H. W. L. [H. W. Lee?]    |   |    | 3  |

It is noteworthy that a number of these contributors were friends of Morris and that some did not, definitely, belong to the Social Democratic Federation. Their contributions evidently represent, therefore, funds solicited by Morris personally. It is also noticeable that Hyndman went no further in this particular sort of charity than did any of the ordinary members, many of whom were workers of small income. Miss Morris states that her father, on the other hand, "spent regularly more money than he could afford on the expenses of the paper," and that he often had a difficult task collecting dues and promised contributions. Thus, when he approached Miss Helen Taylor, one of the so-called "founders of the Federation," he received no aid or encouragement. "I asked Miss Taylor for money, very civil, by letter," he wrote, "but she nay-said me, adding many hard words on the crimes of *Justice*. I don't think that she is cut from the wood of the Socialist tree."

Shortly after the Democratic Federation declared for Marxism, Morris's contributions and activities began to fall off noticeably. During the latter half of 1884 no further Socialist Chants and very few articles, notes or editorials appeared from his pen. Peter Kropotkin's *Appeal to the Young*, poorly translated by Hyndman, began to be run serially, while friends of Hyndman and Hyndman himself began a more and more intensive campaign for "scientific" measures, based more and more upon Marxian formulæ. Indeed, only four important articles were written by Morris after the name-changing episode of August 4, 1884. These were "Uncrowned Kings," in which Morris suggested that the hungry "ask Mr. Gladstone . . . if he can't help them," and if he can't, "let them do without him." A spirited article on "The Hammersmith Costermongers" appeared on September 20, "An Appeal to the Just" on October 11, and a final article on "The Philanthropists" on December 20. In this last article he laboured heavily against the hypocrisy and the half-measures of bourgeois reformers who believed in Christian Charity for the underlings.

It is evident that as the autumn of 1884 drew on, the membership of the S. D. F. was becoming more and more divided. Also it is evident that Morris was either growing lax in his efforts for "Practical Socialism," which is unthinkable, or else that he was being deliberately and systematically forced out of the columns of the paper by Hyndman and Quelch. More and more Hyndman and his immediate friends received the space which Morris's pen had previously filled, while Morris spent his time gathering trifling sums of money and contributing large sums from his own purse to keep the enterprise running.

If this state of affairs existed, and there is reason to think that it did exist, then it becomes evident that Hyndman did not understand the basis of Morris's philosophy or his arguments. Morris's "Practical Socialism" sprang from his philosophy of art and history; Hyndman's from the "new science of economics." Morris's ideas were innately English; they had been conceived from the core of British history; they could appeal to the understanding of the common British citizen. Hyndman, on the other hand, wanted Marxism. All his efforts fostered a Socialist movement that was Continental rather than English in its origin.

It is all the more noteworthy, therefore, that when the final split came, the Continental group as a whole followed Morris. This was more than a tribute to Morris's personality and to his broadminded humanity.

The articles which replaced Morris's consisted largely of Hyndman's own translations of Marx and of Kropotkin, but especially of Marx. Only now and then did an editorial by Morris find its way into *Justice*, almost as if by accident—or perhaps as a sop to wounded vanity—for Morris also was a proud man, and not incapable of anger by any means. In this respect also, Morris and Hyndman were not unlike.

Thus, as the year 1884 drew to its close, there were clouds in the Socialist sky. It looked as if the ground were being surreptitiously prepared for a definite clash between the two "heads" of the Social Democratic Federation.

The story of that clash will be told in the following chapter.

## CHAPTER VI

MARXISM IS NOT ENOUGH, AND MR. HYNDMAN IS A

DOMINEERING FELLOW

ALTHOUGH the time was soon to come when members of various English Socialist groups were to denounce one another in scathing terms and when they who did not see eye to eye were grouped among the outcasts, such a situation did not pertain in the early 'eighties. At best, the Socialists of that day were a mixed crowd, and to many it seemed that fellowship and joint activities were completely in order, if only to hasten their *coup de grâce* to the evil of capitalism. What really mattered to them was that a social revolution should be effected. For Anarchists, Marxists and all "True Radicals," as Morris defined them in *Justice*, were, in those days, Socialists. There can be very little reason for not believing that Morris's own attitude, throughout most of the year 1884, was conciliatory, not only with regard to members of the S. D. F. but also toward Hyndman, its avowed leader, and toward other Socialists.

It is also evident that Morris had striven to please Hyndman. He had subscribed to Hyndman's ideas regarding Socialism both in *Justice* and in the pamphlet which they published as a nominal collaboration, *A Summary of the Principles of Socialism*. Yet the internal evidence of this pamphlet suggests that it was, as Hyndman later claimed, almost exclusively the work of Hyndman. Morris's rôle in it must have been small indeed; and one cannot help wondering if the greater part of that rôle did not consist of financial backing to defray the cost of publication. Certainly, there is nothing in it which jibes with views expressed by Morris elsewhere.

As early as August, 1884, Morris wrote confidentially to a friend that the Federation, small as it was in membership, was not without dissensions. "I find myself drifting into the disgraceful position of a moderator and patcher-up." And again: "The time which I have feared and foreseen from the first seems to be upon us. . . . More than two or three of us distrust Hyndman thoroughly: I have done my best to trust him, but cannot any longer. Practically, it comes to a contest between him and me. . . . I don't think intrigue or ambition are amongst my many faults; but here I am driven to thrusting myself forward and making a party within a party." Yet Morris was not, at this time, to regard a schism as a serious blow to Socialist prestige, for again he writes, toward the close of the year, that a half dozen people who agree as friends "are worth more than a hundred jealous squabblers."

One thing that bothered Hyndman was the growing prevalence of other organizations which called themselves Socialist. There was the Christian Socialist Movement, a resurrection of the old Christian Socialism of Maurice and Kingsley, which had grown out of the Guild of Saint Matthew, founded in 1877 by Stewart Headlam, W. E. Moll, and other earnest church workers who had declared that "Socialism and Christianity are one." This organization was far too clerical, however, to appeal to men such as Hyndman, Morris and Bernard Shaw. Aside from it there were a number of radical organizations which were now claiming to be socialistic, and also the newly organized Fabian Society, which emerged early in 1884 from a group of social and ethical uplift workers who called themselves at first The Fellowship of the New Life. Not until 1889 were the Fabians to become important, however, and for a while their members, notably Bernard Shaw, Annie Besant, Bland, Keddel and others, were members of the S. D. F., the Fabian Society, and, later, of The Socialist League, simultaneously.

But Hyndman did not like them. Their tactics, their creeds and their character were not Marxist and therefore not Hyndman's. The S. D. F., as built by Hyndman, had evolved its creed, its tactics and its chief character from *Das Kapital:* "abstrusely theoretical, bitterly class-conscious, international, intolerant of compromise or partial reform, and apparently anti-Christian." It could make little appeal to the native British proletariat.

The things which bothered Hyndman were not so much the letters and protests from members and correspondents, questioning everything from the morality to the atheism of his organization, but rather the events which were now happening in Scotland. For Andreas Scheu, whose business had taken him to Edinburgh in the summer of 1884, had there been instrumental in founding a branch of the S. D. F. which allowed itself to be called by the popular Georgist name of The Scottish Land and Labour League, instead of "The Edinburgh Branch" of the S. D. F. In Hyndman's eyes, Scheu immediately became a traitor to the cause. Recriminations were flung back and forth. "Tyranny, treachery and corruption" were words bandied about the meeting rooms of the Federation. Morris sickened at the prospect of having to become the leader of an opposition group, but he defended the action of his friend, Scheu. An impasse was at hand. But the impasse was to drag on for four more months.

Meanwhile, strong efforts were made to organize new branches of the S. D. F. and during the year 1884 the establishment of twenty-six such branches was recorded in *Justice*. Strangely enough, only fifteen sent representatives to the annual conference the following year. A number of these groups evidently followed Morris and his friends out of the Federation.[1]

Hyndman apparently did little to mollify branch bodies, or to gain the respect of new members. Judging from his replies to objections and queries which questioned one or another aspect of S. D. F. policy, it might be presumed that he did not care whether members were retained or not. They could follow

---

[1]Edward Carpenter, for example, began to organize his Sheffield group as a branch of Morris's later Socialist League in that year.

instructions or else go to. Thus, when E. Nesbit, an authoress, wrote to *Justice* to inquire whether "we cannot be Socialists without being so bitter," the reply was that "we must hate them" (the *bourgeoisie*) and our bitterness "should be as gall and wormwood to the soul."[2] This view, Hyndman explained, came from a compositor who, as a wage earner, was much better qualified to speak than E. Nesbit, an authoress.

Morris, in a letter to a young American candidate for admission, explained the Socialism of the S. D. F. as follows:

Petitions to Parliaments have long been considered poor instruments of agitation. [Parliament, he adds, is "a dying thing."] We will by all means have a mass meeting in Hyde Park . . . but it would be a great mistake to be in a hurry with such a meeting. . . . A great demonstration must be nothing but the sign of our having a great and closely-knit organization. Otherwise even its apparent success would bring about languor and reaction. . . .

We cannot turn our people back into Catholic English peasants and guild-craftsmen, or into Heathen Norse bonders, much as may be said for such conditions of life: we have no choice but to accept the task which the centuries have laid on us of using the corruption of 300 years of profit-mongering for the overthrow of that very corruption. . . .

Whatever Socialism may lead to, our aim, to be always steadily kept in view, is to obtain for the whole people, duly organized, the possession and control of all the means of production and exchange, destroying at the same time all national rivalries.

The means whereby this is to be brought about is first, educating the people into desiring it, next organizing them into claiming it effectually. Whatever happens in the course of this education and organization must be accepted coolly and as a necessary incident, and not discussed as a matter of essential principle, even if those incidents should mean ruin and war.

It is noteworthy again that in this letter Morris fell in line with Federation policy as laid down by Hyndman. It was also in this letter that he declared Ruskin no "Practical Socialist," and expressed the opinion that Ruskin's idea of national workshops "could only be realized in a state already socialized." He

[2]*Justice*, I, II, III, *passim*. Cf. Godfrey Elton, 83, 88.

also asserted that "ordinary commercial competition is doomed to fail, just as the co-operative scheme is failing: it will be sucked into the tremendous stream of commercial production and vanish into it, after having played its part as a red-herring to spoil the scent of revolution."[3]

As the year progressed Morris continued his toil for the S.D.F. May Morris estimated that during 1884 he gave some forty lectures in London, Edinburgh, Glasgow, Leeds, Manchester, Birmingham, Bradford, Newcastle, Sheffield, and other places. Deficits also were appearing in the accounts, and these he had to make good. In October he reported that "the Federation had had to rely mainly upon the financial contributions of a few middle-class men, one of whom [*i.e.*, Morris] had contributed that month 100 pounds to printing expenses. But contributions from the membership at large, he added, did not seem to be forthcoming—not even in twopences and threepences. It began to look, in the eyes of many, as if *Justice* depended mainly upon "the generosity of an Honorary Fellow of Exeter College, Oxford."[4]

Meanwhile, as Hyndman and his more intimate friends preached the coming revolution, Morris and young Bernard Shaw, who had been attending meetings for several months, irregularly, held that education and organization must precede any radical alteration in the structure of society. One day, in the autumn, a visitor, calling on Harry Quelch to ask him to lecture before a Sunday-school audience, found that worthy in the backyard of the Federation hall, drilling half a dozen men with broomsticks! Although one John Burns might declare, as he did later in Hyde Park, that "The seeds of a bloody revolution are germinating.—Will the middle and upper classes help us to organize it peacefully?—If not, be theirs the responsibility for the lives and property destroyed!"—Morris and Shaw, with whom he was slowly becoming intimate, would be de-

[3]Morris to R. Thomson, July 24, 1884. Identical letters to Yewen and others.
[4]*Justice*, October 18, 1884. Elton, pp. 85–86.

nouncing fervidly the mistaken idea of viewing Marx's *Capital* as a proletarian document instead of regarding it as the "jeremiad against the bourgeoisie" that it was.[5] Needless to say, these activities did not promote friendly relations between the Marxist and the anti-Marxist factions within the S. D. F.

A new series of incidents now took shape which was to split the S. D. F. and cause it to pass from the forefront of the British Socialist stage. Some members would go with Morris to found the Socialist League; some would remain faithful to Hyndman and his Federation; others would join the Fabians, the Socialist Union, and various other radical or humanitarian societies.

[5]Elton, 82, 86, 94. W. S. Sanders, *Early Socialist Days*, 27–33. Hyndman, Bax, Henderson, Shaw, May Morris, *passim*.

# CHAPTER VII

## SCHISM IN THE S. D. F.

THE chief cause of disturbance within the S. D. F. sprang from opposition to Hyndman's arbitrary rule. Among the more bitter malcontents were Doctor Edward Aveling and Eleanor Marx. The fact that they refused, on principle, to be married annoyed Hyndman. Moreover, they were "ruthless critics of the current morality," according to their own pamphlet, *The Woman Question,* and according to Belfort Bax's *Reminiscences and Reflections.* Thus, private feuds augmented the inner dissension. Mr. W. J. Clarke and the Avelings talked against Hyndman in various meetings, and Clarke was accused of disparaging Hyndman's dictatorial attitude before members of the Council. Hyndman, on his part, denounced Clarke, Scheu, and the Avelings on various occasions, and eventually he brought up a motion for Clarke's expulsion from the S. D. F.[1]

A little later Hyndman, acting with Champion and Frost, circulated a story of "the forging of a letter from a French Socialist by Mrs. Aveling" which seemed, to Morris, "quite unfounded and ridiculous."[2] It seemed to Morris that such a charge should have been "made publicly": but in such a case the entire quarrel between the warring factions would have burst out at once, and Morris "dreaded it," still "trying to persuade" himself that "the wounds might heal over."[3]

There was also the bitter question of the control of *Justice,*

[1]Morris to Messrs. Yewen and Thomson, January 1, 1885. Morris to J. L. Joynes, December 25, 1884. May Morris, II, 587–8.

[2]Morris to Joynes, *op. cit.,* n. 1 *supra;* May Morris, II, 588.

[3]*Ibid.*

and on this point Morris's correspondence makes it quite clear that Hyndman was determined to have its policy controlled by Hyndman alone, even to the extent of forcing Morris to give up his financial support of the paper, which, by the close of the year, was rapidly becoming self-supporting. Morris's own contributions had been falling off and both Hyndman and Morris resented the attempts of the other to "dominate" it.

At the Tuesday evening meeting of the S. D. F. Council, December 9, 1884, Clarke was publicly charged with misbehaviour and, according to Morris, "made a poor show of his defense." Yet, since the other side also had been guilty of defamatory remarks, Morris believed that Clarke was being unfairly treated and therefore "determined to vote for him" when the expulsion vote came up at the following Tuesday meeting.

The oncoming schism was further hastened at this time by events in Scotland. A month or so previously Hyndman had inaugurated a Glasgow Branch of the S. D. F. following his lecture before 1200 people in Albion Hall. One W. J. Nairne, who was to become a devoted disciple of Hyndman and a leading exponent of Marxism in Scotland, was named secretary of the new body. Bruce Glasier, who attended the lecture, described Hyndman at this time as "striking in appearance, with his long, flowing, senatorial beard, his keen, restless, searching eyes . . . his whole manner alert, pushful, and, shall I say, domineering? His arguments were racy, argumentative, declamatory, bristling with topical allusions and scathing raillery. . . . The reverberating note, in feeling if not in phrase, was 'I accuse, I expose, I denounce!' . . . Mankind appeared in his view compounded of oppressors and oppressed, fleecers and fleeced, dupers and duped. . . . He appealed for better things —for justice and democracy—for a new system of politics and economics. . . . But his lecture, though it excited, did not inspire. There was hardly a ray of idealism in it. Capitalism was shown to be wicked and wasteful, but Socialism was not made to appear more practical or desirable. There was, in fact, very little Socialism in the lecture at all—it was an anti-capitalist ejaculation."[4]

Shortly afterward The Scottish Land and Labour League, founded by Morris's friend, Scheu, appealed for a joint membership of the two Scottish bodies. "Of course the Edinburgh people must have known," wrote Morris, "that Glasgow would have led as the more important body: however, the Glasgow Branch demurred . . . and some of the members wrote to Hyndman for *orders* as to what to do. Accordingly, when I came to Glasgow (on December 14) I found the executive divided, and in fact quarrelling: at the meeting I attended a letter from Hyndman was read attacking Scheu in what I am compelled to call a treacherous manner: accusing him of being an Anarchist, a friend of Johann Most, and disloyal to the cause of Socialism; in short saying just what the writer thought would injure Scheu the most with the Glasgow people. These charges I knew to be untrue and I saw therefore that it was no longer any use trying to smother the smouldering discontent in the Federation."[5]

It had been Andreas Scheu and Bruce Glasier, working through the influence of Shaw Maxwell, an ardent Land Restorationist, who had induced Morris to come to Scotland over the week end of December 13–14 and lecture before the Edinburgh and Glasgow groups. Glasier attended both meetings, and it was on these occasions that Morris not only began a long and lasting friendship with Glasier, but also discovered the Hyndman-Nairne machinations to which he referred in the letter above quoted.

At this time Morris was fifty years of age. According to Bruce Glasier, "His splendid crest of dark, curly hair and his finely textured beard were brindling into grey. His head was lionlike, not only because of his shaggy mane, but because of the impress and strength of his whole front. There was in his eyes, especially when in repose, that penetrating, far-away,

---

[4]Glasier, 28–33. Morris to Yewen and Thomson, January 1, 1885.
[5]Morris to Yewen and Thomson, January 1, 1885.

impenetrable gaze that seems to be fixed on something beyond that at which it is directly looking." Years afterward Glasier wrote: "I gathered that he was reckoned a man of uncommon mould among men of genius: something of a prophet and heresiarch as well as a poet and artist. . . . One who, somewhere on the higher altitudes, was striking out towards new hopes and endeavours for mankind."[6]

St. Andrews Hall, where Morris lectured in Glasgow, had an audience of about 3000. It was a lecture, says Glasier, that was something more than a lecture, a kind of parable or prediction, in which art and labour were held forth as the very act of living. Whereas Morris's doctrine was true, "universally and forever," Hyndman's was based upon "a temporary and conditional appeal . . . to the more groundling and selfish instincts of the race."

After Morris spoke, the members of the Glasgow Branch of the S. D. F. who were present retired to their meeting hall—the attic of a low-ceilinged warehouse in Watson Street—"a dingy little hall in the slummiest quarter of the city," whither Morris accompanied them. Here, W. J. Nairne, acting as chairman, conducted a discussion of current social problems and theories.

Nairne, unschooled and earnest, a stone-breaker, somber and class-conscious, with a wife and five children to support, could understand the physical unrest inherent in Hyndman's program. Morris he could not understand. Consequently the meeting developed into a heckling match between Nairne and Morris. For the most part, the members cheered Morris heartily, and Nairne, after shaking hands coldly, ventured the remark that he supposed Morris would like to say a word in closing to the assembled comrades. Morris then alluded vaguely to the recent difficulties with the S. D. F. and expressed the hope that they would soon be healed; yet, should a breach prove unavoidable, he hoped that relations between the two groups might continue on a friendly basis.

After this speech, Nairne proceeded to submit him to a Marx-

[6]Glasier, pp. 20, 21, 23, 30.

ist catechism, to which Morris answered quite good-naturedly, for the most part, although his face was growing red with suppressed anger. At last, on his rising to depart, Nairne delivered "as a sort of parting shot," the question: "Does Comrade Morris accept Marx's theory of value?"

At this Morris lost his temper momentarily, vouchsafing a reply that has stood as one of the best-remembered sayings in the history of British Labour politics: "To speak quite frankly, I do not know what Marx's theory of value is, and I'm damned if I want to know! It's enough political economy for me to know that the idle class is rich and the working class is poor! And it doesn't matter a rap whether the robbery is accomplished by what is termed 'surplus value' or by means of serfage or open brigandage!"

It was at this meeting that Morris had discovered how Hyndman had "deliberately attacked Scheu by letter." He wrote that "the spectacle of the discord so deliberately sown among these new recruits fairly swept away all doubt in my mind as to what was necessary. . . . I saw that the fight *must* come off, and that it must be fought out on the true grounds, namely, resistance to H.'s absolutism."[7]

In another letter to Yewen, January 1, 1885, Morris stated that he could easily understand the exception taken by Hyndman to Scheu's Edinburgh organization. "But," he added, "the Edinburgh Branch, under that name, was accepted as an affiliated body by the Council, and at the Annual Conference (August, 1884) Scheu represented it and explained in the open meeting why they had added to the name of the Branch; and no objection was made to it either by Mr. Hyndman or anybody else." Therefore, he (Morris) recognized Hyndman's present charges to be "unfounded, indeed untrue," and saw that he was bound "either to accept Hyndman's charges against Scheu, whom I knew to be trustworthy, or to declare against Hyndman."

Morris returned to London in time for the weekly meeting

[7]Morris to Joynes, January 1, 1885. May Morris, II, 589.

of the Council, December 16, 1884. On this occasion the charges of Clarke's insubordination came to their climax in a vote of the Council. "Clarke this time defended himself on the true ground of opposition to Hyndman and his expulsion was nay-said by 8 votes to 7."[8]

That evening also marked the climax of the schism in the S. D. F., for Morris, in reporting his Edinburgh-Glasgow trip, took the opportunity to say plainly what he thought of Hyndman's conduct . . . "and we were thenceforward two and not one."

"Hyndman," said Morris, "has been acting throughout as a politician determined to push his own advantage . . . always on the lookout for anything which could advertise the party he is supposed to lead; his aim has been to make the movement seem big; to frighten the powers that be with a turnip bogie which, perhaps, he almost believes in himself: hence, all that insane talk of immediate forcible revolution, when we know that the workers of England are not even touched by the movement; hence the founding of branches which melt away into mere names, and the neglect of organization; and, worst of all, discreditable intrigue and the sowing of suspicion among those who are working for the party. Amidst such elements as this I cannot and will not work: I and those that agree with me could only stay in the body as Hyndman's agents or as members engaged in perpetual conflict with him: and remember that in spite of abolition of the perpetual or annual chairmanship, he has in his hands the means of manipulating the body; he has the paper of which he is Editor, through Fitzgerald, his henchman almost: he has the secretaryship and the means of controlling the branches: Champion indeed thinks he can turn him his way: but to speak plainly I think that it is just the other way.

"In short, he made the Federation, and it must be either his property or be in revolt against him: we say, let him keep his property, with all its 'increment,'—'earned and unearned'—but we won't be a part of it."[9]

[8]Morris to Joynes, December 25, 1884.    [9]May Morris, II, 590–591.

Even after this apparent break, however, it seems likely that a last-minute attempt may have been made to patch things up; for at the next weekly meeting of the Council (Tuesday evening, December 23, 1884) Andreas Scheu came down from Edinburgh and "defended himself triumphantly in a very noble speech." Even this, Morris thought, "was scarcely needed," as Scheu's antecedents and activities "had been known to Hyndman all along, and yet he had treated him as trustworthy till the moment came when he found it convenient to attack him, Scheu having done nothing afresh in the meantime to inspire any want of confidence. . . . To my mind Hyndman's tendencies have led the S. D. F. into a futile and even dangerous policy. . . . It has meant adventure, show and advertisement, which would have found us out in the long run and shown us to be a small party without organization and with no very clear aims. Hence all these theatrical boasts and warnings about immediate violent revolution, which frighten those who are ignorant of our condition away from us, and disgust those who know how weak we are. . . . Hence also the perpetual sneers at, and abuse of, the radicals who, deluded as we must think them, are after all the men from whom our recruits must come. Hence attacks on foreigners as foreigners, or at least sneers at them; coquetting also with jingoism in various forms, all of which mean waiting about to see what can be made out of the political situation—if, perhaps, at the best, they can attain to a sort of Bismarckian State Socialism, or as near to it as they can get in England. . . . I cannot stand all this; it is not what I mean by Socialism either in aim or in means: I want a real revolution, a real change in Society: Society a great organic mass of well-regulated forces used for bringing about a happy life for all. And the means of attaining it are simple enough: Education in Socialism, and organization for the time when the crisis shall force action upon us: nothing else will do any good at present; the revolution cannot be a mechanical one. . . . I finish by saying that whatever faults I have, I am by no means a quarrelsome man; and if I could have avoided this quarrel I would have done so. In fact, I have gone on hoping against hope for the last six months that the differences might heal up: but the truth is that Hyndman is determined to be master, and will not accept any other place: he cannot change his nature and be otherwise than a jingo and a politician even if he tries."[10]

On Wednesday, December 24, following the third straight week of Tuesday evening bickerings, Morris wrote to another friend: "Last night came off to the full as damned as I expected . . . and the worst of it is that the debate is adjourned till Saturday, as we couldn't sit any later than midnight yesterday. It was a piece of degradation, only illumined by Scheu's really noble and skilful defense of his character: all the rest was a mere exhibition of backbiting. . . . However, Saturday I *will* be out of it. Our lot agreed beforehand, being, I must say, moved by me, that it is not worth fighting for the name of the S. D. F. and the sad remains of *Justice* at the expense of a month or two of fighting: so, as Hyndman considers the S. D. F. his property, let him take it and make what he can of it, and see if he can really make up a bogie to frighten the Government, which I really begin to think is about all his scheme amounts to. . . . The worst of our new body, as far as I am concerned, is that for the present at least I have to be editor of the paper, which I by no means bargained for, but it seems nobody else will do."[11]

If this letter proves anything, it proves that the real split within the ranks of the Social Democratic Federation had developed into an open rupture on the evening of December 16, 1884, and that just prior to the meeting of the 23d, Morris and his adherents had decided to found a new body, to be known as The Socialist League, with its own organ edited by Morris, if Hyndman refused to co-operate.

The next meeting of the Council was called for Saturday evening, December 27, at 6 p.m. It lasted for four and one-half hours. "There was a good deal of speaking, mostly on

[10]Morris to Yewen and Thomson, January 1, 1885.
[11]From a family letter, quoted also by Mackail, II, 127–128.

our side," wrote Morris, and the formal meeting was finished by a "long, clever, and lawyerlike speech" by Hyndman, after which a vote of confidence was taken. Eight members voted in support of Hyndman and ten in support of the opposition. Thereupon, Morris "got up, and after a word or two in defense of my honour, honesty, and all that, which had been somewhat torn ragged in the debate, I read our resignation from the paper prepared thereto; and we solemnly walked out. This seemed to produce what the penny-a-liners call 'a revulsion of feeling,' and most of the other side came around and assured me that they had the best opinion of me and didn't mean all those hard things: poor little Williams cried heartily and took a most affectionate farewell of us."[12]

Here follows a copy of the resignation of Morris and his friends, as recorded in the minutes of the Social Democratic Federation for December 27, 1884:

Since discord has arisen in this Council owing to the attempt to substitute arbitrary rule therein for fraternal cooperation, contrary to the principles of Socialism, and since it seems to us impossible to heal this discord,

We, the undersigned, think it better in the interests of the cause of Socialism to cease to belong to this Council, and accordingly hand in our resignation.

(Signed)

William Morris; Edward (Dr., Sc.B.) Aveling; Robert Banner; J. Lane; Eleanor Marx Aveling; E. Belfort Bax; John C. Hahon; S. Mainwaring; W. J. Clarke; J. Cooper.

Afterward a brief was prepared by the remaining members of the Executive Council, denying the allegations and calling for a general unity of the Federation. This counterstatement was signed by John Burns, H. H. Champion, Herbert Burrows, H. Quelch, and J. E. Williams.[13] According to the testimony

[12]S. D. F. Minutes, December 27, 1884, and Morris's Merton Abbey letter of December 28, 1884, quoted by Mackail, II, 129.

[13]*Loc. cit.*, December 30, 1884.

of one man who had recently become a member of the S. D. F., the bulk of the membership at the next general meeting "somewhat noisily expressed their disapproval of the action of the minority in breaking away."[14]

Bernard Shaw believed that "constitutional precedent" would have necessitated Morris's holding his ground and voting down the Council on every succeeding issue, employing tactics later made famous by Keir Hardie. Morris himself, however, was of the opinion that he and his followers had done the right thing: "the alternative would have been a general meeting, and after a month's squabble for the amusement of the rest of the world . . . would have landed us in deadlock and ultimately where we are now, two separate bodies."

The apology of Hyndman and his sympathizers was that the quarrel was greatly exaggerated; that discipline was needed in so young an organization; and that Morris, Bax, Scheu and the Avelings, together with their supporters, represented undisciplined and anarchistic elements. Morris, one is led to presume from this testimony, wanted to shape the policy of the organization, or at least have a prominent part in so doing, and hence discord arose. But the real truth is, I suppose, that neither man was subject to control; each personality differed intrinsically from the other; and certainly Morris must have resented his virtual exclusion from the pages of *Justice*. But underlying these aspects of the question there remains the fundamental difference in the philosophies of the two leaders: and only those who recognize the innate hostility of Morris to all forms of centralized bureaucratic control can appreciate the real enmity which, for a few years, broke the peculiar friendship of these two acknowledged leaders of English Socialism.

"Both men were right after their fashion," says Mr. George Bateman, an old member of the S. D. F., "but from now on it was apparent that the Jews would have no dealings with the Samaritans."[15]

[14]From an anonymous correspondent, who points out that while Morris controlled the Council, a majority of the common membership remained faithful to Hyndman.

[15]Letter of George Bateman to the author, February 7, 1936.

Meanwhile, Hyndman was to continue to wave the red flag of Communism until, in 1917, his innate "Tory instincts" turned aghast at the victory which it was to achieve, not in England but in Russia, and from the stage of Bolshevism he finally turned back, a disappointed old man, to that national and political "jingoism" which Morris had detected in him some thirty years before.

But for a few years after the Hyndman-Morris rupture, the public would regard the S. D. F. with something akin to awe; and the term Socialist would become a new epithet, a new rallying point for Liberal-Conservative governments to agree about, even in Parliament. In reality, however, as Lord Elton has so fittingly expressed it: "The Federation, as such, had shot its bolt."[16]

[16]Elton, *England, Arise!*, p. 98.

# V

## THE SOCIALIST LEAGUE—AND BLOODSHED

*Lo, Faithful, lo, the door of my abode*
*Wide open now, and many pressing in*
*That they the lordship of the World may win!*
*Hark to the murmuring round my bannered car,*
*And gird your weapons to you for the war!*
*For who shall say how soon the day shall be*
*Of that last fight that swalloweth up the sea?*
*Fear not, be ready! Forth the banners go,*
*And will not turn again till every foe*
*Is overcome as though they had not been.*

The mill pond, with the weaving and printing sheds, Merton Abbey

## CHAPTER I

## THE SOCIALIST LEAGUE BUSTLES INTO HEADLONG
### ACTIVITY

IMMEDIATELY after leaving the Social Democratic Federation, Morris went to his suite of private rooms in the Merton Abbey "works," just seven miles from Charing Cross (in those days) whither the firm of Morris & Company had transferred its manufactory in 1881. Here, on Sunday, December 28, he wrote his first letters telling of the final results in the S. D. F. "split." On this same day—he must have spent a sleepless night—he rented new and "very humble" quarters for the Socialist League, and authorized by telegraph the purchase of Windsor chairs and a kitchen table. "Tomorrow," he wrote, "we meet to inaugurate the League."

On the evening of January 1, 1885, there were "loud voices in hot discussion" at Morris's London home, Kelmscott House in Hammersmith. There the members of the newly founded Socialist League were drawing up a program. They intended to found a new paper, *The Commonweal*; and within the next month the first issue of that famous periodical was destined to appear. At the moment Morris was unable to turn it into a weekly, as he desired. "Paying for *Justice* has somewhat crippled me," he explained to a friend, "and I shall have to find money for the other expenses of the League first." So, for fifteen issues, *The Commonweal* was to remain a monthly, with occasional supplements; thereafter it became a weekly.

Within a few days after the disruption of the S. D. F. and the founding of the new Socialist League, Morris began to feel "like a dog with a tin kettle tied to his tail." Perhaps it was a premonition of the coming anarchy; perhaps it was only a natural reaction to the storm of abuse that was now flung at him and at "the menace of Socialism."[1] It seems, in any case, that the schism within the Socialist ranks had been noised about considerably, and both the press and the public were taking alarm at the spread of Socialist organizations. Morris was commonly referred to as a "poet-upholsterer" or as a "Capitalist Socialist," who, while remaining a Socialist in principle, continued to remain a Capitalist in reality. Some of the charges he ignored; others required refutation. "I have been living in a storm of newspaper brickbats, to some of which I had to reply," he wrote early in January.

Thus, to *The Standard* he freely admitted that if he surrendered his own income and the interest on the whole capitalized value of Morris & Company (about 15,000 pounds) "and took in lieu of it a foreman's or a highly skilled workman's wage of only 4 pounds a week or 200 pounds a year, there would be left a sum divisible which would represent 16 pounds a year, or about 6 shillings a week for each of the workmen. . . . That would, I admit, be a very nice thing for all of them; but it would not alter the position of any one of them in the least. . . . Further, if I were to die or be otherwise disabled, the business could not get any one to do my work for 200 pounds a year, and would at once be forced to take back the extra 16 pounds a year from each of the workmen."

Morris was not, in short, an exceedingly wealthy man any longer. The failure of many shares in the industrial depressions of the 'eighties, and his own devotion to his main interests and hobbies, rather than to his business, had eaten into his share of the family fortune. Times had changed, both for him and his family, since the prosperous days of the Great Devons Consols.

In the first issue of *The Commonweal* a "Manifesto of the Socialist League" was printed. Forms of State Socialism, of Co-operation, and of Land Nationalization were denounced as mere palliatives, comparable with Parliamentarianism and Constitutional Democracy. The new Manifesto called for a

[1]May Morris, II, 169–170; Mackail, II, 139.

complete revolution in the basis of existing society. In addition to these broad principles, the Manifesto declared for Decentralization, with each political unit taking the form of local *communes* (or cantons) rather than that of a national bureaucracy. Unfortunately, it pointed out, there are two different and opposing views among Socialists: one, merely the Socialism of the Centralized State; and the other the Socialism of a *Federation of Communes* which "would hold all wealth in common, and would use that wealth for satisfying the needs of every member, only exacting from each that he should do his best according to his capacity towards production for the common wealth. . . ."

"To my mind," wrote Morris, "the latter (form of Communism) is simply the necessary development of the former (form of State Socialism) which implies a transition period. . . ."

Under the present régime Morris feared "the danger of the community falling into bureaucracy," with its accompanying "multiplication of boards and offices."

The Manifesto of the Socialist League ended with an appeal for "frankness and fraternal trust in each other and single-hearted devotion to the religion of Socialism, the only religion which the Socialist League professes."

Twenty-three persons were listed as members of the Provisional Council of the Socialist League; in their hands control of the "journal" was vested. Morris was named Treasurer of the League and Editor of *The Commonweal*.

Within less than six months the League was progressing to such an extent that its offices were moved from No. 27 to No. 13 Farringdon Road, where much larger quarters, including a printing office and a lecture hall, were available. Numerous branches had sprung up in various parts of the country and the organization soon boasted an active membership of more than two hundred ardent workers. Immediately thereafter the first annual conference of the League was summoned, on July 5, 1885. An Executive Council of twenty was chosen and annual conferences were ordered at which delegates from all branches were to be present. The Report of the Proceedings of the old Provisional Council of twenty-three was tendered and from this it appears that Morris had attended twenty-four meetings and missed only four because of "duty elsewhere on behalf of the League."[2]

At this meeting a New Manifesto of the Socialist League, slightly altered from the original, was drawn up and approved by the Executive Council. This stated that since absolutism, constitutionalism, and republicanism "have all been tried in our day and have all failed," and since incomplete schemes such as "co-operation, so-called; *i.e.*, competitive co-operation for profit . . . nationalization of the land . . . State Socialism . . ." or any other scheme of government which embraced "merely administrative changes" can *not* be counted upon to secure the rights of the workers, "the Socialist League therefore aims at complete Revolutionary Socialism." The League is aware, it admits, that this can never happen satisfactorily, or in any one country, "without the help of the workers of all civilization," wherefore, neither race nor creed, neither history nor geography, must be allowed to stand in the way. "For us there are no nations, but only varied masses of workers and friends whose mutual sympathies are checked and perverted by groups of masters and fleecers whose interest it is to stir up rivalries and hatreds among the dwellers in different lands."[3]

Two factors stand out clearly and are indications of the way the wind was blowing. First, the checkered membership of the Socialist League was rapidly giving it an international rather than a native British colouring. Secondly, the influence of the more revolutionary members was already coming to the front. Miss May Morris hinted at the influence exercised upon Morris by Doctor Edward Aveling, while that of new members, inducted from God-knows-where, such as Victor Dave and other pronounced Anarchists, has been commented upon

[2]*The Commonweal*, Nos. 6 and 7. *Cf.* Mackail, II, 140; 145–146; Vallance, 331–332.
[3]*The Commonweal*, No. 7; *Manifesto;* Vallance, p. 332.

by numerous other writers and correspondents. Moreover, the fact that revolutionary ideas based upon force were coming into ascendancy within the League is indicated also by the gradual rapprochement that took place between the more radical members of the League and the more ardent spirits of the Social Democratic Federation. For a while, at least, Morris was carried along on the general current. But the earlier split within the ranks of the S. D. F. had had its effect upon him; hence he usually acquiesced and worked for compromise within the Socialist League, doing his best to achieve unity.

## CHAPTER II

## "THE COMMONWEAL"—THAT ADMIRABLE PUBLICATION

ON February 10, 1885, less than six weeks after the organization of the Socialist League, Morris announced that 5000 copies of the first issue of *The Commonweal* had been sold, and that the magazine was then in a second edition. The new body and the new organ had got off to an unprecedented start.

For the following issue he wrote the longest, and probably the best, of his *Socialist Chants*. It was "The Message of the March Wind," the theme of which was later expanded by him to comprise the proletarian narrative poem, *The Pilgrims of Hope*, which appeared in successive installments during the following year. "The Message of the March Wind," representing the first part of the poem, contains some effective stanzas, for example:

> The singers have sung and the builders have builded,
> The painters have fashioned their tales of delight;
> For what and for whom hath the world's book been gilded,
> When all is for these but the blackness of night?
>
> How long, and for what is their patience abiding?
> How oft and how oft shall their story be told,
> While the hope that none seeketh in darkness is hiding,
> And in grief and in sorrow the world groweth old?[1]

The first issue of *The Commonweal* contained Morris's best-known Socialist chant, "The March of the Workers," written to the tune of "John Brown's Body," and since called "the tocsin of the social revolution."

[1] *The Commonweal*, No. 2. There were 18 stanzas in all.

What is this the sound and rumor? What is this that all men hear,
Like the wind in hollow valleys when the storm is drawing near,
Like the rolling on of ocean in the eventide of fear?
                'Tis the people marching on!

.    .    .    .    .    .    .    .    .    .    .

On we march then, we the workers, and the rumor that ye hear
Is the blended sound of battle and deliv'rance drawing near;
For the hope of every creature is the banner that we bear,
                And the world is marching on!

*(Cho.)*
        Hark the rolling of the thunder!
        Lo! the sun! and lo! thereunder,
        Riseth wrath and hope and wonder,
            And the host comes marching on!

One other song, usually included among the *Socialist Chants*, was written to the tune of the old English drinking song, "Down Among the Dead Men." It seems worthy of quotation in full:

Come comrades, come, your glasses clink;
Up with your hands a health to drink,
The health of all that workers be,
In every land, on every sea.

    And he that will this drink deny,
    Down among the dead men, down among the dead men,
    Down, down, down, down,
    Down among the dead men let him lie!

Well done! Now drink another toast,
And pledge the gathering of the host,
The people armed in brain and hand,
To claim their rights in every land.

    And he that will this drink deny, *(etc.)*

There's liquor left; come, let's be kind,
And drink the rich a better mind—
That when we knock upon the door,
They may be off, and say no more.

And he that will this drink deny, (*etc.*)

Now, comrades, let the glass blush red,
Drink we the unforgotten dead
That did their deeds and went away,
Before the bright sun brought the day.

And he that will this drink deny, (*etc.*)

The Day? Ah, friends, late grows the night;
Drink to the glimmering spark of light,
The herald of the joy to be,
The battle torch of thee and me!

And he that will this drink deny, (*etc.*)

Take yet another cup in hand
And drink in hope our little band;
Drink strife in hope while lasteth breath,
And brotherhood in life and death;

And he that will this health deny,
Down among the dead men, down among the dead men,
Down, down, down, down,
Down among the dead men let him lie!

These sentiments, as Mr. Glasier has observed, receive small encouragement from the events of the present-day "class struggle." But class struggle was abhorrent to Morris. He was willing to extend the hand of fellowship to any one, regardless of station, who recognized social injustice, and who was willing to try to do something about it.

The first issue of *The Commonweal* had its cover stamped in plain black letters; the second was decorated with Morris's familiar willow-leafage. In the April and May issues the designs of Walter Crane were substituted, together with his Socialist League insignia—a group of figures bearing the legend: "AGITATE, EDUCATE, ORGANIZE."

These early issues of the magazine contained Morris's poetry and editorials; an article by Belfort Bax on "Gordon and the Soudan"; one by Stepniak (a prominent philosophical anarchist) on "The Actual Position of Russia"; a short article by Paul Fafargue (a son-in-law of Karl Marx's and also a prominent leader of the French Collectivists) on "The Political Game of the Police in France"; a long essay by Friedrich Engels on "England in 1845 and in 1855," and a report by George Bernard Shaw on the Industrial Remuneration Conference in London of that year.

For a while, at least, *The Comonweal* bade fair to be England's liveliest Socialist periodical; indeed, there are critics who have stated unequivocally that throughout Morris's editorship it was far and away the best of the British radical publications.

It would be too huge a task to attempt to treat in brief space the heterogeneous mass of writing which went to swell the pages of *The Commonweal* during the next few years. Suffice it to say that Socialist chants and Socialist romances, essays on internal policy and on external politics and economics, dramas, jokes, news items and declamations representing nearly all shades of advanced opinion, appeared at one time or another. All told, more than two hundred and fifty issues of the magazine passed through Morris's hands, and almost every issue contained two or more of his own contributions and editorial notes. The important thing is that Morris did not, in any of these writings, attempt to define Social Revolution in words other than those employed by him in "How We Live and How We Might Live" (his first essay for *The Commonweal*) in which he said "it does not necessarily mean a change accompanied by riot and all kinds of violence, and cannot mean a change made mechanically and in the teeth of opinion by a group of men who have somehow managed to seize on the executive power," —but rather it means "a change in the basis of society" that will make of individual and of social needs a co-operative enterprise with the machinery both of industry and of government decentralized for the attainment of a happier, a more equitable and a more beautiful world, with all development programs based upon sound historical knowledge and healthy mental and physical programs.

## CHAPTER III

AGITATION AND REVOLUTION: THE PROSPEROUS MIDDLE
CLASSES GO INTO HIDING

WHILE Morris and his cohorts were trying to put *The Commonweal* on a paying basis and "make Socialists" by agitation, education and organization —while Anarchists and Communists began to gravitate toward the League—and while the newly founded Fabians, as yet hardly more than a name, were beginning to grope for new methods of securing parliamentary reforms—the members of the S. D. F., led by Hyndman, Burns, Williams, Champion and Quelch, were turning to force.

The period of the Free Speech Disturbances and the Trafalgar Square Riots (1886–1887) was about to begin, and Hyndman could assure his faithful followers with greater enthusiasm than ever before that "things are getting hot."

Since about April, 1885, the leaders of the S. D. F. had been conducting open-air meetings at the corner of Dod Street and Burdett Road, in Limehouse. As the summer progressed members of the Socialist League began to lecture there also, and shortly thereafter some arrests were made. Socialist speakers were charged by the police with "obstructing a public thoroughfare." Word spread among the populace that the hated police, who had long been accused of accepting bribes from brothel-keepers, were now engaged in suppressing the right of free speech and of unnecessarily harassing the poor. The Sunday audiences increased and on September 20 a mob estimated variously at from 1000 to 7000 jeered and hustled the police. Afterward, when most of the crowd had disappeared into pubs (which opened at 1 P.M.) the police arrested six of the speakers.

256

Morris and numerous other members of both the League and the S. D. F. were in the courtroom on the following morning, while outside a crowd cheered the accused and booed the police. Justice Saunders sentenced one man to two months at hard labour and fined all the rest. Cries of "Shame" were heard and there was considerable confusion. One policeman had his shoulder-strap broken and accused Morris of having assaulted him.

"Who are you?" said the Justice.

"I am an artist and a literary man, pretty well known, I think, throughout Europe," replied Morris, evidently angry enough to try to impress the court with his importance.

"I suppose that you did not intend to do this?" said Justice Saunders.

"I never struck him at all," Morris shouted.

"Well, I will let you go."

Morris was accordingly discharged, and in some newspapers the "notorious artist and literary man" was mocked. But on the whole the episode resulted in a victory for the Socialist cause. The Socialist League and the S. D. F. both received new publicity and new popularity as a result of the incident; and on the following Sunday a crowd of 30,000 packed Dod Street from end to end.[1] A later meeting at the West India Dock packed the Dock Road for half a mile. Yet no untoward incidents occurred. Correspondents protested to the press that police interference had created more disturbance and more sympathy for Socialism than had a year's Socialist activities.

From these episodes the police learned their lesson; Free Speech continued unabated and for the most part undisturbed; and the multitudes went their devious ways, leaving open-air orators to their own meager audiences and meager devices. Only *The London Times*, as the year drew to a close, pronounced the talk of Socialists to be both dangerous and ominous.

Morris must have had some forebodings of what was coming. On October 31, he wrote to Mrs. Burne-Jones that he had no

[1]*Daily News*, Sept. 28, 1885; Vallance, 336; Elton, 119–122; Mackail, II, 145–148.

great confidence in the stability of his new organization and had always said to himself that when the League broke up, he and some half-dozen others must immediately found a new organization. Certainly differences of opinion with regard to methods of agitation and revolution were agitating the membership; but they usually managed to "make it up."

One very important episode that was to have important consequences for the Socialist League was the struggle concerning parliamentary action, or political action of any nature. For certain members of the League, despite the circumstances under which it organized, were indulging in a campaign to secure the adhesion of the League to a program of parliamentary action as an avowed means of agitation. Time and again, both in his speeches and in his *Commonweal* notes, Morris opposed this course. He had been opposed also to the Free Speech Demonstrations on the ground that Socialism was not ready for demonstrations. He wrote that "the whole thing smacks too much of trying to force on palliatives by parliamentary measures, and we don't believe in palliatives or in Parliament."[2]

None the less the agitation continued and the thing that brought it to a head was the series of Trafalgar Square Riots in 1886–1887. Hyndman, having drunk the wine of success in the Dod Street affair and found it to his liking, believed that "the day" for the uprising of the proletariat was not far off. During the preceding year there had been almost unbroken slumps in trade, and unemployed agitation was increasing the membership of various radical clubs. Two little-known organizations, the Labourers' League and the Fair Trade League, called for mass meetings of their membership in Trafalgar Square, February 8, 1886, whereupon Hyndman issued orders for a mass meeting of the S. D. F. Members. The Socialist League, getting wind of the proposed demonstrations, voted for participation and it was agreed by a vote of the League Council that they who wished could take part in the demonstration.

On the afternoon of February 8, 1886, violent speeches

[2]Morris to Thomson, February 25, 1886.

were made by Burns, waving a red flag from a stone platform near the National Gallery, and by Champion, Williams, and Hyndman, all speaking for the S. D. F. Such words as "revolution" and "penalties" were heard; but most of the crowd turned to the uncouth speakers of the Labourers' League, whose orators were complaining loudly that they were honest workingmen, while Hyndman and his followers were ex-stock-exchange brokers and ex-officers. Meanwhile, a huge crowd from the East End engulfed the Fair Trade speakers, and during this lull in the S. D. F. program the police requested Hyndman to lead his following to Hyde Park. The result of this attempted manœuvre was a movement *en masse* in which leaders and led became separated into different groups. One mob, largely composed of radicals, followed Burns, who still waved his red flag above his head, along Pall Mall. Here, stones and epithets went back and forth between the members of wealthy Club Land and the overwrought marchers, after which Club Land was windowless. St. James Street, Half Moon Street, South and North Audley Streets and Oxford Street also suffered. Shops were raided, vehicles overturned, and property rights—the most defensible rights of all Englishmen—were openly mocked. The police, who should have been in Pall Mall, were in the Mall.

By evening the episode of revolutionary activity was ended. But that night and all the next day London trembled. Not since 1848 had anything approaching such violence been seen. To add to the apprehension, threatening meetings and utterances were reported from half a dozen industrial centers. To many persons it seemed as if the revolution of Hyndman's wishful prophecies were at hand. It was even said that several notorious capitalists of London prepared red flags with which to placate the proletarian mobs when the hour of general pillage should arrive.[3]

An eye-witness of the affair wrote in his diary:

I am glad I saw this. It may be the first battle in a world revolt. And again, it may be a fizzle. But the glorious incongruity of it! There were

[3]*Cf.* Elton; *Justice*, February 13, 1886; Vallance; *London Times* accounts, and various works dealing with early labour troubles.

four men on the plinth of Nelson Monument in Trafalgar Square. Hyndman in frock-coat and silk hat, bearded and handsome . . . stood beside Jack Williams, a labourer in corduroys. . . . Then there was Champion, trim and soldierly, ex-artillery officer, nervously buttoning and unbuttoning his coat as he talked, bidding the unemployed to "Join the Volunteers, learn how to drill, and get possession of a rifle." Beside him stood John Burns holding a red flag. The audience of unemployed seemed to be listening apathetically. How the mess started I don't know, but presently the crowd, all helter-skelter and confused, poured across the square toward Pall Mall. I saw the first overt act. It was before a club. Some young aristocrat at one of the upper windows mocked the marchers. That much was plain. The poor fellows were singing a marching song, one playing a tin whistle, and a man at an upper window waved his hand mockingly, as though beating time. He was well-dressed, a flower in his buttonhole, high collared, with mustache à la Churchill, and those below were ragged, cold, and hungry, doubtless. Then something was thrown from the club window. My sympathies went with the mob. A stone was cast and the jeerer promptly disappeared. Then came more stones, an irregular volley, and the crowd went mad. Policemen started clubbing men here and there and that turned the trick. Force begat force. Soon a window of a jewelry store was broken and a hundred hands went to work. I was sorely tempted to take something myself as a memento, but some inherent prejudice forbade. . . . Tradesmen began locking doors and putting up shutters. Scared men, white faced. An ill-advised coachman tried to drive through the crowd and some got busy and cut the traces. Then my silly sympathy jumped again and was with those in the carriage and against the crowd. Later I saw them raid a baker's place, eating as they marched. Then a clothing store was stormed; men dressed themselves in stolen clothing as they walked. My sympathies hopped again. . . .

My landlady, poor, shabby thing, said this evening, "The Poor's rose at last, Sir. I ses, ses I, to my husband, Lord knows we're poor, but you keep out of it. What with 'Indman breaking up the government, and Bradlaugh breaking up the Church, it's awful."

At eight met H. S. and went to theatre. H. S. tells me that Hyndman and the rest were arrested. Coming out after the show, newsboys were yelling: " 'Orrible riots by Socialists. Four men hung! All about the 'anging!" Buying an *Evening News*, found that the " 'anging" had nothing to do with the riot, but related to the execution of four murderers at Carlisle. We walked along talking, and getting into White-chapel, wandered around until 3 A.M., and so, as old Pepys would have put it, "to bed with the milk maid," metaphorically speaking.[4]

Two days later thousands of middle-class London families went into hiding when it was reported that John Burns was marching on the West End at the head of 60,000 rioters. *The London Times* was informed that 30,000 more were marching on Trafalgar Square. Shops closed in many districts, additional constables were sworn into service, and troops were ordered to stand to arms. But the day passed without disorder. The press demanded action against the malcontents, and members left the S. D. F. by the hundreds. The Nottingham Branch seceded from the London body *in toto*, declaring that it would not tolerate the unbecoming activities of the London leaders.

The following week Morris, speaking for the Socialist League, printed a long article in *The Commonweal* condemning incidents and provocations and declaring that "at the risk of being misunderstood by hot-heads, I say that our business is more than ever education." Even if aimless revolt were temporarily successful, he said, "the men thus floated to the surface would be powerless, their attempts at legislation would be misunderstood, disappointment and fresh discontent would follow, and the counter-revolution would sweep them away at once. But, indeed, it would not even come to that. History teaches us that no revolts that are without aim are successful even for a time. . . . The educational process, therefore, the forming of a rallying point for definite aims, is necessary to our success. . . . *Education towards Revolution* seems to me to express in three words what our policy should be."[5]

To Burne-Jones he wrote that the current excitement would soon die out, although the result upon the public mind might be beneficial for propaganda purposes.

[4]Rosalind Travers Hyndman, *The Last Years of H. M. Hyndman*, Brentano's, 1924. Appendix VIII, pp. 308-309. "A Note on Hyndman, Veteran Radical," by Charles J. Finger, 1920, who quotes from a diary.
[5]*The Commonweal*, loc. cit.

On February 21, 1886, another huge meeting was held in Trafalgar Square, carefully guarded by plain-clothes men and police. Burns and Hyndman talked of the inevitability of revolution in the interest of the proletariat; Hyndman quoted Latin and even attempted to explain the theory of surplus value according to Marx. But since there seemed to be no prospect of imminent revolution, and since the expected rioting did not occur, the ardour of the crowd soon diminished.

A week later, on February 28, Hyndman, Burns, Champion and Williams were tried in court and acquitted. It is noteworthy that the ringleaders escaped without punishment. Minor offenders were usually jailed for a month or two, or else fined. Less than three weeks before *The Times* had reported nineteen such cases.[6]

To his engineering friend, John Carruthers, who was then employed in Venezuela, Morris sent a long account of the recent events. Writing on March 25, he told Carruthers how the Federation had had much more to do with political activity than had the League, and that "Hyndman got into a mess, as I was sure he would."

John Burns stood for Nottingham: his candidature was genuine, and though he had no chance of being elected he had a chance of making a good fight for it. Well, in the midst of this a go-between offered Champion money from the Tories to put up candidates in two places . . . to "make running" for the Tory candidates. Hyndman couldn't resist this and so J. E. Williams stood for Hampstead and Fielding for Bermondsey (I think it was) and moreover there was a Federationist named Parker standing for Hackney; none of these men had the faintest chance; but Hyndman seems to have lost his head and committed the folly on the strength of this help of going to Chamberlain and threatening him with Socialist opposition to the Liberal candidates (John Bright at Birmingham amongst others) if he, Chamberlain, did not promise to support an eight hours bill in the forthcoming house. Well, of course Chamberlain showed him the door; also the whole thing got about and offended the Radicals mortally, and injured such chances as Burns had at Nottingham. Moreover, many of the members of the S. D. F. were

[6]*The London Times*, February 10, 1886.

much displeased, as the whole transaction had been done over their heads. The result was that Burns was badly beaten at Nottingham, got only about 560 votes, and the others were absurdly beaten, only polling some 50 votes amidst the tee-hees of the bourgeois press. The Socialists generally were much discredited, and there has been a split in the Federation, some of the branches remaining independent, one joining us, and some members setting up a new organization under the name of the Socialist Union: which latter I don't think will do much.

Meantime, as you know, the distress in this country has gone on increasing. . . . State work for the unemployed was always a *cheval de bataille* for the S. D. F., and after the split they went into this matter with special ardour . . . a few days before February 8th they had an excited meeting at Holborn Town Hall, where it was determined to meet again and take fresh action. For amidst all this a set of discredited 10th rate politicians (backed up by Tory money) had been busy making capital for the so-called Fair-Traders out of this unemployed business; they called a meeting for February 8th to Trafalgar Sq. and the S. D. F. determined to try to take the meeting from them: we determined to take no part officially in what seemed likely to be a faction fight; though many of our members went there. The meeting came off, and was very big, the people were clearly very much excited: the S. D. F. completely beat the Fair Traders, and Hyndman, Williams and (specially) Burns spoke in their usual way—not overwisely I fear. One or two of our people also spoke. As far as the speeches went they were (as I hear, for I wasn't there) of the usual type. However, the result was widely different from the usual one. . . . Burns and the others led the mob up to Hyde Park, doubtless meaning nothing more than an ordinary demonstration by it: all went well till they got to the Carlton, where they stopped to hoot, and where some fools in the windows fell to jeering them: this led to stoning the windows, and the crowd got quite unmanageable and in Piccadilly they turned out two or 3 shops. Well, they got up to Hyde Park where the others including Champion addressed them again, bade them go home quietly and so forth. There some of the crowd behaved very ill, frightening old ladies, upsetting carriages and the like, but the more part seem to have listened quietly. And so the Socialist leaders went home. But meantime a return wave of the crowd went back from Hyde Park down Audley Street where they broke nearly all the windows, and so into Oxford Street where they sacked several shops (as also in Audley Street) and broke much plate-glass (my own shop, 449, only escaping by about one-half a minute). Well, this was all the rioting, but the next day and the next, foggy dreary weather by the way, the shopkeepers and others had a regular panic, and behaved as though London were on the point of being carried by storm; nothing can be conceived more absurd than their cowardice. . . . The next Sunday the S. D. F. held a very orderly meeting in Hyde Park attended by 50 to 60 thousand people. . . . [Note: this was the computation of *Justice*.] Next act was the arrest of the leaders and after a wearisome time before the Bow Street magistrate in which I assisted as bail for Burns and Williams (Bax bailing Champion, and Joseph Cowen, Hyndman) they were committed for trial which comes off on April 5th. . . .

Well, this matter has rather drawn us and the Federation together, though some of us hardly approve of their defending themselves by law quibbles.

For the rest, contemptible as the riot was, as a riot, it no doubt has had a great effect, both here and on the continent: in fact the surprise of people that the British workman will not stand everything is extreme. . . . I fancy there will be another attempt on our meetings this summer and I rather expect to learn one more new craft—oakum-picking to wit, though I assure you I don't want to—far from it.

The League is going on pretty well; our Branch is much livelier than it was, and our meetings have been well attended throughout the winter. . . .

On March 18th we had a meeting in Commemoration of the Commune at South Place: that was a great success. . . . Kropotkine, new come from prison, spoke, and I made his acquaintance there: I like him very much: had a long talk with him yesterday evening at a gathering of the S. D. F. So you see, as far as meeting goes, the old quarrel is patched up.[7]

Morris's expectation that there would be other attempts to

[7]Morris to Carruthers, March 25, 1886. May Morris, II, 595–599. This is especially interesting for a number of reasons other than Morris's lively account of the First Trafalgar Square Riot. It furnishes a clear account of Hyndman's further efforts to secure political recognition for his group—as a political party designed to be influential in Parliament; and it places Morris's first meeting with Prince Kropotkin as of March 18, 1886—despite the speculations of many other authors. The reference to "our own branch" of the League is to the Hammersmith Branch, founded by Morris in the long shed back of Kelmscott House in Hammersmith.

suppress open-air meetings of Socialists was to be confirmed. On June 2 he writes that he "saw in *The Daily News* that our men had been 'run in' at Stratford, and expected what followed: namely, that as soon as I got home I had to go off to West Ham Police Court . . . and see about cash for paying their fines." On that day it cost him about 5 pounds and 17 shillings.

Again, on June 15, he himself went to speak at the disputed place. Here, C. W. Mowbray, one of the more anarchical members of the Socialist League, had been arrested and fined 20 shillings and costs only the day before. Nothing happened to Morris on this occasion, however, and he reported afterward that the meeting was orderly and brief.

But on July 18, while speaking in the Edgeware Road, he was not so fortunate. An Inspector of Police approached and requested Morris to stop speaking. Upon Morris's refusal to comply the officer took his name and address and he was summoned two days later to appear before the Marlebone Police Court on the technical charge of obstructing the highway. This was Morris's last appearance in court. According to Messrs. Vallance and Shaw the "counsel for the crown, appalled by the eminence of the prisoner, loaded him with compliments and appealed to him to overlook the formality of a shilling fine."

On Sunday, June 13, 1886, there was an attempt on the part of the Anarchists to change the Platform—the Constitution, Morris called it—of the Socialist League. Those favouring more political action were finally defeated; but Morris reported a long and weary day, "May and I getting home about 11:30 P.M. . . . But I am very glad there is a respite of a year before we can have another."[8]

After some efforts to patch up an understanding with the S. D. F. in the interest of Socialist unity, Morris wrote, "Well, I think I have done enough for that lot." He was tired unto death of "political action" and resumed some of his old interests: pattern designing and a translation of Homer.

His return to literature was presaged to some extent by the

[8]From a letter to his elder daughter, June 15, 1886.

change in the nature of his writings for *The Commonweal.*
Picking up the thread of thought begun with "The Message of
the March Wind," he evolved *The Pilgrims of Hope,* an
ideal narrative in verse which aimed at a restoration of the
native idealism of the common man. During 1886 twelve new

*From a copy in the British Museum Manuscript Collection, by permission of Miss May Morris
and Basil Blackwell, Ltd.*

Mr. Morris reading poems to Mr. Burne-Jones

A drawing by E. Burne-Jones

installments appeared: "The Bridge and the Street"; "Sending
to the War"; "Mother and Son"; "The New Birth"; "The
New Proletarian"; "In Prison—and At Home"; "The Half of
of Life Gone"; "A New Friend"; "Ready to Depart"; "A
Glimpse of the Coming Day"; "Meeting the War Machine,"
and "The Story's Ending." In the opinion of many critics this
series of connected verse is one of the finest of Morris's poetic
efforts: a view in which Messrs. Vallance, Spargo, Glasier, Miss
May Morris and the Countess Warwick all seem to concur.
There have been few, if any, valid criticisms of it. Says Mr.
Glasier: "Of all his [Morris's] poetic writings it is the most
modern in ethical sentiment. It is a narrative poem, which

might be classified as a saga or small epic, and has for its theme
a tale of frankly conventional love-melodrama blended with
the story of modern working-class revolt and the tragedy of the
Commune of Paris. . . . It is the first and as yet, so far as I
know, the only poetical narrative of modern proletarian revolt
which we possess."

Morris himself did not seem to regard the work as important.
But since others do, perhaps the following brief excerpts, telling of the mother's advice to her son, and the feeling of the
son after losing her, may give a fair idea of its nature and display the stream of proletarian rebellion which runs through it:

Now therefore, while yet thou art little, and hast no thought of thine
        own,
I will tell thee a word of the world; of the hope whence thou hast
        grown;
Of the love that once begat thee, of the sorrow that hath made
Thy little heart of hunger, and thy hands on my bosom laid.

.    .    .    .    .    .    .    .    .    .    .

Many a child of woman tonight is born in the town,
The desert of folly and wrong; and of what and whence are they
        grown?
Many and many an one of wont and use is born;
For a husband is taken to bed as a hat or a ribbon is worn.
Prudence begets her thousands; "Good is a housekeeper's life,
So shall I sell my body that I shall be matron and wife."
"And I shall endure foul wedlock, and bear the children of need."
Some of them born in hate, many the children of greed.
"I, I too can be wedded, though thou my love hast not."
"I am fair and hard of heart, and riches shall be my lot."

And all these are the good and the happy, on whom the world dawns
        fair.
O son, when wilt thou learn of those that are born to despair,
As the fabled mud of the Nile, that quickens under the sun
With a growth of creeping things, half dead when half begun?
E'en such is the care of Nature, that man should never die,

Though she breeds of the fools of the earth, and the dregs of the
　　city sty.

　·　　·　　·　　·　　·　　·　　·　　·　　·　　·　　·　　·

O fool, what words are these? Thou hast a sorrow to nurse,
And thou hast been bold and happy; but these, if they utter a curse,
No sting it has and no meaning, it is empty sound on the air.
Thy life is full of mourning, and theirs so empty and bare,
That they have no words for complaining; nor so happy have they been
That they may measure sorrow, or tell what grief may mean.

　　At this time Morris also wrote two of his Socialist Romances,
"An Old Story Retold," later reprinted as "A King's Lesson,"
which appeared in *The Commonweal*, No. 36, and which dealt
with a legend concerning Matthias Corvinus of Hungary; and
the famous semi-historical romance, *A Dream of John Ball*,
which ran in the issues from November 13, 1886, to and including that of January 22, 1887. There can be no doubt that these
Socialist Romances, as well as his proletarian epic, were intended to instill the native quality of proletarianism into the
hearts of his readers. In Morris's own words, *A Dream of John
Ball* concerned "the struggle against tyranny for the freedom
of life, how that the wildwood and the heath, despite of wind and
weather, were better for a free man than the court and the
cheaping-town; of the taking from the rich to give to the poor;
of the life of a man doing his own will and not the will of another man commanding him for the commandment's sake."

## CHAPTER IV

## BLOODY SUNDAY ON TRAFALGAR SQUARE

FURTHER agitation for political action came with the famous "Bloody Sunday" of November 13, 1887. The leading Socialist groups planned a monster Free Speech Demonstration, in which Morris agreed to take part. In spite of the celebration of the Queen's Jubilee, the depression in business had continued and economic conditions seemed to be growing worse. Not only that but the agitation for free speech had grown more popular and members of the Socialist League were particularly insistent upon it. During that extremely hot summer of 1887 Morris had remained in London working busily on League affairs. "I am trying to get the League to make peace with each other and hold together for another year. It is a tough job; something like the worst kind of pig-driving, I should think, and sometimes I lose my temper," he wrote. And in view of his known attitude toward parliamentary action, it may reasonably be assumed that his participation in the Trafalgar Square demonstration was a concession to the more ardent members of the League.

Meanwhile, despite the refusal of the police and of the Home Secretary to allow the meeting, plans were made, and on the appointed day crowds converged on the Square, which was lined with Foot Guards, fully armed.

Members of the Socialist League assembled at Clerkenwell Green to address the crowds assembling there. Among the speakers, according to *The Times* report, were Mr. William Morris and Mrs. Annie Besant, "both of whom delivered speeches of a determined character. Mr. William Morris began . . . by expressing sympathy with Mr. O'Brien [the Irish

National League agitation being then at its height]. He then proceeded to say that wherever free speech was attempted to be put down, it was their bounden duty to resist the attempt by every means in their power. . . . At about half-past three the procession started from Clerkenwell Green. . . . When the procession reached the Bloomsbury end of St. Martin's Lane, the police attempted to disperse it . . . mounted and on foot (the police) charged in among the people, striking indiscriminately . . . and causing complete disorder in the ranks. . . . In a short time the police had captured the remnants of the banners, which were torn and destroyed, and carried them off as trophies of the encounter."

According to Messrs. Vallance and Shaw, Morris marched with Shaw for some time, until, realizing that there was trouble ahead he went to the front of the procession just in time to see the rout of the advance guard of paraders. "If the men who had had the presumption to call themselves his 'comrades' and 'brothers' had been in earnest about cleansing and beautifying human society as he was in earnest about it, he would have been justified in believing that there was a great revolutionary force beginning to move in society. Trafalgar Square cured him and many others of that illusion."

"Our comrades," said Morris afterward, "fought valiantly, but they had not learned how to stand and turn their columns into a line, or to march on to the front . . . there was no rallying point . . . and all that the people composing our once strong column could do was to struggle into the square as helpless units."

For the time being, however, London was in a state of siege. "In fact," wrote Morris, "this affair, as far as it has gone, has been an ominous flash from the smouldering volcano of class war which underlies modern sham-society." A panic set in, similar to the one "caused by the last great demonstration of waning Chartism in 1848." More than three hundred persons were arrested, many were sent to prison, several were condemned to penal servitude, and it was thought that at least three persons died as the result of injuries received on "Bloody Sunday."[1]

Funeral rites for Alfred Linnell, who had been run down by the police and mortally injured, were held the following month. Morris wrote a death-song for the occasion and delivered a speech at Linnell's grave in Bow Cemetery on December 18.

"It is our business," said Morris in his speech at the grave, "to begin to organize for the purpose of seeing that such things shall not happen. . . . Our friend who lies here has had a hard life; and he has met with a hard death; but if society had been differently constituted, his life might have been a delightful, beautiful and happy one."

Two stanzas from Morris's memorial song, which was reprinted in full in numerous Socialist circles, are widely known:

> We asked them for a life of toilsome earning,
> They bade us bide their leisure for our bread,
> We craved to speak to tell our woeful learning,
> We come back speechless, bringing back our dead.
>
> They will not learn; they have no ears to hearken.
> They turn their faces from the eyes of fate;
> Their gay-lit halls shut out the skies that darken.
> —But lo! This dead man, knocking at the gate.

Then, at the next great Socialist demonstration following Bloody Sunday, when the enormous crowd poured out of the Square down Parliament Street, William Morris marched out in front, in the midst of those who bore the red flags, marching as the crusaders must have marched, his face the face of a crusader.

[1] *Justice*, November 19, 1887. Mackail, II, 191–193; Vallance, 340.

# CHAPTER V

EVERY JOHNSON HAS HIS BOSWELL: GLASIER REPORTS
ON WILLIAM MORRIS

DURING these years Morris travelled over much of the British Isles, lecturing on art and Socialism. He made several tours of Scotland and visited Dublin on at least one trip. Bruce Glasier and his friends in the Glasgow Branch of the S. D. F. had followed Morris, Bax and their supporters at the time of the great schism and organized a Glasgow branch of the Socialist League. And the best account of the work of Morris for the League is contained in Glasier's *William Morris and the Early Days of the Socialist Movement*. That work, like Boswell's *Life of Johnson*, contains anecdotes and personal reminiscences galore.

Mr. Glasier has told of Morris's first visit to the new League Branch, early in 1885, and of Mrs. Neilson's ardent "preceptorial address, in which she gently rebuked us for the warlike tone of some of our Socialist utterances, and pressed upon us her view that only by the extension of the franchise to women could Socialism ever be attained, as men were too stupid and selfish ever to do away with a system that satisfied their fighting and predatory instincts." Morris she admonished against becoming conceited, and he, in turn, assured her that if she but knew of his experiences for one week as editor of *The Commonweal*, "or as a member of the Council of the League with Joe Lane and Frank Kitz as colleagues and monitors, she would have no anxiety."

March 25, 1888, was another memorable occasion in the Socialist career of Glasier, for again Morris spent an entire day at the Glasgow Branch and discussed many things, among them the question of whether Revolutionary Socialism involves Anarchism.

I call myself a revolutionary Socialist [said Morris] because I aim at a complete revolution in social conditions. I do not aim at reforming the present system, but at abolishing it. . . . But, mark you again, what I aim at is Socialism or Communism, not Anarchism. Anarchism and Communism, notwithstanding our friend Kropotkin, are incompatible in principle. . . . I don't want people to do just as they please: . . . the fact that at present many laws and customs are bad, does not mean that we can do without good laws or good customs. . . . In a word, then, I tell you I am not an Anarchist, and I had as lief join the White Rose Society, or the so-called "Liberty and Property Defense League," as join the Anarchist organization.[1]

Once again it becomes evident that Morris's Socialism is neither an individualistic nor a communistic belief, but is, in effect, to be founded upon human nature and social instincts rather than upon laws and formulæ as such. He wants to convince his hearers that there really are such things as the social custom and the social mind. Hence, his insistence, ever increasingly, that men must first be educated to Socialism before they can have it forced upon them. Indeed, he felt the same way "about Democracy, so-called." According to May Morris, the education of the workmen was in many respects "the true root of his Socialism."

With the turn of the year, internal troubles in the Socialist League again came to the fore and in February Morris stated that if the Socialists were strong enough to send men to Parliament, he "certainly wouldn't be one of them." Once again he affirmed that he saw no use for action that was not organized, or for competition for political victories that was not the outcome of very definite policies for which the people had first been well prepared.

It was at about Whitsuntide, in 1888, that the trouble between the "Parliamentarians" and the "Practical" Socialists in the League came to a head. Bruce Glasier, who attended the

[1]*Loc. cit.*, pp. 61, 63–65.

annual conference at that time, has told the story of the expulsion of those who favoured parliamentary action.

"For the life of me," said Morris the night before the meeting, "I can't see what possible object they can have in all this business of theirs. If they succeed . . . then I and our side will leave the League: and what then? We have all the speakers that count, we have *The Commonweal*, and I have the money—more's the pity, maybe. They will have a few penniless branches, and no object or policy to justify their existence apart from the S. D. F. It is a sheer faction racket."

On the following day, Whitsunday, the Conference lasted from 10:30 in the morning until 10 P.M., and when the "parliamentary resolution" was finally voted down at about 9 P.M., Morris made an earnest appeal for unity and for continued good-fellowship. Well could he say to Bruce Glasier afterward, "the damned business is over for at least another year," and once again, to seek relief from his pent-up feelings, give vent to a characteristic outburst on the state of art:

This infernal civilization has no capacity to understand either nature or art. People have no eyes to see, no ears to hear. The only thing they understand is how to enslave their fellows or be enslaved by them, grubbing for a life lower than that of the brutes. Children and savages have better wits than civilized mankind today. Look at your West-End art—the damnable architecture, the damnable furniture, and the detestable dress of men and women. Look at the damnable callosity of the rich and educated, who swill themselves in the rottenness of their wealth, in the face of the horrible want and misery of the poor: and the poor who not only suffer the misery and the insult of it, but grovel before the ruffians who souse them in it! They haven't the sense or the pluck of rabbits. But we must "think about environment!"—Oh, must we! Damn environment! Don't think if the devil pulls me by the ears I'm going to hell without kicking!

Well might Morris lament the failure of both rich and poor to grasp his principles of art and of social regeneration. After a decade of preaching he had not yet found one man who seemingly comprehended either the significance of art as he saw it, or those relationships which Morris knew to exist between art and society on the one hand, and art and Socialism on the other.

Meanwhile, the Socialist League was at last rid of the Parliamentarians. Most of them were to seek the fulfillment of their political ambitions elsewhere. There remained, however, the Anarchists and the Anarchistic-Communists.

## CHAPTER VI

### SIGNS OF CHANGE—FROM GLASGOW TO HAMMERSMITH

IT is sometimes claimed that Morris was not opposed to violence in order to gain his ends, and it must be admitted that there are certain statements in his writings which would seem to indicate that at heart he was a violent revolutionary. Thus, as early as July, 1881, he had written of those conditions in society which "make thinking people so sick at heart that they are driven from all interest in politics," and yet, he adds, "the hope in me has been that matters would mend gradually, till the last struggle, which must needs be mingled with violence and madness, would be so short as scarcely to count."

It is not unlikely that as he had played with the idea of a "Twilight of the Gods" in his earlier days, so the idea of a similar twilight of the present world may have appealed to him from time to time. He still believed, no doubt, that the last great act in the transition of society might be played out in blood. There is no evidence, however, that he ever advocated this sort of play in his own lifetime. Always it was to come after due preparation on the part of society, and society was not yet prepared.

The best-known monument to his propaganda activities in these years is the volume entitled *Signs of Change* which he published through Reeves and Turner in 1888. In this volume were contained his lectures and essays on "How We Live and How We Might Live"; "Whigs, Democrats and Socialists"; "Feudal England"; "The Hopes of Civilization"; "The Aims of Art"; "Useful Work *vs.* Useless Toil" (which was reprinted separately by The Socialist League Office in 1885 as *The Socialist Platform, No. 2*), and "The Dawn of a New Epoch."

276

What did he have to say on matters of violent revolution and on his own particular kind of Socialism? Apropos of the proletarian revolution he states that "it is not revenge we want for poor people, but happiness; indeed, what revenge can be taken for all the thousands of years of sufferings of the poor?" In the coming society, as he visualizes it, "there will be no non-working class, the organized workers will be the whole community, there will be no one left out. Society will be recast."

With regard to the matter of individualism as opposed to common welfare, he says that "Socialism bases the rights of the individual to possess wealth on his being able to use that wealth for his own personal needs; and, labour being properly organized, every person, male or female, not in nonage or otherwise incapacitated for working, would have a full opportunity to produce wealth and thereby to satisfy his own personal needs."

Labour, under his scheme, would never be wasted by war, commercial or political, by lack of freedom, or by individual labour competition. National rivalries would be eliminated by the new federated systems of communes or cantons, and for the "worn-out superstition" of Nationalism there would be substituted *"a system of free communities living in harmonious relations with each other, managing their own affairs by the free consent of their members; yet keeping some kind of center whose function it would be to protect the principle whose practice the communities should carry out."* (*Italics* mine.)

As far as the workers of society are concerned, Morris still believed that it should be the birthright of every man to enjoy social and economic freedom as well as political. "It is right and necessary," he states (for perhaps the four hundredth time in his career), "that all men should have work to do which shall be worth doing, and be of itself pleasant to do; and it should be done under such conditions as would make it neither over-wearisome nor over-anxious."

Not all conflicts among the ranks of reformers were to be solved so easily as Morris thought possible, however, and many a time he was to wonder whether it would not be better to withdraw from the League and band together with half a dozen faithful followers in some new organization. Yet by 1888 he had emerged victorious in each important matter of policy. The advocates of political action had been defeated; the basic program of *Education, Agitation and Organization* remained, for the time being, at least, unchanged. Now and again, however, Morris was glad to escape from the conflicting atmosphere of the League offices and seek recreation in new literary and artistic tasks. He spent more time upon them now, and sometimes he may have rejoiced at discussions with congenial spirits among the branches in Scotland and elsewhere. Mr. Glasier tells many anecdotes of Morris's Scotch journeys: of how he loved to exchange views with the workers and toilers of Glasgow and neighboring towns, and of the atmosphere of homely cheerfulness that pervaded their gatherings. Whatever the nature of the questions addressed to him, Morris replied with unfailing willingness, even when, as in some instances, the question was of a directly personal nature, such as "Why don't you carry out your Socialist principles in connection with your own business?"—"Why does the firm of Morris & Company object to advertise its wares?"—"Do you dress unconventionally as you do in a blue-serge suit and discard white linen on principle as a Socialist or as a craftsman, or simply as a matter of personal taste?" These questions usually came from the visitors and not from the members, most of whom had known the answers now for several years.

On one occasion Morris remarked to the members of the Glasgow Branch that he was not surprised at the manner in which the Scotch workers had come to Socialism of their own accord "without even being in contact with foreign revolutionary influences." He went on to state that most of them, and indeed most people, by nature and temperament, had always been Socialists at heart, and that there had always been "a making of Society towards Socialism, since human history began. I have recently been looking a good deal into the literature of the Middle Ages and earlier periods, and have been struck with the definiteness of Socialist feeling, and even of Socialist customs, among the people and the monkish sects of those days. I am writing some chapters for *The Commonweal* on 'The Revolt of Ghent' and on 'John Ball' of the Peasants' Revolt in England in Richard II's time, and so hope to make the movement better understood."

On one of Morris's Scotch trips he addressed a small gathering of mining people on a cinder-heap outside Coatbridge. One old woman, according to Mr. Glasier, listened with prophetic interest and then said: "He's a guid man onyway; for he looks an honest man, and he speaks the guid truth. My ain father, who was a great Radical, used to say muckle the same thing as this gentleman here; but the working folk round aboot thocht he was cracked. The working folk noo-a-days hae awfu little gumption in their heads, and I'm sorry to think a gentleman like this should waste his pains trying to put some common sense into them."

On the same occasion a gentleman who had been standing near by, approached at the close of the speech and took his stand upon the cinder-heap, addressing the surrounding crowd in this wise:

You people don't, I suppose, know who the gentleman is who has been addressing you. He is one of the leading men of literature and art in our day, and it is one of the greatest surprises of my life to find myself so unexpectedly listening to him address a meeting of this kind in Coatbridge. I am not a Socialist and don't share his hopes for improving society—I wish I could, but all my experience denies them—but I greatly admire his works, both his poetry and his art, and I wish to say that I am sorry I did not know of his coming, for I am sure that he is entitled to a much better hearing and to much more comfortable conditions for speaking than he has here on this cinder-heap.

For these expressions Morris thanked the gentleman, but assured him that he had every reason to be delighted with his visit to Coatbridge:

And after all, my friend, I wish to remind you that this is just the sort of way that Diogenes and Christ and, for all we know, Homer, and your own Blind Harry the Minstrel used to get their crowds; so I am not so far out of the high literary conventions after all.

The occasion of the Edinburgh Art Congress in 1889 proved to be a triumph for the members of the Socialist League. For, as at the Liverpool meeting shortly before, Morris, Walter Crane, Emory Walker, Cobden-Sanderson, all prominent members of the new Socialist organization, gave lectures at the various sectional meetings; and at least one newspaper accused "Morris and his friends" of having "turned the Congress into a Socialist Demonstration," while another paper "lamented the regrettable intrusion of revolutionary Socialist politics into the peaceful republic of the arts."(!) The headline "Art and Socialism" flourished in the columns of all the Edinburgh newspapers during the week of the Congress, and became a subject of numerous clerical remarks on the following Sabbath.

It was from the Edinburgh Art Congress, says Mr. Glasier, that we must date the beginning of that remarkable bent toward Socialism among the students of the Glasgow and other art schools which soon afterwards became one of the most significant facts in the culture of the period. Within the next few years more than half the art students in Glasgow, Edinburgh, Birmingham, Manchester, Leeds and other industrial centers were socialistic in their professions or in their sympathies.

Of public opinion, either in private or in public, Morris was always indifferent. Mr. Glasier has told how, while walking down a busy thoroughfare, or crossing an intersection, Morris, to illustrate some tale he was telling, would pause to imitate the antics of a drunken man, much to the amusement or to the indignation, as the case might be, of passers-by. On one occasion, while approaching the Glasgow Cathedral, from which a number of people were emerging from a Sunday morning service, Morris caught sight of a huge sculptured memorial in shining white marble jammed into the old, grey stonework of the aisle, "cutting through the string-courses of the base, projecting up into and completely cutting off a portion of the stained-glass window above."

At the sight of this grotesque abomination in mixed art effects Morris stopped dead in his tracks, "as if struck by a rifle ball, his eyes fixed furiously on the object in front of him. As he glared at it he seemed to crouch like a lion about to leap at its prey, his whiskers bristling out. 'What the hell is that? Who the hell has done that?' he shouted, to the amaze, alarm and indignation of the people near by. 'What infernal idiot has done that?' Morris again demanded, and heedless of the consternation around him he poured forth a torrent of invective against the unknown perpetrators of this atrocious crime. . . . Meanwhile, the scandalized onlookers, believing that they were witnessing the distraction of some unfortunate fellow creature bereft of his reason, resumed their way, remarking compassionately about him to one another."

It was on these Scotch journeys that we have recorded many of Morris's most hostile criticisms of education, pedantry, and of the jargon of the scientific exponents of Communism, State Socialism and Anarchy. "Fancy," he once remarked, "a Carlylean aristocracy of talent: the country under the benevolent rule of Senior Wranglers and LL.D.'s!" Or, "fancy a democracy educated up from, or rather down to, the level of Oxford and Cambridge, as some, even of our Socialist friends, would have it!"

Again, in tramping the streets of the Glasgow slums, he often remarked upon the cleverness, wit and ingenuity of children in their play, "especially in the poorer districts where they are freer from the tutelage of the grown-ups. . . . But the faculty soon withers," he added, "the poor things become dull and vacant-minded once they grow out of childhood and lose the sap of the common stem. The natural well-springs of their imagination become soiled and soon run dry."

## CHAPTER VII

ANARCHY DISRUPTS THE SOCIALIST LEAGUE:

ANARCHY *À LA* VALENCIA

D URING the last two years of Morris's association with the Socialist League (1888–1890) the formal meetings frequently degenerated into arguments among Socialists, Anarchists and Anarchist-Communists. Tochatti, the Anarchist tailor, would discourse on the superiority of Anarchy over State Socialism; Mordhorst, a Danish Socialist, would insist that "not less, but *more* law" was needed; Munsey, a postal telegraph official, would then complain that the lectures and discourses were becoming too technical and too far-fetched: "The Social Revolution depended solely upon the working class. 'Who would be free, themselves must strike the blow.' What was wanted was plain statements."

Answering a series of attacks from "Comrade Blackwell" in *The Commonweal* for May 18, 1889, which were based upon some resolutions recently passed by an Anarchist Congress at Valencia in Spain, Morris clearly defined his own position, showing therein how his Socialism differed from Marxian Communism on the one hand and from Anarchism on the other, as well as from that strange blend of the two which was, in those days, sometimes called Anarchistic-Communism.

"I will begin [he says] by saying that I call myself a *Communist*, and I have no wish to qualify that word by joining any other [such as Marxian, or Anarchistic] to it. The aim of Communism seems to me to be the *complete equality of condition* of all people; and anything in a Socialist direction which stops short of this is merely a compromise with the present condition of society, a halting-place on the road to the goal. This is the

only logical outcome of any society which is other than a closed
company sustained by violence for the express purpose of the
'exploitation of man by man' in the interests of the strongest.—
Communism also [he says] will have to keep itself free of superstition. Its ethics will have to be based upon the recognition of
*natural* cause and effect, and not on rules and formulæ derived
from *a priori* ideas of relations of man to the universe. Today
most people who can be said to think at all are now beginning
to see that the realization of Socialism is certain; although
many can see no further than a crude and incomplete *State
Socialism*. All genuine Socialists admit that Communism is the
necessary and natural development of Socialism; but, I repeat,
further than this everything must be speculative. And here I
join issue with our Anarchistic-Communistic friends, who are
somewhat authoritative on the matter of authority—of the ad-
visability or possibility of an individual man doing what he
pleases always and under all circumstances. This is an absolute
negation of society and makes Communism as the highest expression of society impossible; yet when you begin to qualify
this assertion of the right to do as you please by adding 'as long
as you don't interfere with other people's rights to do the
same' the exercise of some kind of authority becomes necessary.
If individuals are not to coerce others, there must somewhere
be an authority which is prepared to coerce .them not to coerce;
and that authority must clearly be collective. And there are other
difficulties besides this crudest and most obvious one."

Proper collective action, he believes, can only be built up
when you have first built up a proper "public conscience" in
each community—and this "community will" then will replace
the individual will and the collective will of the State as a
whole.

This pronouncement, in which Morris took issue with Fabian,
Marxian and Anarchist tenets, shows clearly and positively the
philosophy which underlay Morris's Socialist activity. It
summed up, in a few words, many scattered ideas which hitherto
had been expressed at random in his various writings and

speeches; but for the doctrinaires within the Socialist League it marked the beginning of a rupture.

Shortly afterward Morris attended an International Socialist Congress at Paris. During his absence the Anarchistic elements within the League were clamouring for new aims and for new leadership. And much the same sort of thing was happening among the diverse cliques of radicals who had assembled in Paris. It seemed that no two parties could agree, although there were only some four hundred delegates from the various nations. Edward Carpenter, one of the twenty-one English delegates, wrote later how "After the glib oratorical periods of Jules Guesde and the others, what a contrast it was to see Morris . . . fighting furiously . . . hacking and hewing the stubborn English phrases out. . . . Something in the solid English way of looking at things, the common sense of it, and the practical outlook on the world, the earnestness and tenacity of Morris made that speech one of the most effective in the session."[1]

At the Paris Congress Morris wished to put a resolution that would pledge the meeting definitely to Socialism; but as agreement seemed impossible and as the members were already divided between *"Possibilists* and *Genuine Socialists,"* as Morris afterward wrote, he gave up his attempt at unity and left the Congress several days before its formal conclusion.

Upon his return to London he was faced again with the matter of dissension and prepared a lengthy answer to the Anarchist complaints. This answer, entitled "Communism and Anarchism," appeared in *The Commonweal* on August 17, 1889. In it he stated that they who suppose his use of the word Communism to mean nothing more than what the Owenites meant by it are definitely mistaken: "I use it as a more accurate term for Socialism, as implying equality of condition and consequently abolition of private property. . . . Equally, of course, the living in small communities is not in theory an essential of this great change, though I have little doubt that

[1] *Cf. Vallance,* 348.

it would bring about such a way of living and abolish big cities, which, equally with Comrade Davis, I think much to be desired. . . . As to the matter of majority rule. . . . If, at any time, the minority rules it is because they are better organized, better armed, less stupid, more energetic than the mere nose-counted majority: this effective 'majority' therefore coerces the 'minority.' . . . The time may come when the Social Conscience will be so highly developed that coercion will be impossible, even on the part of the community. But I do not consider myself a pessimist because I am driven to admit that such a condition of things is a long way ahead:

I must repeat practically also what I said in my first article: however much the unit of association may be divided, people will have to associate in administration, and sometimes there will be differences of opinion . . . *e.g.*, a community may discuss the building of a bridge; some say Ay and some say No, and persist in that opinion after all possible arguments have been examined. What is to be done? Which party is to give way? Our Anarchist friends say that it must not be carried by a majority; in that case, then, it must be carried by a minority. And why? Is there any divine right in a minority? I fail to see it, although I admit that the opinion is held by the Absolutists."

He concluded by saying that "whatever will give us equality, with whatever drawbacks, will content me, and I find that at bottom this is the ideal of all Socialists. So I think that the fewer hyphenated party names and distinctions between persons of different temperaments, the better."

This article, August 17, 1889, marked the beginning of the end of Morris's connection with the Socialist League. The Anarchistic element was now in a majority and they determined to make use of their opportunities. Henceforth, Morris could use his powers of persuasion to no avail. The members would not agree that the question was one of mere verbal expression; they saw clearly that they favoured principles essentially different from those of Morris. Therefore, they refused to be conciliated.

## CHAPTER VIII

## THE WORLD-REDEEMING AMERICANS

THERE was one way in which Morris did not wish the world to move forward, and that was by the extension of rights to the centralized bureaucratic State power. He was very much afraid of the loss of individual rights under the kinds of State Socialism advocated by many exponents of the "American Socialist" doctrines of Henry George and, later, of Edward Bellamy. When his discontent was beginning to turn into action Morris had hailed George's *Progress and Poverty* as a potent force in spreading discontent. But as time went on he studied George's idea of land nationalization more carefully and came to the conclusion that it represented an artificial panacea which did not go to the root of the matter: *viz.*, human nature. Therefore, as early as April 5, 1884, he had written in *Justice* on the subject of Henry George, "that eloquent and enthusiastic American" who has been working hard to push "what he believes" to be the true remedy for our "terrible ills."

The phrase "what he believes" suggests Morris's opposition to the single tax as a valid solution of the evils of civilization. Just as he disagreed with Christian Socialism, and disagreed later with Marxian Scientific Socialism, so he disagreed with George's ideas and with those of his confreres. "It is impossible," he added, graciously, "not to feel sympathy and regard for a man of this kind." But, "while we heartily chant Amen" to Mr. George's anathema, "we cannot finish, nay, we cannot even begin here, because the worst enemies are left untouched by our prophet."

Morris thought that George's success was due largely to his

emotional appeal, stating that "it is not unlikely that a more logical and correct thinker, a more rigid economist, would have failed where he has succeeded. People read between the lines of his book, not his economical errors, but his deep love of truth and his never-ceasing desire to benefit his fellow-men." It was useless, he felt, to talk about repairing the roof of the capitalistic system when it was the foundations that leaked.

Therefore, said Morris, "we look upon Mr. George's visit with misgiving," fearing that the capitalists, especially the Whig liberals, "would make common cause with Mr. George, and, anxious to save the proceeds of their own still worse methods of plunder, would show a tendency to throw the landlords overboard as Jonahs from a craft now owned and chiefly manned by themselves, and on the other hand would pit Mr. George as the reasonable and moral reformer against the unreasonable and immoral revolutionists, of which we form a part."

Nevertheless, George's work made a tremendous impression upon all classes in England and many recruits of the Labour movement owed their chief inspiration to him. Meanwhile, as Morris's difficulties with the Socialist League expanded, another American began to attract attention with his depiction of a "brave new world" that would come in the year 2000, or thereabouts. This man was Edward Bellamy and his book was entitled *Looking Backward*. In 1888–1889 *Looking Backward* was the latest mania among the "parlour-pinks" of the English-speaking world. Morris reviewed the volume in the June 22 issue of *The Commonweal*.

This critical essay is particularly interesting and it presents intelligently the distinction between the purely mechanized brain of the analytical Socialists who advocated Scientific State Socialism and the kind of brain which envisaged what Morris called constructive or "Practical" Socialism, which ardently opposed all forms of centralization, monopolization and robotization.

A few years ago, said Morris, few people in England knew

more about Socialism than Messrs. Bradlaugh, Gladstone and
Admiral Maxse know now—*i.e.*, nothing—yet today it is "fashionable for even West-End dinner-parties to affect an interest
in and knowledge of it." This indicates, he adds, with delightful sarcasm, "a wide and deep public interest." He also ob-
serves that recently it has become fashionable for "a watery
tincture of proletarianism" to form an ingredient in any novel
which is supposed to be "serious and life-like." Ten years ago,
he thinks, Edward Bellamy's *Looking Backward* would hardly
have been noticed. Certainly its romantic aspects do not account
for its popularity, despite the author's acknowledgment that
"he has only given it this form as a sugar-coating to the pill,"
for these aspects have often been handled in less popular books
with many times Mr. Bellamy's skill. It is the subject matter,
therefore, which accounts for the attention of the public.

He said that there was a twofold danger in books such as
this:

> For there will be some temperaments to whom the answer given to
> the question How Shall We Live Then? will be pleasing . . . others
> to whom it will be displeasing. . . . The danger to the first is that they
> will accept it with all its errors and fallacies. . . . The danger to the
> second is that they will be inclined to say, If *that* is Socialism, we won't
> help its advent . . . it holds out no hope to us.

Of course, said Morris, there are many thousands of people
who have a temperament like that of Mr. Bellamy, "admiring
due economical knowledge and adroit construction." This temperament he terms "unhistoric and unartistic." It may be
called, he says, "the unmixed modern one" and makes its
owner "perfectly satisfied with modern civilization, if only the
injustice, misery and waste could be got rid of—which half-
change seems possible to him." Morris pointed out, in passing,
that "Bellamy has his mind fixed on the mere *machinery* of
*life*." As for its idea of monopoly, its primary essential is, "I
warm myself by the fire which you have made, and you (very
much the plural) stay out in the cold."

In brief, Morris objects to the author's idea of and definition of monopoly. It is what he terms "ahistorical" in its reasoning. Presumably, if you remove the element of personal interest
and substitute merely a public interest that operates through
bureaucracies, "you don't get happiness for everybody, you
get inefficiency and graft." Morris very definitely prefers his
own kind of "Socialism," which demands "Decentralization"
and *the maintenance of that individuality which creates self-
respect in both personal and public obligations.*

To go on. The hope of the developments of trusts and rings to which
the competition for privilege (*i.e.,* for monopoly) has driven commerce,
especially in America, is the distinctive part of Mr. Bellamy's book;
and it seems to me to be a somewhat dangerous hope to rest upon. . . .
It may indeed be the most logical outcome of the most modern side of
commercialism: *i.e.,* the outcome that *ought* to be; but then there is its
historical outcome to be dealt with: *i.e.,* what *will* be; which I cannot
help thinking *may be* the recurrence of break-ups and re-formations of
this kind of monopoly, under the influence of competition for privilege,
or war for the division of plunder, till the flood comes and destroys
us all.

He closes this aspect of the problem by saying that the
"economical semi-fatalism of some Socialists is a deadening
and discouraging view."

Bellamy's idea of the organization of life after the great
change has taken place, says Morris, is "nothing less than
State Communism worked by the very extreme of national
centralization. The underlying vice in it is that the author
cannot conceive of anything else than the machinery of society."
He tells us, says Morris, with thinly veiled disgust, that material goods will be so increased under this new efficiency that
terror of starvation will disappear. He tells us that every man
will be "free to choose his own occupation and that work is
no burden to any one": but, Morris adds, "the impression he
produces is that of a huge standing army, tightly drilled, compelled by some mysterious fate to unceasing anxiety for the

production of wares to satisfy every caprice, however wasteful and absurd, that may be cast amongst them."

As an illustration it is mentioned that everybody is to begin the serious work of production at the age of twenty-one, work three years as a labourer, and then choose his skilled occupation and work till he is forty-five, when he is to knock off . . . and amuse himself (improve his mind, if he has one left him). Heavens! Think of a man of forty-five changing all his habits suddenly and by compulsion! It is a small matter after this that the said persons . . . should form a kind of aristocracy (how curiously old ideas cling) for the performance of certain judicial and political functions!

In short, Morris thinks that Mr. Bellamy's knowledge of life and his ideas concerning it "are curiously limited." His ideal for the life of the average citizen of the future "is Boston (U. S. A.) beautifed." To Mr. Bellamy, the inhabitants of villages, which come into his picture only in one passage, "are mere servants of the great centers of civilization. This seems strange to some of us, who cannot help thinking that such aggregations of urban population afford the worst possible form of dwelling place, whatever the second worst might be." To Morris's mind, the multiplication of machinery will lead only to more machinery. The real ideal, says Morris, should point "to the reduction of *pain in labour* to a minimum." Such a gain to humanity, he believes, "can only be dreamed of till men are even more completely equal than Mr. Bellamy's Utopia would allow them to be."

He then goes on to point out that Mr. Bellamy, having established the supremacy of lazy virtue, "worries himself with obvious failure" over the matter of finding an incentive to make men work—an incentive which would replace their present fear of starvation. Here Morris points out that the only incentive to good and useful work of any sort must be *pleasure in the work itself*.

It will be necessary for the unit of administration to be small enough for every citizen to feel himself responsible for its details, and to be interested in them: that individual men cannot shuffle off the business of life on to the shoulders of an abstraction called the State, but must deal with it in conscious association with each other: that variety of life is as much an aim of a true Communism as equality of condition, and that nothing but a union of these two will bring about real freedom.

Morris closed his condemnation of Mr. Bellamy's *Looking Backward* (and incidentally the above statement of his own principles of Socialism) by saying that in any such ill-considered portrait of "the mere economical reconstruction of society, however much courage may be displayed by its author, there are sides to the problem which such an author evidently does not consider, such, *e.g.*, as the future of the family"; and that instead of seeing "the necessity for the equality of all labour," he sees only "the necessity for the equality of the reward of labour"—which is "always a stumbling-block for would-be Socialists!"

His final verdict on the importance of *Looking Backward* is that "it will be read and considered seriously" by many persons, because "incomplete systems impossible to be carried out, but plausible on the surface, are always attractive to people ripe for change, but not knowing clearly what their aim is."

To answer more completely the challenge of *Looking Backward*, Morris wrote a long essay, *How Shall We Live Then?* in which he described minutely the plans for his own type of decentralized communes, acting together under a federated, but decentralized, government. It was this essay, written for *The Commonweal*, which explained most clearly the practical mechanism of his new idea of the modern State.

## CHAPTER IX

BUT MORRIS'S LITERARY EFFORTS STILL CONTINUE

THE method used by Morris to conciliate the members of the Socialist League and incidentally to enlighten them on various aspects of social change during the ages of history is one that has given rise to much of the thoughtless criticism directed against his particular brand of Socialism: *viz.*, that he was a Utopian and a Romantic rather than a real Socialist. For had he not written the "pseudo-historic" *Revolt of Ghent* and *A Dream of John Ball?* Now, in addition, there appeared in the pages of *The Commonweal* the so-called Utopian Romance, *News from Nowhere*. Like *The Pilgrims of Hope* this ideal narrative in prose, rather than in poetry, did not admit of further controversy. It, too, was based upon human sympathy and sentiment, but it aimed at the restoration of native British idealism.

*News from Nowhere* (which ran in *The Commonweal* from January 11 to October 4, 1890) portrays one aspect of Morris's idea of a Utopian life—and it was offered in contrast to Edward Bellamy's idea of an ultra-modern mechanistic paradise, *Looking Backward*, which Morris had reviewed in *The Commonweal* shortly before. This most recent English "Utopia" was to be his last prose contribution to the Socialist League with the exception of his farewell letter.

The story opens with a man leaving his Socialist Club meeting after a discussion of what society will be like after the "Morrow of the Revolution" is past. He goes to his bed with the words "If I could but see it!" on his lips. He awakens in the future and discovers what the perfection of a true society is like. The days of inequality are over and man is now free to engage in pleasurable activities.

As he progresses through this "Utopia," this land of *Nowhere*, which has replaced his native Hammersmith and his native Thames-land, he learns the story of how the "great change" has been brought about—of the final breakdown of the old régime. The peculiar thing about this history is the similarity it bears to that of the recent breakdown of the old régime in Russia[1] but apparently with less bloodshed in London. (Another remarkable similarity lies in the description of riots which bear striking resemblance to the Trafalgar Square Riots.)

Now that the revolution had succeeded, England had become "the fair, green garden of the North." Machines were still used, but they were now used wisely; and the old estates and buildings that had been deemed worthy of preservation were turned into workers' clubs (as is the case today in Russia).

There were now no political parties, and hence nothing could create party divisions. Neither did crime exist, for private property including landed and personal possessions—and also women (who were no longer regarded as property) were merely integral parts and appurtenances of the various communes. Now, at last, as in the days when John Ball preached to the men of Kent and Essex, the great object in a man's life was to do great and worthy and noble things for the sake of the deed, and not of the reward.

Good work and praise of work abounded everywhere, the chief object being to encourage all things which redounded to the benefit of your fellow men. In brief, the entire state of this new society is one in which the individual feels his responsibility to his fellow men; he has become a *social* rather than an *unsocial* being.

Here, in *"Nowhere,"* shops could be entrusted to children; money did not exist; communities were largely self-supporting,

[1]*Loc. cit.*, Ch. XVII, How the Change Came, *passim.*

although bound by certain threads of organization to the Federation of which they formed a part; and wants were few and pleasures many.

The latter part of *News from Nowhere* describes a journey up the Thames into the picturesque region of the upper valley, near Lechlade (the site of Kelmscott Manor). The particular point connected with this account of the "new life" is not that the story represents a "rural fantasy," but that it presents *a very true account of Morris's own life among his own friends*. These passages, therefore, are not Romantic, they are Realistic, and the life that Morris himself lived in his own leisure moments he wanted to be possible for others. The old manor which the friends visit is indeed none other than Kelmscott Manor. The entire scene, in abbreviated form, may be visualized in the following brief excerpts:

Presently we saw before us a bank of elm·trees, which told us of a house amidst them, though I looked in vain for the grey walls that I expected to see there. As we went, the folk on the bank talked indeed, mingling their kind voices with the cuckoo's song, the sweet strong whistle of the blackbirds, and the ceaseless note of the corn-crake as he crept through the long grass of the mowing-field; whence came waves of fragrance from the flowering clover amidst of the ripe grass. . . .

I disentangled myself from the merry throng and looked about me. The river came down through a wide meadow on my left, which was grey, now, with the ripened, seeding grasses; the gleaming water was lost presently by a turn of the bank, but over the meadow I could see the mingled gables of a building where I knew the lock must be, and which now seemed to combine a mill with it. A low wooded ridge bounded the river plain to the south and the southeast, whence we had come, and a few low houses lay about its feet and up its slopes. I turned a little to my right, and through the hawthorn sprays and long shoots of the wild roses could see the flat country spreading out far away under the sun of the calm evening, till something that might be called hills with a look of sheep pastures about them bounded it with a soft blue line. Before me the elm-boughs still hid most of what houses there might be in this river-side dwelling of men; but to the right of the cart-road a few grey buildings of the simplest kind showed here and there.

There I stood in a dreamy mood, and rubbed my eyes as if I were not wholly awake. . . . But no change came as yet, and my heart swelled with joy as I thought of all the beautiful grey villages, from the river to the plain and the plain to the uplands, which I could picture to myself so well, all peopled now with this happy and lovely folk, who had cast away riches and attained to wealth. . . .

As I stood there Ellen detached herself from our happy friends who still stood on the little strand and came to me. She took me by the hand, and said softly "Take me on to the house at once; we need not wait for the others: I had rather not. . . ."

Once again Ellen echoed my thoughts when she said: "Yes, friend, this is what I came out for to see. This many-gabled old house, built by the simple country-folk of the long-past times, regardless of all the turmoil that was going on in cities and courts. . . . It seems to me as if it had waited for these happy days, and held in it the gathered crumbs of happiness of the confused and turbulent past. . . ."

I could not answer her or say a word. Her exaltation and pleasure were so keen and exquisite; and her beauty so delicate, yet so interfused with energy, that any added word would have been commonplace and futile. I dreaded lest the others should come in suddenly and break the spell she had cast about me; and no one came. I heard the merry voices some way off, and knew that they were going along the river to the great meadow on the other side of the house and garden.

We drew back a little and looked up at the house: the door and the windows were open to the fragrant sun-cured air; from the upper window-sills hung festoons of flowers in honour of the festival, as if the others shared in the love for the old house.

"Come in," said Ellen. "I hope nothing will spoil it inside; but I don't think it will. Come! We must go back presently to the others. . . ." She led me on to the door, murmuring little above her breath as she did so, "The earth and the growth of it, and the life of it! If I could but say or show how I love it!"

We went in and found no soul in any room. . . .

Everywhere there was but little furniture, and that only of the most necessary and of the simplest forms. The extravagant love of ornament which I had noted in this people elsewhere seemed here to have given place to the feeling that the house itself and its associations was the ornament of the country life amidst which it had been left stranded from old times, and that to re-ornament it would but take away from its use as a piece of natural beauty.

We sat down at last in a room over the wall which Ellen had

caressed, and which was still hung with old tapestries, originally of no artistic value, but now faded into pleasant grey tones which harmonized thoroughly well with the quiet of the place, and which would have been ill-supplanted by brighter and more striking decoration.

I asked a few rambling questions of Ellen as we sat there, but scarcely listened to her answers, and presently became silent, and then scarce conscious of anything but that I was there in that old room, the doves crooning from the roofs of the barn and dovecot beyond the window opposite me. . . .

She looked at me kindly, but as if she read me through and through. She said: "You have begun again your never-ending contrast between the past and the present. Is it not so?"

"True," said I. "I was thinking of what you, with your capacity and intelligence, joined to your love of pleasure and your impatience of unreasonable restraint—of what you would have been in that past. And even now, when all is won, and has been for a long time, my heart is sickened with thinking of all the waste of life that has gone on for so many years."

"So many centuries," she said, "so many ages!"

There follows an account of a hay-makers' feast, but the narrator is bound to "go off into another dream," as Ellen fears, and in one of them he steps at last out of the house into the drabness of the nineteenth century. "Was it a dream?" he asks, and answers "Yes" for those whom he has seen only in his dream. He will "go back and be happier" for having seen them, "for having added a little hope" to his struggle. But at the end he poses the real problem for himself and for his people:

To go on living while you may, striving with whatsoever pain and labour needs must be, to build up little by little the new day of fellowship, and rest, and happiness.

Yes, surely, and if others can see it as I have seen it, then it may be called a vision rather than a dream.[2]

It may fairly be supposed, perhaps, that only those who knew Morris's life and work and thought could venture to interpret his *News from Nowhere*. In any event, we can be cer-

[2]Morris, *News from Nowhere*, loc. cit. (N. Y., ed. 1926, pp. 244–258.)

tain, by this time, that the tale is not that of a "fool's paradise on which all the world is off on a May-day."[3] Neither can we believe that in this book, "religion and philosophy disappear," that "science and poetry supply the background—art, exercise and an abundance of beautiful and innocent girls supply the foreground."[4]

There is one other significant writing which should be examined in this chapter. Perhaps more than any other of his distinctly literary productions it bears directly upon Morris's philosophy of life and of history. It is "the narrative in prose and verse" called *The House of the Wolfings,* in which is to be found some of the finest writing that Morris ever attempted. But its chief importance lies in its expression of all that William Morris ever felt regarding "the period of greatest historical change in the world"—the transition period when the Romans were fighting the barbarians, when Christianity was battling with Paganism, when the approaching death of ancient Classical civilization was heralding the approaching birth of European civilization.

This carefully written literary work, voluminous as it was, meant to Morris the depiction of a barbarism that was not barbarous: the depiction of a simple society, loosely joined together by social ties, each community more or less self-sufficing, and each having its own moot and its own council hall. To Morris it meant the superiority of a life lived close to nature, and the superiority of the Medieval Northern "barbarians" over the decadent, urbanized, cosmopolitan civilization of the South and East.

Morris was now concerned more with impressing his ideas upon his readers by a subconscious appeal in the sheer beauty and truthfulness of his picture than with dramatizing a narrative. He had already evolved a prodigious amount of rapidly moving and melodious poetry in *Jason, The Earthly Paradise,* and in *Sigurd,* but in most of it his thought and his feeling had

[3] Paul Elmer More, *The Shelbourne Essays, Seventh Series,* p. 117.
[4] Vallance, p. 347, paraphrasing the criticism of Mr. Frederic Myers.

been somewhat deadened by the rhythmic effect of that poetry upon the ear—by the very monotony of its melody. For his later *Sigurd* he had evolved an heroic, epical meter of his own, slower in tempo and more inspiring. But *Sigurd* had failed to make any great impression upon the public mind, and most of the contemporary critics had succeeded beautifully in misunderstanding its entire message. A decade later, during his early labours with the Socialist League, he had composed his prose rhapsody on the Medieval spirit of British proletarianism, *A Dream of John Ball*, originally published in *The Commonweal*; but it also had failed to produce any immediate or profound effect. Now, however, in *The House of the Wolfings*, he set out very carefully to improve both *métiers*—to produce a narrative in combined poetry and prose. In so doing he proved himself a master not only of technique but also of prosody. For he succeeded in weighting his prose sentences with a new emphasis that slowed the lightness of their movement to the point at which one could not only read them but also think about them; and in so accenting them as to produce a measured cadence that gave an effect of simple and natural blank verse without possessing the usual monotony of it. And in the poetry of *The Wolfings* he introduced some subtle changes of emphasis which tended to slow the reading and the effect of over-rapid movement, while at the same time retaining both the dramatic and the epical effects of his earlier poetry.

But beyond that, and surpassing it, this book shows the core of Morris's view of historic development—the most striking aspects of that "whole view" of a society which Morris himself had had for so many years. It portrays his own philosophy of the individual life not losing itself in the social network, but rather aiding that society and being aided in turn by it. It suggests, moreover, his political view of Decentralization, and the urgency of his demand for a return to nature and to the simplicity of nature in living the full and the good life.

Morris begins his story slowly, with artistry in every line:

The tale tells that in times long past there was a dwelling of men beside a great wood. Before it lay a plain, not very great, but which was, as it were, an isle in the sea of woodland.

He then builds a picture of the pristine natural beauty in the environment of this "isle," where:

On either side, to right and left the tree-girdle reached out toward the blue distance, thick, close and unsundered, save where it, and the plain which it begirdled, was cleft amidmost by a river about as wide as the Thames at Sheene. You must know that this great clearing in the woodland was not a matter of hap-hazard; though the river had driven a road whereby men might fare on each side of its hurrying stream. It was men who had made that isle in the woodland.

For many generations the folk that now dwelt there had learned the craft of iron-founding, so that they had no lack of wares. . . .

There, then, in the clearing of the wood that for many years grew greater yearly, they drave their beasts to pasture in the new-made meadows, where year by year the grass grew sweeter as the sun shone on it and the standing waters went from it; and now in the year whereof the tale telleth it was a fair and smiling plain. . . .

In such wise had that folk made an island in the midst of the Mirk-wood, and established a home there, and upheld it with manifold toil.

They were the men of the Mid-Mark, and up and down the Mirkwood-water lived their kinsmen, the men of the Upper-Mark and the Nether-Mark. Among these kindred of the Mark there were many Houses, or tribes, and the tale tells especially of one such House, the Wolfings of the Mid-Mark. It describes their way of life and something of how these people governed themselves, and of how their customs grew, in love, in marriage and in council.

If any one compares this opening with those in most of Morris's prose romances of his later years, he will note a great difference. In *The Wood Beyond the World* and *The Story of the Glittering Plain*, action, romance and adventure begin immediately; there is in them no careful building up of social atmosphere. They are largely composed of words of imagination, fire and beauty, and suggest no moral. But *The House of the Wolfings* suggests a social as well as a romantic purpose at the very start.

The argument of the tale is as follows: The Germanic tribes are threatened by the expansion of Roman power and fear the loss of their freedom. The sorceress of the Wolfing tribe describes the wealth of the Romans, their excessive riches, their military prowess, and the folk who "are sitting about them in dumb, down-trodden peace," slaves to Roman power. Thiodolf, war chief of the Gothic tribe known as the Wolfings, leads his warriors to battle against the Roman legions.

> Glistening of gold
> Did men's eyen behold;
> Shook the pale sword
> O'er the unspoken word;
> No man drew nigh us
> With weapon to try us;
> For the Welsh-wrought shield
> Lay low on the field.

But the Romans hold many cities and peoples in subjection, and so great are their "kindreds" that "each liveth in a garth full of mighty houses, with a wall of stone and lime around it . . . but as to each city being the habitation of one kindred, it is otherwise; for rather it may be said of them that they have forgotten kindred, and have none, nor do they heed whom they wed, and great is the confusion amongst them. And mighty men among them ordain where they shall dwell, and what shall be their meat, and how long they shall labour after they are weary, and in all wise what manner of life shall be amongst them; and though they be called free men who suffer this, yet may no house or Kindred gainsay this rule and order. In sooth, they are a people mighty, but unhappy."

The Folk-Mote of the Markmen is well described, and the goddess Hall-Sun prophesies a coming battle:

I see the hail of battle and the onslaught of the strong,
And they go adown to the folk-mote that shall bide there over long.

I see the slain-heaps rising and the alien folk prevail,
And the Goths give back before them on the ridge o'er the treeless vale.
I see the ancient fallen, and the young men smitten dead,
And yet I see the War-Duke shake Throng-plough o'er his head,
And stand unhelmed, unbyrnied before the alien host,
And the hurt men rise around him to win back battle lost;
And the wood yield up her warriors, and the whole host rushing on,
And the swaying line of battle, until the lost is won.
Then forth goes the cry of triumph, as they ring the captives round
And cheat the crow of her portion and heap the warriors' mound.

The Romans, unable to drive back the Goths in the ensuing battle, try trickery, and flanking them by detouring through forests and mountains, attempt to carry out a surprise attack from the rear by night; but Hall-Sun, foreseeing this move, sends out the women to guard the passes in the mountains. Then follow in rapid succession the battle on the ridge, the story of what befell Thiodolf, and of his second meeting with Wood-Sun, the mother of Hall-Sun.

Now and again, as the narrative progresses, there is recounted some tale, some happiness or dream, which bears upon the joy of work and of fellowship, of individualism saved even in union through the simple virtues of these naïve people, all working for one and one for all. But there is no attempt here to idealize utterly; rather the poet attempts to keep faith with human nature and with history, telling the good with the evil, and indulging in no milk and water dream of pacifism for a world in which pacifism is unknown. For sometimes, it appears, virtue may be found even in battle, as when he says:

> In the acre of battle the work is to win,
> Let us live by the labour, sheaf-smiting therein;
> And as oft as the sickle we sang in times past
> When the crake that long mocked us fled light at the last,
> So sing o'er the sward, and the sword-hardened hand
> Bearing down to the reaping the wrath of the land.

In *The Wolfings* as in *Sigurd* the great struggle and the

descent of Doom are to clear the way for a better time. They mark the death of the old world and the beginning of the new.

It shall soon pass over, and we shall fare afield,
And reap the wheat with the war-sword and winnow in the shield. . . .

Lo ye! whoever follows I fare to sow the seed
Of the days to be hereafter, and the deed that comes of deed.

Then they all shouted loudly and gladly; nor were they otherwise than exceeding glad; for now had they forgotten all other joys of life save the joy of fighting for the kindred and the days to be.

To Thiodolf, upon whom the Doom of the Gods has finally come, there is the same fate as that reserved for Sigurd. His triumph in the hour of death—his clinching of the ultimate victory—brings on, symbolically, the "new order." Thiodolf symbolizes the leadership of the new Germanic race that is, for a while, to purify again the putrefied air of the decadent ancient world, and help to bring to birth the new ideals of the race, and the new order that is to dominate Europe for the next thousand years.

But neither the members of the Socialist League nor the populace of England were willing to admit that there might be some importance in William Morris's historical and Utopian moralities.

## CHAPTER X

THE DYNAMITE PLOTS AND OTHER DASTARDLY ACTIVI-
TIES—MORRIS RETIRES IN DISGUST AND FOUNDS THE
HAMMERSMITH SOCIALIST SOCIETY

UNDOUBTEDLY," said Mr. Glasier, "the presence in the movement of a large number of foreign refugees, particularly from Russia, Poland and Spain, afforded Anarchism a stimulating soil for growth. These exiles, possessing no attachment to British traditions, and often failing to acquire any deep sense of civic responsibility, were naturally disposed to favour 'autonomist' and insurrectionary ideas." And it was this element within the League which, in the annual conference of 1889, finally won control of the Executive Council. It was decided that David Nicol, author of several workers' songs, including "The Workers' Marseillaise," should be editor of *The Commonweal.*

Morris was now definitely out of control. His offices, his periodical and his money were to be placed in the hands of the agitators of violence, several of whom had already expressed a preference for dynamite as an enforcer of their arguments. But Morris did not contest the issue. He resigned from the Executive Council and from the editorship of *The Commonweal,* which soon declined into a "flaming red" periodical; and these actions were to be followed shortly by his resignation from the League.

On November 15, 1890, his final contribution to *The Commonweal* appeared. It was a sort of farewell address, entitled "Where Are We Now?"

To some among us [he wrote] the past few years have seemed many and long, and crowded with disappointments. For what was it that we set out to accomplish? To change the system of society on which the stupendous fabric of civilization is founded, and which has been built up by centuries of conflict with older and dying systems. . . . It cannot be said that great or unexpected talent for administration has been developed amongst us, nor any vast amount of foresight. . . . We have between us made about as many mistakes as any other party in a similar space of time. When I first joined the movement, I hoped that some working-man leader, or perhaps leaders, would turn up, who would push aside all middle-class help and become great historical figures. I might still hope for that, if it seemed likely to happen. . . . But, to speak plainly, it does not seem so at present. . . . When we first began to work together there was little said about anything save the great ideals of Socialism, and so far off did we seem from the realization of these that we could hardly think of any means for their realization. . . . But our very success has dimmed the great ideals (and we have fallen into political methods and subterfuges).

These Morris classified as the method of palliation through the acceptance of half-measures, and of futile revolt against authority, which had been easily suppressed.

Just as Morris had opposed State Socialism, Land Nationalization, the Class Struggle, and the wilder theories and forms of Anarchism, Marxism and Anarchistic-Communism, so also he opposed the methods of those labour agitators who had advocated disturbances. Let Trade Unionists, disturbance-breeders, and "what not" go their own way also: as for "Complete Socialists"—"or let us call them Communists"—the only thing for them is to proselytize and make converts, publicizing only "the simple principles of Socialism, regardless of the policy of the passing hour,"—let them make the public at large know that Socialism is both possible and good. "Until we have that mass of opinion, action for a general change that will benefit the whole people is impossible!"

Morris's withdrawal brought upon his head a storm of abuse from those who remained behind. But the usurpers were doomed to disappointment. No rosy path lay ahead of their united zeal for violence and rabble-rousing. Branches dropped away, most of them joining other Socialist bodies—preferably the Fabians—and finances grew smaller and smaller. Success did not attend their efforts.

It has been claimed, sometimes, that these Anarchists were mild, docile men, for the most part: ideologists rather than real Anarchists. Yet the manner in which they threw caution to the winds, after Morris's withdrawal, hardly supports that view. One member wrote that "Even the ordinary criminal is an unconscious revolutionist, and is doing good work for us." Another specifically advocated the use of dynamite "to help abolish political corruption." As Mr. Vallance has pointed out, the League had grown far beyond Morris's control, and beyond the control of any other man.

So Morris withdrew—on principle. Without resistance, he permitted his former "comrades" to "appropriate" the resources of the Socialist League, including the plant, type and copyright of *The Commonweal*. They even appropriated the name of the periodical, although, beginning with the issue of December, 1890, it became a monthly magazine and bore the subtitle *A Journal of Revolutionary Socialism*. A little later, in February, 1891, a notice appeared stating that it had become the property of the newly constituted London Socialist League. In May, 1891, a new issue was printed *on red paper*, with the subtitle *A Revolutionary Journal of Anarchist-Communism*. On November 28, 1891, there appeared in *The Commonweal* a letter from J. Creaghe denouncing Morris and Edward Carpenter. Finally, in April, 1892, Charles W. Mowbray and David J. Nicol, the alleged "proprietor" and "publisher," respectively, were prosecuted by the Treasury and charged at Bow Street with inciting to murder and Anarchism, for having published, on April 9, 1892, an incendiary article.

It may be interesting to note a few ideas of the *Revolutionary Studies* [consisting largely of weird translations of *La Revolte* (*sic*)] which, under the old Socialist League Emblem designed by Walter Crane, were issued from the office of *The Commonweal*, 145, City Road, E. C., in 1892. Here are a few samples:

These revolutionary heroes who are not stopped in their revolt by a hundred thousand men have not one single revolutionary thought. They know nothing but previous revolutions. . . . They dreamed of the Commune, reproducing in miniature the State which they overthrew. . . . Had not Marat dreamed, before them, and Marx, the modern God of the Socialists, had he not also preached popular dictation!

.     .     .     .     .     .     .     .

Are we prepared to face the revolution which approaches? Shall we have the audacity of thought which our fathers lacked, to frankly decide the immense economic, politic, and moral problems in face of which history has placed us?

.     .     .     .     .     .     .     .

All dream of dictatorship: the dictatorship of the Proletariat, said Marx,—that is to say, of Tribunes, of Ourselves, say the majority of the Blanquists and Possibilists, which comes to the same thing.

All dream of revolution as the legal massacre of their enemies. . . .
All dream of acquiring new power in an omnipotent, omniscient State. . . .

All dream of representative government as "crowning of edifice" which is to succeed the revolution after a period of dictatorship.

All preach obedience to the laws made by dictators.

All have but one dream, that of Robespierre: to massacre whosoever dare to think otherwise. . . .

This is the dream of 99 per cent of those who usurp the name of revolutionists. The Jacobin tradition stifles them. . . .

To massacre the bourgeoisie is always easier said than done. . . . Thus it is seen that Jacobinism reduces itself to absurdity. . . .

Thanks to the fables set up by the Jacobins, the people have learned nothing of their own history.

The abolition of the State is, we say, the task imposed upon the revolutionist. . . .

The revolutionist will have to employ a boldness of thought, an energy of action, an eagerness for work of which people have given no proof in previous revolutions. . . .

To remit this cause to others would be to betray the cause of the Revolution.

It was these and similar writings which brought about the seizure of *The Commonweal* plant and the arrest of several of the ring-leaders in "The Anarchist Conspiracy." It was said that police agents and *agents provocateurs* played their accustomed parts in the arrests.

According to Mr. Glasier, Morris, before leaving the Socialist League, had discharged the debts of the paper and of the organization, and continued to meet their deficits for several months thereafter. On the occasion of Mowbray's arrest, it so happened that his wife died and he applied for a release in order to attend her funeral. His plea having been refused with typical bourgeois indignation, Morris went to the court in person and gave surety to the extent of 500 pounds.

David Nicol, the editor of *The Commonweal*, was imprisoned. Mowbray later became a tool of the police; while Charles, Deakin and two other members received "long terms of penal servitude" as the result of the contemporaneous Walsall Anarchist Plot, instigated by Coulon, a spy in the service of the French government!

Thus did the old Socialist League membership slowly vanish and leave no trace! Several of the members found it convenient to change their names—and at least two of them are now wealthy, respected citizens, entirely unconcerned with revolutionary agitation. They who were wise decided, so they said, to "play cricket."[1]

For Morris, the Hammersmith Branch of the Socialist League, of which he was the head, had long been a center for his kind of Socialism. And at the close of 1890 he turned it into a still newer kind of Socialist organization, known as the Hammersmith Socialist Society. Here his old friends and many of their converts met regularly.

---

[1]Glasier, pp. 129–130; Vallance, 336–357; Letters from an anonymous correspondent who knew the members personally.

# VI

## THE HAMMERSMITH SOCIALIST SOCIETY—AND VICTORY IN SIGHT

*—Is the house finished? Nay, come help to build*
*Walls that the sun of sorrow once did gild*
*Through many a bitter morn and hopeless eve,*
*That so at last in bliss ye may believe;*
*Then rest with me, and turn no more to tears,*
*For then no more by days and months and years,*
*By hours of pain come back, and joy passed o'er*
*We measure time that was—and is no more.*

## CHAPTER I

### NEW FRIENDS AND OLD RALLY IN THE NEW PRACTICAL SOCIALISM

T HE breaking up of the Socialist League left Morris more melancholy than had the earlier rupture with the Social Democratic Federation. The most discouraging thing about Socialists, to his mind, was their ever increasing desire for action in the present. "All Socialist organizations seem to be affected with ambition to 'do something,' " he wrote. "The main cause of failure (which was obvious about two years ago) is that you cannot keep a body together without giving it something to do in the present; and now, since people will willingly listen to Socialist doctrines, our rank and file have nothing to do."[1]

But Morris distrusted the activists. He planned, therefore, that in the Hammersmith Socialist Society there should be evinced intellectual leadership, and that the new body should be controlled by men capable of discussing Socialism and of propagating Socialist doctrines without undertaking either political adventures or militant measures. In other words the Hammersmith Society was to be an Academy, or a Lyceum, of thinkers. In that respect it would resemble, in some measure, the newly organized Fabian Society. But unlike the Fabian group it was not to be an organization devoted to political and economic *permeation:* it would depend for its appeal upon humanity, nature, art, history and philosophy, hoping that when a true knowledge of these fundamental factors in the making

[1]May Morris, II, 324. Quoted from a letter by Morris shortly after the Socialist League split of November 21, 1890.

of civilization and culture became thoroughly known and appreciated, society would then be in a position to enforce its demands by the strength of its own will.

The Hammersmith Socialist Society was officially founded as an independent organization on November 23, 1890. Yet it had, in effect, been functioning as an organization promoting Morris's own views and doctrines for at least four years, and the Sunday meetings which had been held there—as well as occasional week-day meetings—were different, to say the least, from those of the Socialist League headquarters.

Kelmscott House, the Morris city home on the Upper Mall, Hammersmith, was the site of the invention of the telegraph in England. Sir Francis Rolands, the inventor, had run his first wires around the garden, from the house to the stables and coach house, which had been built into one large workshop. Here he had experimented during the period from 1838, when Wheatstone's bridge was perfected, until 1843. It was this workshop, first used by Morris in 1878 for carpet-weaving, that was now converted into the meeting hall of the Hammersmith Socialist Society.

It was a long hall with a raised dais at the far end, where a table and chairs for the speakers and the chairmen of the meetings were placed. The hall itself was filled with rush-bottomed chairs for the audiences, and with several long wooden benches. Near the entrance there was a bookstall, and here Mr. Cosmo Rowe, the literature secretary, held forth until Morris's death in 1896, selling all varieties of English Socialist literature.

The plain, whitewashed walls of the hall were covered with rush matting and were decorated with one or two prints of early Socialist leaders and pioneers, such as Sir Thomas More. Opposite them hung a couple of Walter Crane's famous Socialist cartoons. Outside the entrance door there was a large sign, painted by Mr. Rowe, bearing the insignia of the Hammersmith Socialist Society—a figure of Labour and one of Justice, with the scales of justice between them—and the name of the Society. Behind the deal table, from which the speakers addressed the audiences, there was a banner of the Society on the wall, and on the platform were a piano and some copies of Roman mosaics.[2]

To the hall of the Hammersmith Socialist Society at Kelmscott House came many well-known visitors and speakers from Europe and the United States, to lecture upon, or to learn about, the New Socialism. Here many Americans heard their first Socialist addresses: scholars, artists, politicians, and the president of Harvard University, among others. During the period from 1890 until 1896 some of the more famous speakers included George Bernard Shaw, Prince Peter Kropotkin, Sergius Stepniak, Lawrence Gronlund, Sidney and Beatrice Webb, Mrs. Annie Besant, Graham Wallas, John Carruthers, J. A. Hobson, Philip Webb, Henry Mayers Hyndman, Herbert Burrows, John Burns, T. J. Cobden-Sanderson, Pete Curran, R. B. Cunninghame-Graham and Ramsay MacDonald, besides Morris himself. The lectures and discussions centered largely upon art, economics, and Socialism: and the more frequent lectures, as well as the most popular, were those of William Morris and George Bernard Shaw.[3]

[2]From Cosmo Rowe's description; letters to the author, May–June, 1936. *Cf.* Glasier, p. 117.

[3]Glasier, and letters to the author by May Morris, Cosmo Rowe and Arthur Mackmurdo, 1935, 1936, 1937.

## CHAPTER II

## MORRIS'S LATEST PRINCIPLES OF DISCONTENT

IT is very probable that Morris's lack of hope of effecting any notable degree of unity within the ranks of British Socialists turned him more strongly than ever from the violent sort of agitation in which he hitherto had sometimes indulged. He spent more spare time in literary occupations than he had done in many years, interesting himself more than ever in the production of fine works of art and in the making of beautiful books. And his attitude toward Socialism itself now became more philosophic and resigned than heretofore. Having lived in Pluto's cave, he could at last adjust his vision to the upper spheres of human thought and activity. Indeed, there is good reason to believe that Morris, now entering upon a new stage of Socialist activity, had come to the conclusion that perhaps the wisest course was to adopt a Socratic method when dealing with Socratic audiences, and produce something akin to Platonic dialogue when propagating those elements of Socialism which he had referred to in his *Statement of Principles of the Hammersmith Socialist Society*. It is all the more noteworthy, then, that in his first propagandist publication for the new body he adopted the form of a dialogue which resembles in all respects the work of a modern Plato; and afterward he kept it up, at least for a while. This first dialogue was entitled *The Reward of Labour: A Dialogue by William Morris, Author of "The Earthly Paradise,"* Being No. 1 of the Hammersmith Socialist Society.

The personæ of the dialogue are an Earnest Enquirer, an East End weaver, and a West End landowner who is also an M. P. The latter has just emerged from a philanthropical meeting and is accosted by the Earnest Enquirer about the speaker,

who spoke so "elegantly" on the "compensation which the
working classes have for their apparently inferior position; and
how necessary it was for the progress of civilization that there
should be this division of labour and life; and what a noble
position it was for the workers to hold; and how the slight
sacrifices they had to make they ought to make cheerfully and
as a matter of religion, that new religion of Humanity, con-
sidering their position as the foundation of all the culture,
thought, light and leading which is the glory of Humanity."[1]
He then asks the weaver what he thinks about the speech.

To this the weaver replies that what he thinks about it might
just as well not be stated—"don't waste your time by asking me
what I think of a vote-of-thanks speech." So they continue to
discuss the matter, asking many pertinent questions and answering in their respective fashions of thought. The landowner and
M. P. admits that he takes "a good deal out of the stock of
the wealth of the world," but claims that in return he is "much
respected, looked up to—liked even." He adds: "I am respected
because of my property, my position," and the argument leads
him further to state that "there must be rich and poor or there
would be no society. . . . I know it always will be so, that's
all."

Meanwhile, a small crowd has gathered, and others, mistak-
ing the scene for an "open air meeting of Socialists," hover near.
A policeman then bustles through the crowd, grabs the harm-
less and unoffending weaver, "gives him a rough shake, and
says, 'Come, *You* get out of this.' Exit weaver, hurriedly, glad
to get off so lightly. The policeman turns to the Landowner,
who is very nicely dressed, touches his helmet, and says, 'Shall
I get you a cab, Sir?' "

The Earnest Enquirer wanders slowly away on foot, asking
himself why society exists when it is merely an organized injustice.

After Morris and his friends had decided to transfer their

[1]Morris, *The Reward of Labour*, p. 2.

allegiance from the Socialist League to the Hammersmith Socialist Society, they were bitterly attacked by certain League members. One member, at least, even ventured the opinion that Morris's final financial report had been "insufficient or unsatisfactory," to which Morris had retorted: "Well, Mr. Chairman, I can't see that it matters a damn; for I receive ten pounds in one hand, and with the other I pay out fifty pounds."[2]

But in order to clear the atmosphere, after the final parting, the membership decided to send to the League a letter of explanation. This was accordingly done. Afterward they drew up a *Statement of Principles* for the new Hammersmith Socialist Society. It was subsequently published in an eight-page pamphlet with a headblock designed by Walter Crane.

In the *Statement of Principles* certain rules and conditions of membership were defined. No chances were to be taken with candidates for membership: each new member's name had to be proposed in advance, discussed, and voted upon at the following weekly meeting at Kelmscott House—and the minimum membership fee was set at one shilling per year. All money received was to be used specifically for the advancement of Socialist propaganda, which would consist of occasional pamphlet literature, reprints of special lectures from time to time, and the publication of a monthly, four-page leaflet which was to be known as *The Hammersmith Socialist Record*. Mr. Samuel Bullock was to edit *The Record* and to act also as Lecture Secretary for the Society.[3]

The *Statement of Principles* constitutes a Manifesto of Morris's measures for the attainment of the socialized society of the

[2]May Morris, II, 323–24.

[3]*The Hammersmith Socialist Record* continued to be published until Morris's illness in 1895 began to cause the gradual breakdown of the organization. It was discontinued in August, 1895. Mr. Bullock, the editor, married Bruce Glasier's sister, and the frequent notations A. B. and S. B., in the publication, testify to their activities in editing and writing the monthly. Glasier himself and Morris made most of the literary contributions to the periodical and to the publications of the Society. *The Record* had no cuts, only a small map of the Hammersmith section, with directions for reaching the hall, and also Hammersmith Bridge, where open-air meetings were conducted every Sunday. Glasier, Rowe, *Record,* etc.

future. Aside from certain stock phrases that were common to most Socialists of the time (in an endeavour to appeal to the working classes) there is little, if anything, in this manifesto which differs from those principles which Morris had been expounding for fifteen years. It states essentially the same beliefs that were expressed in his early lectures on art and industry, in his S. D. F. lectures, in his Socialist writings for *Justice*, *To-day*, and *The Commonweal*, in his innumerable lectures for the Federation and for the Socialist League, and in his private correspondence.

Socialism to him still meant, as it first meant, the realization of a society of fellowship, of mutual aid and co-operation; one in which equality of condition would be guaranteed to all persons by the community will, by the social conscience, and hence by the framework and laws upon which the true society of that distant future should rest. In order to attain to this desirable state of affairs it must first be necessary to prepare the minds of all honest men for an honest realization of things as they *might be;* hence their minds must be educated away from the mere idle acceptance of belief in things as they *are;* they must learn that conditions of life are not governed by fixed and immutable laws under which only the fit can survive happily. With things as they are, however, even the fit—the rulers and controllers of society—cannot lead full and happy lives, and hence they, too, must be prepared to yield concessions.

Again it is clear that Morris, carrying through his ideas of historic evolution, believes that privilegism (or oligarchy) on which most societies have sooner or later come to be based, and on which they have sooner or later fallen, must be done away with. He sees the capitalists of the world as men who have usurped the privileges of the controlling classes of the past by virtue of economic ownership of the means of production, instead of by religious or military pressure and by social customs regarding birth and status, as in past times. He sees them as the hierarchy of the modern age, living upon economic privilege, protected by wealth and by State Power, and forming a class of "masters."

He believes that no such organization of society can be either stable or permanent: "it holds within itself the elements of its own dissolution" as did every society of the past that was dominated by a hierarchy founded upon fraud. Hence the whole evolution of society, he declares, and all the "signs of the times" indicate that this "fraudulent" society of "economic mastery" is also doomed to fail and be replaced by a new kind of society which, he hopes, will be a true society controlled by the creators and the producers of social wealth. For whosoever in the past has been denied his just heritage has been thrust out of society and therefore, at present, "owes no allegiance to it."

But granting that the needs of all men are to some extent similar, so also are their obligations and their duties. All men, in order to participate in the satisfaction of their needs, must be prepared, through education and training, to assume their roles in the organization and in the administration of the new society. It is not enough that they merely demand new rights and privileges, as do the Anarchists and the Marxists, for such concessions will prove, at best, but temporary abatements of their misery. Hence it is not the "dissolution of society" for which we should strive, but the *regeneration of society*."

In the meantime, he adds, it may be of some advantage to "sap the strongholds of privilege" and to attempt "various crude experimentations in the direction of State Socialism," but there is also the danger that the men who achieve these concessions will prove to be only men who "use the advocacy of them as a political expedient for strengthening their position,"—a slap at Labour leaders.

Moreover, he believes that no good can emanate from "spasmodic and desperate acts of violence" or from those who advocate them, "for their only tendency will result in forcing the timid people to support the old régime,"—a blow at Marxists and Anarchists. He thinks that passive resistance would be far better than violence which cannot be followed by intelligent action based upon a public opinion that is prepared to organize and administer capably its new régime.

In order to create an educated opinion it is necessary, in the meantime, that labour should organize and educate itself for the time when action looking toward "complete control" of the means of production will be possible of achievement. Yet even such control, he adds, will be only "the first step in the realization of Socialism."

This action, however, is not the action of political attrition or of military attrition, he continues; it is an action which, in accordance with the slow and historic evolution of the past, must have a slow and historic evolution in the future. Meanwhile, men must first be educated in the simple elementals of Socialism before any such "general combination" can become effective and achieve its ends.[4]

In view of the several varieties of Socialism that were coming to the front in England, and in view of Morris's own experiences with Socialists and others who did not see eye to eye with him or with some other types of reformers, one can easily accept the statement of Mr. Glasier that "Morris never had much hope of, or belief in, what was termed 'Socialist Unity.' " Nevertheless, he was to continue to work and to agitate for unity and for combination. It was this attitude which led him to attempt again a rapprochement with the members of the S. D. F., occasionally lecturing for their audiences and inviting members of the S. D. F., especially Hyndman and Quelch, to lecture at the hall of the Hammersmith Socialist Society. This attitude of conciliation on his part also accounts for the frequency with which Fabians, Anarchists and other types of social reformers were invited to lecture at Hammersmith. If Socialist and Labour leaders in England failed to agree among themselves, if, sometimes, jealousy and animosity prevailed, as it did later —for example, between Keir Hardie, who edited *The Labour Leader*, and Robert Blatchford, who edited *The Clarion*,—such disagreements were certainly no fault of Morris's. To the end he continued to work for mutual forbearance, understanding, and co-operation.

[4] *A Statement of Principles of the Hammersmith Socialist Society*, pp. 3–8.

## CHAPTER III

MORRIS AND BAX REWRITE HISTORY: THEY MAKE A
GLORIOUS BOOK, WHICH IS, UNFORTUNATELY, NOW
OUT OF PRINT

EDWARD BELLAMY'S *Looking Backward* had had a pronounced effect in turning Morris away from all doctrines envisaging a higher degree of State Centralization. Instinctively he hated those forces which tended toward the mechanization of either human or material "units" in society. His philosophy of history forced him to believe in a free art and a traditional art which would shape all the works of men—not only in art itself, but in ethics, literature, politics, and economics as well. Hence, he never lost sight of the human factor in dealing with the social organism. Therefore, he became an advocate of *Decentralization,* and of *Equality* of human conditions. In his vision of the society of the future he fell back once more upon those visions of the Icelandic Federation and of the Hellenic Federations of past times, as well as of the village communes of medieval society in Western Europe at a time when men were not haunted too frequently by sordid economic fear. He became, in a very real sense, the forerunner of the Distributist school of thought of post-war times. There was a large element of truth and of insight in Gilbert K. Chesterton's words when he said: "Modern England will never exhaust her debt to William Morris. He was a very great Distributist. There seems to be a curious idea prevalent that he was a Socialist. Indeed, it was so prevalent that he was partly deceived by it himself."[1]

[1] G. K. Chesterton. *William Morris: An Appreciation.* Walthamstow, The Library, 1934.

While still members of the Socialist League, Morris and Belfort Bax had composed a series of articles on *Socialism from
the Root Up*. In a diary kept by Morris during the first three
months of 1887 there is entered, February 23, the following
passage: "Yesterday all day long with Bax trying to get our
second article on Marx together: a very difficult job; I hope it
may be worth the trouble." These *Commonweal* articles were
used later to form the gist of a book by Morris and Bax, entitled *Socialism: Its Growth and Outcome*. The chapter on
Karl Marx and his theory is the nineteenth of the twenty-one
chapters, and the footnote at the end indicates that the original
of this article must have been written shortly prior to the publication in 1885 of the third volume of Karl Marx's *Das Kapital*.
This article, with others, was rewritten in 1887–88, and finally,
in 1893, a complete book was issued on the subject of Socialism.
Internal evidence shows that the historical sections—particularly
the first twelve chapters, the twenty-first, and part of the closing chapters—must have been written by Morris, for they are
in his language and in accordance with his thought. The volume
is important, therefore, in showing what Morris thought of
human history in 1893, at the height of his association with the
Hammersmith Socialist Society.

The first task essayed in *Socialism: Its Growth and Outcome*
is a complete slaughter of evangelicalism, after which the subject changes to "the crowning sham of modern politics under
its absurd title of Representative Government . . . a mere
term used to cloak an oligarchy." Under such conditions, he
asks, how can "Art, the expression of the life of society" be
more than a sham also?

In the chapter on "Ancient Society," a new interpretation of
history is justified on lines similar to those laid down by Morris
in his essay on *The History of Pattern Designing*. Prevailing
notions of historic progress, says Morris, have been elaborated
for an ignorant society by middle-class historians. Liberalism,
the accepted state form of nineteenth-century civilization and
progress, tends to make the state a capitalistic factotum—as

Carlyle implied—controlling individual activity in much the same fashion that it might control mechanized units.

Unlike the historians of the liberal tradition, Morris did not view the decline and fall of the Athenian and Roman "democracy" and "republic" as calamities to progress. Morris believed that the oligarchies which became masters of the ancient social states "were self-destructive"—therefore giving way to the absolutist power that was the core of them. Hence their place was taken in the Greek world by Tyrannies and in the Roman by Cæsarism (the Principate).

Ancient civilization used to be considered as the direct parent of modern society, with nothing between them but a chaos of merely negative lapse of time. . . . But it is now recognized that this supposed chaos had an order of its own, and was an integral and necessary part of the evolution of modern life.

Thus, he says, the "classical system of production" was founded on chattel-slavery, the medieval on serfdom, and it was the change from the one labour system to the other which was the special characteristic of the transition (from Classical to Medieval civilization).

As for medieval civilization, he adds, "the great epical and mythological poems of the Teutonic race have been kept alive solely by those tribes which never crossed Roman civilization."

Besides Morris's low opinion of Roman and Classical civilization, supported by scores of arguments, one finds here a strong aversion to all Eastern influences, as expressed in art, in religion, and in social customs, and his preference for Western, or European, culture. For he thought that these Western Lands required an art and a mode of life that grew from their own traditions and that was not borrowed from the eclectic arts of other lands and other peoples.

His love for medieval civilization is shown by his references to the "true" literature of those peoples who "had not made the mistake of crossing Roman civilization," and by his preference for "progressive barbarism" in contrast with "decaying Roman civilization."

Medieval towns, he believes, had two origins: first, the survivals of Roman times, found mostly in the South, and secondly, the new towns which grew up for reasons of convenience out of the Germanic Mark, and which were largely incorporated into the feudal manorial system. The merchant guild, he has discovered in advance of his time (among English historians), was not derived from the old Frith Guild. "Nor was it identical with the Corporations of the Towns, since non-residents could be members of it; whereas the members of the Corporation (*Les Lineages, Geschlechte, Porterey, Ehrbarkeit, Patricians, etc.,*) were bound to be holders of the lands which were once tribal."

Carrying on the idea of association, Morris points out that one must note the relations between corporations and the kings and their nobles. For as feudalism became paramount, the tribal Mark lost its independent position and came under the domination of a feudal baron or lord of the manor. Under such conditions, it was to the interest of the kings or monarchs, as the case might be, to favor centralization of power. Thus, nationalism was favored.

Morris disagrees with the interpretations of medieval life as reflected in the pages of those whom he terms the "bourgeois historians."

The shortcomings of the life of the Middle Ages [he concludes] resolves itself in the main, firstly, to the rudeness of life and the absence of material comforts: secondly, to the element of oppression and violence in which men lived; and thirdly, to the ignorance and superstition which veiled so much of the truth from their minds.

Yet he explains these by pointing out that as for rudeness, "men do not suffer from the lack of comforts which they have never had." As for ignorance and superstition, this was rather a naïveté in their conception of the universe and not a matter of brutal choice. As for misery and violence, it was often because of their appearance under dramatic conditions, wars and plagues, that they have seemed to overshadow everyday life. The misery of our own times, on the other hand, "is not spasmodic and accidental, but *chronic* and essential to the system under which we live. . . . In medieval times the violence and suffering did not spare one class and fall entirely upon another. . . . The unsuccessful politician did not retire to the ease and pleasure of a country house, flavoured with a little literary labour and apologetics for his past mistakes, but paid with his head. . . ." In any event, he concludes, the misery, whatever it came from, was "totally unlike the misery of modern Whitechapel, from which not even the faintest scintilla of art can be struck, in spite of the idealizing of slum life by modern philanthropic sentimentalists and the impressionist novels and painters."

Morris marked the beginning of the gradual decline of the Middle Ages at about the year 1350, "when craft guilds had received all the development possible to them as societies of freemen and equals." Then came labour troubles and proletarian revolts over much of Europe, on the heels of the Black Death. He hailed John Ball's movement as the first proletarian expression of hope in England and of opposition to the traitors who ran the government behind the king's back for their own profit. And meanwhile, the development of commerce created two classes of capitalists and free workmen.

During the next two centuries the modern age arrived swiftly. New "casuistical forms of Christianity" sprang up to justify the profit system and usury; they were essentially allies of the rising bureaucratic system. Meanwhile, national monarchies evolved swiftly, the old feudal nobility was crushed and a new nobility created to be dependent on the king, serving him as mere courtiers and functionaries. By the middle of the sixteenth century, after the failure of the last native English proletarian revolt of Kett in Norfolk, the animating spirit of the Middle Ages and of feudal society was dead, though its names and forms were retained.

He points out that with these momentous changes in the fun-

damental history of England came the stultifying effects of
the Renaissance with its disastrous influences, foreign and eclectic, upon art, society, politics, religion, and ethics. He saw the
Elizabethan age as one in which English gentlemen, adventurers and common labourers turned to filibustering, converting
a people once "jovial, indolent and generous" into a nation of
"sordid traders and restless money-getters." He follows these
changes through the seventeenth and eighteenth centuries, with
their revolutions in agriculture, industry, and intellect. The
whole history of England was "melting away into money-
privilege; and all was getting ready for the completest and
securest system of the plunder of labour that the world has yet
seen." He denounced bitterly the patronized art of the period,
the *laissez faire* ideas of Adam Smith and the Manchester
School of Whig economists, so-called, and the very idea of the
division of labour. It didn't even make a man into a machine,
he said, but into only part of a machine.

From the post-Napoleonic wars and depressions of the nineteenth century, Morris traces the growth of proletarian sentiment, especially in the Plug Riots of Chartist days.

Yet "in spite of all the suffering caused by the Industrial
Revolution, it was impossible for the capitalists to engross the
whole of the profits. . . . The class struggle took another
form, besides that of mere hunger riots and forcible repression,
the Trade Unions to wit. . . ."

Meanwhile, with the changes occasioned by the abolition of
the corn laws and the consequent cheapening of food, and at
the same time the opening of great gold fields in California and
Australia, and the prodigious increase in the world's riches,
there came an elusive picture of general prosperity which occasioned those typically bourgeois and ignorant views of a coming
and ever continuous wave of progress—and, in an optimistic
moment of triumph, the extension of the hand downward to all
"the thrifty and industrious" among the workers, so that they,
too, might "rise above" their class.

But then came waves of depressions—there was not enough

wealth to go around. "The capitalist mind" even grew to consider this also as a "sign of stability" of the present system.

But within the last few years this latest eternal bourgeois providence has failed us. In spite of the last partial revival of trade, depression dogs us with closer persistence. The nations who we assumed would never do anything but provide us with raw materials, have become our rivals in manufacture, and our competitors in the world-market. . . .

He then goes on to say that for some time "a new commercial revolution" has been on the way. And this means, he adds, that the days of the small merchant and of the small business man are numbered; it also means an increasingly rapid rate of speed in the mechanization of industry. Then will come the rise of gigantic business enterprises which will cause periodic starvation, imperialism and world war!

"The fact is that the commerce of the great industries has entered insensibly into its second stage, and sheer cut-throat competition between the different nations has taken the place of the benevolent despotism of the only nation which was thoroughly prepared to take advantage of the first stages of Industrial Revolution—Great Britain, to wit.

"This second stage is assuredly preparing for the final one, which will end with the death of the whole bourgeois system. Meanwhile, what was the real social product of the Industrial Revolution? We answer, the final triumph of the middle classes, materially, intellectually, and morally. . . . The English Industrial Revolution may be said to have created a new commercial middle class hitherto unknown to the world. This class on the one hand consolidated all the groups of the middle class of the preceding epoch, such as the country squires, large and small, big farmers, merchants, manufacturers, shopkeepers and professional men, and made them so conscious of their solidarity, that the ordinary refined, thinking man of today cannot really see any other class at all. . . . On the other hand, the bourgeoisie has attained such complete domination that the upper classes are merely adjuncts to it and servants of it. In fact, these also are now of the bourgeoisie, as they are all engaged in commerce in one way or other. . . . Moreover, striving ever to extend itself downward as well as upward, the middle class has absorbed so much . . . that it now has nothing left below it except the mere propertiless proletariat. These last are wholly dependent upon it, utterly powerless before it, until the break up of the system that has created it (the signs of whose coming we have just noted) shall force them into a revolt against it. In the course of that revolt this great middle class in its turn will be absorbed into the proletariat, which will form a new society in which classes shall have ceased to exist. This is the Next Revolution, as inevitable, as inexorable, as the rising of tomorrow's sun."

This is Morris's most complete story of what lay behind the more sordid developments of modern times. How right he was has already been proved to some extent by history. Whether he was to be proved entirely right—whether he was the seer that he has been credited with being by various admirers—remains for the future to tell.

## CHAPTER IV

KELMSCOTT PRESS AND MORRIS'S LATER LITERATURE

OF CONTENT

IT is quite understandable that Morris's lack of hope of effecting any notable degree of unity within the ranks of British Socialists now began to turn him more strongly than ever from the violent sort of agitation in which he had hitherto sometimes indulged. He spent more spare time now in literary occupations than he had done for many years—if we may distinguish his pure literature from his socialist literature—and he spent more and more time at his Kelmscott Press, where one by one the finest books then being manufactured in England were being issued. He had, in his spare time, invented a number of new type fonts: *Roman, Chaucer,* and *Golden;* and of these *Golden* was his favourite because it most closely approximated the Gothic. The usual criticism levelled at Morris's Golden Type books is that they are difficult to read. Actually, like modern German or Gothic script, the Golden type can be read very quickly once one has become accustomed to it. This Morris himself knew. "How in hell can any one tell, as some of my critics tell the world, that these books are not readable because the print is not clear?" said Morris to one of his foremen. "The trouble is they merely look at a page here and there, and then, because they aren't used to it, the poor, weak young saplings say it doesn't grow from the common stem. Damn the common stem, and all other Classical remains. Gothic was good enough for our ancestors, and to any one who will take the time to spend more than a minute or two upon it, it should be good enough for any of us."[1]

During the 'nineties Morris produced that series of prose romances and translations of medieval romances and sagas

Sunday gossip at The Grange. By Edward Burne-Jones

which had begun to take shape with *The House of the Wolfings*, published in 1889, and which distinguished his later career in the literary world. Some of these were published in Kelmscott Press editions. Mr. S. C. Cockerell (at present Sir Sydney Cockerell, curator of the Fitzwilliam Museum in Cambridge and a trustee of the Morris estate) became the skilled secretary and manager of the Kelmscott Press, and was largely responsible for its smooth operation while Morris indulged his Hammersmith Socialist proclivities.

[1]An anecdote from an anonymous correspondent who worked with Morris for thirteen years.

Despite ill health, which hampered Morris's spirits in the 'nineties but not his multifarious activities, his interest in literature, art and Socialism never wavered. But he was turning to books and fine manuscripts with renewed zeal. The Merton Abbey works were thriving under the management of F. and R. Smith, who succeeded Mr. George Wardle upon the latter's retirement, and three Kelmscott presses were running full blast. In 1895 Morris undertook a complete translation of the *Heimskringla* Saga, begun twenty-three years before in collaboration with Professor Magnússon. His completed translation of the *Beowulf* had just appeared in January of that year, and three new Kelmscott books were issued during the year. On October 30, he addressed the Oxford Socialist Union; and in November he delivered a funeral oration in the rain outside Waterloo Station for Sergius Stepniak, who had been killed while trying to outrun a train—a characteristic effort, according to some of his friends.

These efforts made Morris ill, and his doctor advised him to take "a *long* rest," but without much success. Rest was one of those things for which Morris had very little use.

## CHAPTER V

A NEW SPIRIT IN THE LABOR MOVEMENT:
ROBERT BLATCHFORD AND THE CLARION CALL

FORGETFULNESS of past animosities seemed to prevail among most members of "honest Socialist organizations" in the early 'nineties. Morris, says Bernard Shaw, was universally respected and looked upon by many besides Glasier as a heresiarch of the coming reign of Socialist virtue. Once more he was invited to contribute to *Justice;* on May Day, 1892, he published in it a poem of ten stanzas, "Once Again Cometh Spring to Deliver," and for May Day, 1894, another of nine. Hyndman wrote that he was again "lecturing before our branches and contributing to our funds." But most of his reform activities centered in the hall of the Hammersmith Socialist Society.

"Of late years," according to *The Pall Mall Gazette,* "Sunday evenings at Kelmscott Hall have been nearly equally divided between Socialistic and Artistic, historic and literary subjects." The favourite speaker, according to that periodical, was Morris himself. On evenings when he spoke the people were "packed into the hall . . . its entertainments were patches of bright colour in the great, drab, dreary, dull, dirty Hammersmith."

Yet people, for the most part, did not seem to understand Morris. They could not see how historical, literary and artistic things could be connected with practical politics of the moment and with necessary social reform. Perhaps they were unwilling to. To most people traditions have little to do with the all-important present—but that very condition, said Morris, "is a symptom of the decay of England." He wrote to Mr. Rowe that "now-a-days, every belief, virtue and tradition is sacrificed to profit and to money-bags." Mr. Rowe himself wrote, some forty years later, of how he and his friends came under the influence of Morris and the Hammersmith Socialist Society:

When I lived in Euston Road I had a College of Science student lodging with me and I decided to hold my place open to young men from the Science and Art Schools on Sunday nights. H. G. Wells lived near and so he came in as often as he pleased. We took in *The Commonweal* during the latter 'eighties and had read a lot about Morris. So we decided to go to Kelmscott House and see what his Socialism was like. Wells regarded Morris as a man who wanted to get back to the reign of Queen Anne! So, for a while, Wells and I joined the Fabian Society as we did not think that Morris was advocating Practical Socialism. . . .

Later I went to live in Hammersmith and being near Morris decided to join his Society. I had often heard that artists were not business men, so I decided to show that it did not apply in my case any more than in his. I bought everything that was saleable on the subject of Socialism and was appointed Literature Secretary. This brought me into personal touch with Morris, as I had to see about pamphlets being published, and thus had talks with him in his study from time to time. . . .

In time I found that I could hold a crowd, and Halliday Sparling (the husband of May Morris) and myself often conducted meetings between us, doing 20 minutes each, two or three times in one night in the open. It was announced that I would give a talk on "What We Want and How We Might Get It." Morris said he would come to hear this one evening and invited me to supper along with three or four others. After supper we all sat around the fire and he told us about the vile state of things in the Middle Ages. . . .

We had business meetings at Kelmscott, that is, in the long hall attached, every Friday Night. Morris mostly presided and he sat at a deal table with a big jar of Latakia from which he filled his big pipe —it surely held half an ounce at a time. He would always invite others to fill, but most of them never did. (Presumably they were a bashful lot.)

Now and then we had theatrical performances (perhaps not more than four) as well as a choir and concerts. I sang duets with Miss

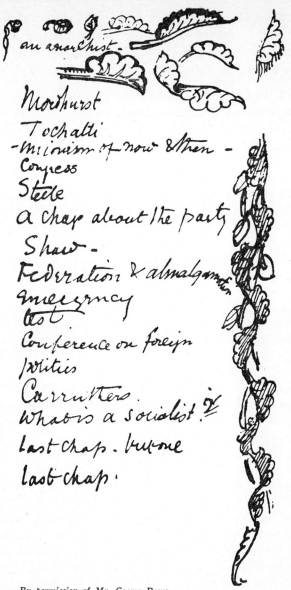

Facsimile notes of Morris's last lecture, January 5, 1896

Harrison. Our choir was conducted and trained by Gustave Holst, who afterward married Miss Harrison. Years later I visited them at Baron's Court. She was very Greek in type—perfect face and figure. (Mr. Bullock says "No, just doll-like!")

Emory Walker, local secretary of the society, and Sydney Cockerell had an office in Clifford's Inn. They were always at Kelmscott. Sir Emory lived close by and had a photo-process works near the Kelmscott Press. Like them, Morris might have been knighted, but he would not accept it on account of his unorthodox views. . . .

The table at which Morris sat in Kelmscott Hall had many drawings on it—of ornament. Morris, like most of his set, was not really a master of figure work. Their figures usually looked ill, washed out. . . .

I usually went with Bullock to Kelmscott House, but on the whole saw very little of Anarchists. The more level-headed men, like Bullock and Morris, used to keep most of them out of their way—"defended himself against them," said Bullock. Tochatti, who had belonged to the League, was most in evidence; I knew him well, but he was never the sort to get himself in trouble with the police. The other Anarchists, two or three only, like Kropotkin, did not cause any trouble at the Hammersmith Socialist Society. They were a more peaceable lot than the average. Morris certainly knew Kropotkin well, but would most likely not have read any of his books. He didn't think any more of Anarchist writings than he did of Marxist. He used to say, "Why should I read Marx? I can see the evils of society without going to him," whenever someone said that he ought to read Marx.

Morris always filled in odd moments drawing bits of ornament on the deal top and blotters, or on scraps of paper. The enclosure is the original note made by Morris on the occasion of his last lecture at Hammersmith. The persons are as follows:

Shaw—George Bernard.

Carruthers—a retired and well to do member who advanced me the money necessary for the literature purchases.

Steele—Secretary to the Chemical Society at Burlington House.

Mordhorst—A German-Danish Socialist.

Tochatti—Anarchist-tailor with a printing press in his cellar—publisher of *Liberty*, a journal of Anarchist-Communism, the cover of which I designed for him. (This cover was used later in Russia for a similar periodical.)

I am nearly seventy-six now and can hardly picture myself being so energetic and prolific in the drawings which I did for Socialism, and for the Land Nationalization Movement also. I have lived on, into an age of rush, speed, and extreme ugliness, and far above all social reforms and their causes, the present generation of young people that I see about me care only for sport—eternal cup finals and racing— racing at Gatwick this day! We have university men highly trained to pull their weight in boats, but who take jolly good care not to do so when they get out into the world and give all their support to the class that will not get off the backs of those who have to pull more than their weight. All the same, there are some splendid fellows amongst them—Morris was one, and many another you will know of. It's our outworn aristocratic tradition that taints the English today and makes so many snobs. Yet please forgive this outburst, as it is not the subject in hand.[1]

Meanwhile, at the Trades Union Congress of 1892 the new leaders of the Labour Unions resolved, at the suggestion of Keir Hardie, to organize an Independent Labour Party. This work was carried through at the Conference of Bradford, January 13, 1893. One hundred and twenty-five delegates were present, including ninety-four from independent labour organizations, twelve Fabians, five members of the S. D. F., two from other Socialist groups, three from Trade Councils, one apiece from the Labour Representation League and the Eight Hours League, and seven from the New Trade Unions which had sprung up since 1889. Thus was the foundation formed for the beginning of a new political party, and in its platform were a number of ideas that were termed socialistic.

The effects of the Great Dock Strike of 1889, the breakdown of the old Unionism, and the emergence of new leaders for a Labour Party in Parliament brought about the "Labour Alliance" for which Keir Hardie had slowly been working for several years. It was to be based upon an ideology which favoured the rise to political power of the working classes and the diffusion of Collectivist ideas. The "Labour Alliance" of

[1]Letter of Cosmo Rowe to the author, February 16, 1936. *Ibid.*, December 8, 1936. They have been slightly abstracted and printed consecutively to conserve space.

the newly rounded I. L. P. was to be a link between the old Unionism and the new creed of active Socialism.

But neither the Fabians nor the S. D. F. joined this new political party: the former insisting upon continued "permeation" and the latter hailing the organization as a compromise with the true principles of scientific socialism. Most of the Socialist groups felt that what was needed was a closer alliance among the Socialists of Great Britain. For this purpose there was planned, for May Day, 1893, a *Joint Manifesto of British Socialists*.

For the purpose of producing this Joint Manifesto a committee of the three leading Socialist groups was formed, comprising delegates from the S. D. F., the Fabian Society, and the Hammersmith Society. The committee, as originally drafted, included, among others, Hyndman and Quelch for the Federation, Shaw and Webb for the Fabians, and Crane and Morris for the Hammersmith Socialist Society.

Morris played a prominent part in all the arrangements and once more was stirred to hope that all Socialists might at last get together. He had been greatly repelled by what was obviously an "intensely electioneering" kind of activity on the part of the newly formed I. L. P., hence his aversion to it and his interest in a new unity for all true Socialists.

The actual meeting at which the "Joint Manifesto" of the United Socialists of Great Britain was drawn up was, according to Bernard Shaw, a sort of afternoon tea at Kelmscott House attended by the delegates and one proletarian member who served as secretary. Hyndman, of course, favoured the omission of the Fabian program of municipal socialism—or "gas and water Socialism" as he termed it—and was equally determined to make the Manifesto Marxist. On the other hand, Morris and Shaw were equally determined not to endorse the platform advocated by the S. D. F. Hence the meeting of the "great leaders" of English Socialism achieved little more than an impasse. Morris, recognizing the impossibility of reaching an agreement, nevertheless worked for compromise and for the

sublimation of tortuous points. Finally he succeeded in drawing up a vague kind fo program, consisting largely of bland
platitudes, to which each of the others was willing to subscribe.
This draft, patched, broken, platitudinous and eviscerated, according to Mr. Shaw, was subsequently adopted as "The Joint
Manifesto of the Socialists of Great Britain." Although Hyndman subsequently and characteristically, managed to convince
himself that he had been the pacificator and the drafter of the
document, the work as a whole was, undoubtedly, that of
Morris. This can be known not only by the wording of the document and the internal evidence, but also by the very serious
testimony of Mr. Shaw. Mr. Buxton Forman, who was later
engaged in attempting to evolve bibliographies of Morris's and
of Hyndman's work, wound up his task, according to Mr.
Shaw, considerably perplexed as to whether Hyndman or Shaw
was the greater liar!

*The Hammersmith Socialist Record* for May, 1893, displayed no trace of dissatisfaction with the result of the meeting. Its leading article began:

FRIENDS AND COMRADES:

"Union is Strength." The organized Socialist bodies of England have
come to the opinion that it is necessary to make it clear to those interested in the forward movement in social politics that the various
English Socialist Societies have identical aims in view, although, for
various reasons, they have chosen to work through several different organizations. On the initiative of the Hammersmith Socialist Society,
a joint committee of the Social Democratic Federation, the Fabian
Society and the Hammersmith Socialist Society was formed a few
months back and has just published a "Manifesto" which contains a
clear and outspoken declaration of the policy of the English Socialist
party. . . .

The "Manifesto" is an eight-page pamphlet in a brilliant red cover.
It lays down all the main points on which Socialists are agreed, while
disavowing both the doctrines and the tactics of Anarchism. . . .

The "Manifesto" also makes it clear that, while Socialists advocate
such measures as an Eight Hours Law, Universal Suffrage, etc., they
are fully aware that these can be in themselves only temporary pallia-

tives of the present evils, and ought only to be regarded as means to the ultimate establishment of a complete Socialist Commonwealth, wherein such laws will be superfluous.

—S. B.[2]

In a letter to the editor of *The Daily Chronicle*, written November 10, 1893, Morris denied that his view of art was pessimistic, although he admitted that he himself would not live to see the blossoming of the New Art because of the ignorance of people who do not grasp the true significance of Art in Society.

Mr. Glasier has written of the enthusiasm with which Morris regarded the work of Robert Blatchford in *Merrie England* and *The Clarion*. Of all Labour editors, perhaps Blatchford's ideas came closer to those of Morris than any one else's did. In any event, Morris thought that Blatchford "had a true grip on the meaning of Socialism as it should be preached, as well as the faculty of understanding and appealing to the minds of the working classes. . . ." "He [Blatchford] has been to see him at Kelmscott House, and they had had an interesting talk together."[3]

On October 24, 1894, Morris wrote to Robert Blatchford to signify his sympathy with those aims of labour which Blatchford was then popularizing over much of Northern England. He urged a new union of labour, without any interference with or from the existing organizations.

That new union was to come, two years later, in the year of Morris's death.

[2]*The Hammersmith Socialist Record*, No. 20, pp. 1–2. S. B., of course, refers to the editor, Samuel Bullock.

[3]May Morris, II, 519–27; Mackail, II, 292 *et seq.*; Glasier, 137–38.

## CHAPTER VI

MORRIS AND BURNE-JONES DISCUSS ART AND REVISIT
THE SCENES OF THEIR YOUTH

TOWARD the end of the winter of 1891 Morris had
endured a severe attack of gout and thereafter he evinced
more and more symptoms of serious illness. Among
other things a diabetic condition set in and he was warned by
his doctor that hereafter he must consider himself a sick man.
In no case was he to overtax his strength.

Morris passed his fifty-seventh birthday almost an invalid.
Late that spring he wrote to his friend, Ellis, "my hand seems
lead and my wrist string." In July of that year he was still
far from recovered. "I am ashamed to say that I am not so well
as I should like," he wrote to Mrs. Burne-Jones, "and am even
such a fool as to be rather anxious—about myself this time.
But I suppose the anxiety is part of the ailment. I hope you
are better, as I have still some anxiety left for the service of
my friends." For three weeks during August he toured northern France with his elder daughter, Jenny, seeking a change
after his convalescence. He wrote on this trip that the beautiful
churches were as charming as they had been thirty-three years
before.

Despite attempts at rest, at change and at medical cures, he
was never fully to recover from the illness of that year. The
intense activity of his varied career and the strain of mental and
physical exhaustion were beginning to prove too much even
for his strong constitution. In physical appearance he was beginning to age rapidly now, and his hair was turning quite gray.
Only continued physical weakness could restrain him from
going on with his many pursuits in his old accustomed manner,

and even that did not retard his efforts. Morris was not the sort
of man who could be restrained easily, and to the end he con-

*From a copy in the British Museum Manuscript Collection, by permission of Miss May Morris
and The Macmillan Company*

Morris and Burne-Jones re-visit the scenes of youth

tinued in defiance of his doctor's orders to work to the utmost
of his capacity.

Yet Morris found some relaxation during these last years in
spending longer Sundays with the Burne-Joneses, sometimes
remaining for week-ends, and occasionally taking trips to scenes
that he had not visited since his boyhood. Thus, on one occasion,
they hired an equipage and drove down to Avebury to see the

great stone dolmens. On other occasions they visited old country houses, ruined castles, and the Berkshire Hills, usually proceeding thence to Kelmscott Manor.

On other days, when they remained at the Grange, they discussed literature and art. Morris still believed in the principles of Pre-Raphaelitism, and he still considered Burne-Jones to be the greatest of the modern English painters. On October 24 of that year he went up to Birmingham to lecture at the Museum and Art Gallery on the subject of Pre-Raphaelitism, defending it strongly for its naturalism of spirit—"a factor that has led many critics into errors of judgment concerning it."

After a sincere and emphatic argument for the Pre-Raphaelites, he made it clear that impressionistic painters and novelists ought to be taboo. His definition of impressionism, he admitted, occupied a low place in his synthesis of art, society and history.

Now I must just say one word about the fact that both Rossetti and Burne-Jones have had very little to do with representing the scenes of ordinary modern life as they go on before your eyes. One has often heard that brought against the "Romantic" artists as a short-coming. But is the short-coming due to the individual artist, or is it due to the public at large? For my part, I think the latter. When an artist has really a very keen sense of beauty, I venture to think that he can not literally represent an event that often takes place in modern life. He must add something or another to qualify or soften the ugliness and sordidness of the surroundings. . . .

That is not only the case with pictures, if you please: it is the case also in literature. Two examples occur to my mind at this moment. Let us take the novels of such a man as Hardy, or of others who write more or less in the same way. They are supposed to represent scenes of modern life in their novels. But do they? I say they do not; because they take care to surround those modern scenes with an atmosphere of out-of-the-way country-life, which we ourselves never by any chance see. If you go down into the Wessex country you won't see Mr. Hardy's heroes and heroines walking about, I assure you. You will see a very different kind of thing from that when you meet the ordinary British agricultural labourers walking about, and, more especially—excuse me—when you see their wives and daughters walking about. I am very sorry, but so it is. Well, I say the difficulty is even greater, perhaps, for the painter. In painting you cannot get so far away from the facts as you can in literature.

He then went on to compare the popular Mr. Walker's Victorian pictures of "real" country life with real naturalism, and declared that "his haymakers, his carters and all the rest of them are not really modern English carters and haymakers: they are figures that have stepped down from the frieze of the Parthenon," with their flowing, clinging robes and classic faces. "The agricultural Briton," he says, "is not built like that."

Meanwhile, between occasional visits to his friends, he kept up his work for the Hammersmith Socialist Society, and interested himself generally in the progress of the arts. "No cause was nearer to his heart," wrote Aylmer Vallance, than that of the Society for the Protection of Ancient Buildings. As time went on, Morris had become a member of the Art Workers' Guild and occasionally lectured before it during the last few years of his life. He became a Master of that organization in 1892 and in 1894 a Past-Master.

Morris was more interested, however, in The Arts and Crafts Exhibition Society, of which he was considered a co-founder. This group had been founded in 1886, chiefly through the activities of George Clausem, W. Holman Hunt, and Arthur Crance. Most of its members in later years also belonged to The Art Workers' Guild, and Morris, among others, was a financial guarantor. Although the chief purpose of this society was to hold and foster national exhibitions of the arts, Morris was not personally ambitious in this matter, his reputation and that of his firm having been established for upwards of thirty years. But he was vitally interested in having other artists make known their work, and in having the public made aware of the great changes which were beginning to affect art in England. Between 1891 and 1896 he helped to arrange a number of exhibitions at the New Gallery in London.

In July, 1893, Morris wrote a Preface for the collection of

*Arts and Crafts Essays,* published by the society, in which he said:

The modern *Impressionists* loudly proclaim their enmity to beauty, and are no more unconscious of their aim than the artists of the revival are of their longing to link themselves to the traditional art of the past. Here we have then . . . a school which is pushing rather than drifting into the domain of the empirical science of today, and another which can only work through its observation of an art which died centuries ago . . . while at the same time the great mass of civilization lives on, content to forego art altogether. . . . Now it seems to me that this genuine eclecticism is all that we can expect under modern civilization; that we can expect no *general* impulse toward the fine arts till civilization has been transformed into some other condition of life.

## CHAPTER VII

MORRIS'S LAST TRIP TO THE HOME OF THE VIKINGS:
THE PROPHET RETURNS TO VALHALLA

DESPITE his busy days Morris carried on unrelent-
ingly with his personal interests, his art, his writing,
his bookmaking and his Socialism. Throughout 1895
he seemed to be doing as many things as he had ever done at
one time. But the drenching which he received while delivering
Stepniak's funeral oration in the pouring rain of November,
caused serious consequences. On January 3, 1896, he lectured
before the Social Democratic Federation at Holborn Town
Hall and returned home feeling miserable. Two days later he
gave what was to be his last speech at the Kelmscott Hall of his
Hammersmith Socialist Society. It was a severe winter and
Morris had been ill now, and overworked, for some time.

"I am getting anxious about him," remarked Burne-Jones
before that month was out, and on the 23d of February his
wife noted in her diary, "No Morris to breakfast,"—"nor did
he ever come again in the old way," she added in after years.

During July and August, Morris made an ill-advised trip to
Norway in company with John Carruthers. The doctors believed that the northern atmosphere might restore his spirit and
vitality. But it was a dreary trip and Morris seemed to have
lost interest in the lands of the Vikings. He must have been
thinking perhaps of their eternal land, in Valhalla, for he returned on August 18, broken completely in health and apparently disinterested in life. "I'm done for, old man," he said
simply to a friend who stopped to inquire about his health.

He was too ill even to be removed to Kelmscott Manor, as he desired.

During the next few weeks, while he lay at Kelmscott House in Hammersmith, he finished his dictation of *The Sundering Flood*, his last work. Thereafter he weakened steadily. Mr. Arnold Dolmetsch, who was just beginning his remarkable efforts to revive the use of old musical instruments, was brought out to play for Morris his favourite Elizabethan airs. But the lung congestion, which had set in at the end of the northern journey, continued to grow worse. The great man weakened steadily, and on the morning of Saturday, October 3, he died peacefully and apparently without pain.

During Morris's long illness despondency had settled gradually over the membership of the Hammersmith Socialist Society. Bruce Glasier and Robert Blatchford made the last addresses there on August 9, 1896. There seemed to be nothing left for any one to do. The organization seemed to fade quietly away, leaving only a long tradition which would continue to live henceforward within the framework of the new Independent Labour Party.

R. B. Cunninghame-Graham, in a little essay entitled *With the North-West Wind*, has told the story of how Morris's friends carried the body of their hero from London to Lechlade, the station for Kelmscott Manor, where the body was to be laid to rest.

The train rolled on through Oxford, but no undergraduates thronged the station, silently standing to watch the poet's funeral. True, it was the Long Vacation; but had the body of some Buluwayo Burglar happened to pass, they all had been there. The ancient seat of pedantry, where they manufacture prigs as fast as butchers in Chicago handle hogs, was all unmoved.

Sleeping the sleep of the self-satisfied were dons and masters and the crew of those who, if they chance once to have a man of genius amongst them, are all ashamed of him.

Sleeping but stertorous, the city lay girt in its throng of jerry buildings, quite out of touch with all mankind, keeping its sympathy for piffling commentators on Menander.[1]

No periodical in England exceeded *Justice* in its praise of Morris. The funeral of the famous former member of the S. D. F. was held on Tuesday, October 6, 1896. On Saturday, the 10th, *Justice* with its heavy black margins looked funereal. Harry Quelch on the first page declared that:

His death has inflicted a loss upon the party which no living man can replace. Loved and revered by all who knew him, no man wielded a wider influence or commanded more universal esteem. . . . Nor was his Socialism, as some of his critics . . . try to make out, a mere sentimental expression of sympathy with suffering—the outcome of the revolt of his artistic sense against the squalor and artificiality of our day. . . . He never did things by halves. He hated shams, and in whatever he undertook he was thorough. Brave, noble and good, it may indeed be that we ne'er shall look upon his like again. . . . He is dead, but his work lives with us, and we know, as he knew and sang, that in the time to come:

We who once were fools and dreamers then shall be the great and wise. There amidst the world new builded shall our earthly deeds abide, Though our names be all forgotten, and the tale of how we died.

On the editorial page, H. M. Hyndman devoted most of three columns—practically the entire page—to his eulogy of Morris. "We have lost one whose place can never be filled," he wrote. "Happily the differences which arose in the autumn of 1884 were composed. . . . Again he wrote poems for *Justice*, again he lectured for our branches, and kindly contributed to our funds. . . . The memory of what he was will ever remain with us—sweet as the music of his verse, and encouraging as the hearty welcome with which he never failed to greet his comrades in the cause."

This editorial was post-dated as of the week before, when

[1] *The Ipané*, by R. B. Cunninghame-Graham. The references to Buluwayo Burglar and to "piffling commentators on Menander" would seem to refer to Cecil Rhodes and Matthew Arnold.

Morris was laid to rest in his oak coffin with the wrought-iron decorations in the little graveyard at Kelmscott.

Seven paragraphs on The Tatler's page of *Justice* were devoted to Morris's part in Socialism. A letter from Leon Caryll was also printed, together with Walter Crane's poem of tribute, reprinted from *The Daily Chronicle* of October 4, and an announcement of the impossibility of printing or even of acknowledging the innumerable expressions of regret which had come from every quarter of the kingdom. There was, however, space reserved for a large portrait of Morris and for a poem about him by a proletarian comrade, J. Leslie, entitled *William Morris: A Proletarian's Tribute,* of which the last three stanzas are worthy of quotation.

> Oh! Noble singer—"wrath and hope and wonder"
>   Arose, as soared your flight, and peal on peal
> Proclaimed through silver trump in tones of thunder
>   The rights of Labour in the Commonweal.
>
> For this we love you and for this revere you;
>   For this your name shall ne'er forgotten be;
> For this our children's children yet will hear you,
>   And love the voice from o'er the sunless sea.
>
> Oh! Of the many who may come anear you
>   A sorrow, greater, deeper, none may tell
> Than we the poor can, for the love we bear you,
>   Our stainless Bayard, brave comrade—Farewell.

"To me," wrote Bruce Glasier, "he was the greatest man in the world."

# EPILOGUE

## "THE SINGERS HAVE SUNG AND THE BUILDERS HAVE BUILDED"

*Lo, saith the World, a heart well satisfied*
*With what I give, a barren love forgot—*
*Draw near me, O my child, and heed them not!*
*The world thou lovest, e'en my world it is,*
*Thy faithful hands yet reach out for my bliss,*
*Thou see'st me in the night and in the day*
*Thou canst not deem that I can go astray.*

# CHAPTER I

## WILLIAM MORRIS AND THE IDEAS OF THE FUTURE

THE Socialism of William Morris differed widely from the accredited forms of Socialism commonly recognized by students of that phenomenon. For Morris did not believe that "political machinery" should be directed mainly at the improvement of temporary economic conditions. He had no faith in demagogues, as he called politicians. Neither was he prepared to help destroy the economic power of the capitalistic class by means of violence and civil war, although at times he thought that the final change would necessitate some violence for a brief moment. We have also seen that Morris's idea of a "true Utopia" was not based on the ideas of other Utopians concerning superstate organizations inconsistently blended with the "natural right" of man to be happy; his idea of Utopia was based mainly on *the natural right of man to work*, and this work, he felt, must be pleasurable—"neither overburdensome nor overanxious"—and capable of satisfying the natural creative instincts of every man.

Morris's philosophy implicitly decreed that all the works of men constituted Art, if properly conceived, with history behind them. No other man in his time—philosopher, artist, economist or historian—had evolved a philosophy of art and of work which was so intrinsically allied with principles governing human progress and with principles that governed the growth and decay of political, ethical and religious concepts and conditions in society.

In an age of ostentatious display and over-decoration Morris almost alone clung to the need for "simplicity." In an address on "The Society of the Future" he said:

What is simplicity? Do you think I mean a row of yellow-brick, blue-slated houses, or a *phalangstère* like an improved Peabody lodging-house; and the dinner-bell ringing one into a row of white basins of broth with a piece of bread cut nice and square by each, with boiler-made tea and ill-boiled rice-pudding to follow? No; that's the philan-thropist's ideal, not mine; and here I only note it to repudiate it!

Yet no one can state positively to what extent the ideas of other social philosophers of the age may, or may not, have influenced Morris. In his lectures he made occasional refer-ences to the works of other men: Fourier, Ruskin, Arnold, Carlyle, Kropotkin, Marx, Gibbon, Green, Freeman, Owen, Saint-Simon, Proudhon, Huxley, and Spencer. But in the final analysis, Morris's views always differed in some respects from those of the others, and to that extent it can be clearly and firmly stated: he had his own message to preach. This message sprang from his own interweaving of history, beauty and æsthetics, as well as the doctrine of human fellowship and work, into a doctrine that sought human equality and that sprang funda-mentally from his own philosophy—in which the arts of life, especially of common life, determined the growth or the decay of cultures. Naturally, he could not imagine Utopia just around a corner, consequent upon the success of some great and sudden revolution or reform which might be effected almost overnight. Naturally, he did not accept the Liberalism of the nineteenth century as an endless extension of merit into the cloudcuckoo land of materialistic progress. Naturally, he did not think that the newly discovered "scientific evolution" of society would necessarily result from educational advantages, progressive po-litical reforms, liberal parliamentary action, or from sociological conclusions. He would not go so far as to admit, with Tenny-son, that we should "doubt not through the ages one increasing purpose runs, and the thoughts of man are widened with the process of the suns." For he knew that sometimes the natural evolution of man took a downward and narrower curve. In his last conversation with Bruce Glasier he remarked: "The truth is that none of us knows what actually is the universe of which we ourselves form a part. Priests, prophets, and philosophers in all ages have puzzled themselves trying to find out God, and are no nearer the end of their quest to-day than five thousand years ago. . . . One thing is quite certain to me, and that is that our beliefs, whatever they be, whether concerning God, or nature, or art, or happiness, are in the end only of account in so far as they affect the right doings of our lives, so far, in fact, as they make ourselves and our fellows happy."[1]

But it must be admitted that few men have evolved all their ideas, or any very important ones, single-handed. So also with phrases and slogans. Thus, Alexis, Comte de Tocqueville (who wrote at great length upon American democracy) employed the phrase "equality of condition" in the same year that Morris was born. But there is no evidence to prove that Morris ever read De Tocqueville. It might be easier to prove that Morris borrowed certain ideas from Gibbon, Saint-Simon, Vico, Leroux, Proudhon, Spencer, or even from Kant.

Thus, one might claim with some reason that his Socialism was more nearly the Socialism of Saint-Simon than of Fourier; his so-called Anarchism more nearly the anarchism of Proudhon than of Kropotkin, especially since the time element would have been more nearly in Proudhon's favour: his "development theory" in history an idea derived from Giovanni Vico (possibly in the French translation of Michelet) rather than from Karl Marx; and his so-called Communism the "communism" of Pierre Leroux. Unfortunately, however, there is very little evidence to indicate that Morris was strongly influenced by any one of these writers. Spencer and Proudhon are mentioned in only one or two of Morris's lectures, and I have found no evidence to indicate that Morris so much as heard of Vico or Leroux.

Gibbon, however, was occasionally mentioned by Morris;

[1] Glasier, p. 172.

and it is noteworthy that Gibbon had certain speculations to make regarding "barbarian" and "enlightened" cultures: *viz.*, that it is unlikely that any people can relapse into barbarism unless the whole face of society is changed. On the other hand, Gibbon admits negatively that perhaps such a view is unfounded, perhaps civilization may once more decay, in which case a new growth will be brought about because "the more useful or at least more necessary arts" . . . would survive. This view, as we have noted, is one that Morris welcomed. He preferred barbarism in order that society might be rebuilt on more secure foundations. At that time he believed also, with Gibbon, in a twilight of the Gods,—a cataclysm,—which might "change the face of society."

The early Socialists of the nineteenth century, such leaders as Owen, Fourier, and Saint-Simon, were motivated largely by eighteenth-century doctrines. Thus it was that they laid the blame for human misery upon social, *i.e.*, man-made, institutions; and in so doing they helped to carry over to the "constructive" and "scientific" Socialists of a later age the revolutionary ideas of the encyclopædists and of the ideologists. Morris may have recognized something of this when he said that John Stuart Mill, in his article on Socialism, dealt only with the older type, such as that of Fourier. Yet Fourier was perhaps a humanitarian mathematician with a flair for imaginative formulæ rather than a Socialist.

As an afterwave of the French Revolution a new spirit was emerging in France. The writings of Madame de Staël (notably *Literature in Relation to Social Institutions*, and her *Germany*) as well as of Chateaubriand (especially *The Spirit of Christianity*) marked the beginning of a new interest in Medievalism and in Romanticism, and the discrediting of the Classicism and the Rationalism of the decadent and mechanical eighteenth-century philosophers. The individual man, said they, must also be the social man; he cannot free himself except in abstract thought. The ideas of Voltaire, Condorcet and other philosophers and ideologues emerged from their treatment as mere abstractions without practical value. It appeared that modern thought, from Descartes to Condorcet, had become degraded; and from a broader understanding of the Teutonic ideas of social life and institutions during the medieval period, much was to be expected.

These writings, together with those of Bonald, De Maistre, and Lamennois, led to new endeavours in art, in history, and in literature. A new respect was created for ideas that had come from other lands, and France began to notice the views of Herder, Kant, Lessing, Fichte, Hegel and Von Schlegel, from Germany; while in 1827 Michelet translated Giovanni Vico's *Principles of a New Science on the Subject of the Common Nature of All Nations*, which had appeared in a German edition in 1822.

Vico's book had originally been published in Naples in 1725, but had attracted little attention, coming, as it did, a century in advance of its time. The *New Science* introduced into modern Europe a new synthesis of history. Vico, like Morris at a later date, regarded the Middle Ages in Europe as analogous in social development with the Homeric age in Homeric civilization, Dante taking the place of Homer. The dawning decadence of the age of Baroque and Rococo, with strong monarchies organized in western Europe, is compared with the decadence of the late Roman Empire. In each a decadent Classicism emerged triumphant as the result of eclectic ideas and ideals. To Vico, history revolved in cycles; and he explained the major cycles of human development since the rise of Hellenic culture. Naturally his cyclical view of history does not preclude the possibility that modern civilization, like that of decadent Greece and Rome in their latter days, is doomed to decay and destruction—after which a new barbarism will emerge and cause the beginning of a new cycle in the development of man. Each new cycle, however, may be regarded as containing within itself the fundamentals of a new resurrection—because the basic arts and traditions of the race remain as a heritage, or *residuum*, of the older culture.

Such views, we know, were held by Morris; but we have

no reason for suspecting that Morris ever heard of Vico, although it may be possible that he had read Michelet's version. But for that matter it is just as probable that Vico's work was known to Gibbon. Of course, Vico's own thought must have been, in turn, partly derivative, as all modern thought must necessarily be; yet no one can affirm positively that because of its similarities to the ideas of later men, later men necessarily borrowed from it.

The emergence of these new (or resurrected) ideas in France, together with the reactionary writings and words of historians and politicians during the Bourbon Restoration, were not, of course, Utopian. But they pointed toward new procedures for the progress of future men and undoubtedly they reacted upon the Socialistic ideas, Romantic visions and Utopian dreams of the early nineteenth-century social reformers—the Utopians proper—who, departing from the ideologies of the revolutionary philosophers, at least in part, turned their attention toward the amelioration of mankind's future lot, and thus became transmitters of both the radicalism of the latter part of the eighteenth century and the Utopianism and Humanitarianism of the early part of the nineteenth century to the Scientific Socialists and Anarchists of the latter part of the nineteenth century. Among the transmitters of this heritage of eclectic radicalism were Saint-Simon, Fourier, Considérant, De Tocqueville, and Leroux, together with others who adopted some of their views.

Thus, Saint-Simon had inherited the traditional views of eighteenth-century ideologues, but added to them elements of the Romantic and Social theory of the new school that was emerging. He held that certain fundamentals of the thought of Condorcet were valid, especially that human progress must depend upon intellectual advancement. But Condorcet had viewed the Middle Ages as a dead period in the forward-looking march of humanity and he regarded religion as an evil. Saint-Simon, on the other hand, held that the Middle Ages represent a valuable lesson, having played a necessary and important part in the evolution of ideas concerning social organization and human relationships, and that the harmony and balance achieved by medieval civilization can set an example in maintaining both temporal and spiritual rights and powers. He looked at history as a series of alternate cycles of organization and of revolution. Thus, the Middle Ages had organized; the eighteenth century had criticized and revolted; the coming age would mark a new epoch in organization for new knowledge, new governmental forms and new religions which will supersede those of the revolutionary cycle just ended. (And history may now be proving how right he was!) Rejecting the catchwords of nineteenth-century democracy and liberalism, Saint-Simon looked forward to the dawn of a new ethical and social consciousness which would abolish war and bring about a new co-operative group of European states—not unlike the United States of America—with a parliamentary régime exercising a certain amount of supremacy and sovereignty over the various small commonwealths.

One can see at once how Saint-Simon's thought must have affected the thought of William Morris; indeed, certain similarities in the thought of these two men account for Morris's acknowledged acceptance of part of Saint-Simon's ideas, among others, in the program of the Socialist League,—which does not mean, necessarily, that Morris thought the Socialist League should become an exponent of the Socialism of Saint-Simon. Morris would have distrusted Saint-Simon's parliamentary régime. Moreover, Saint-Simon had rejected the idea of Equality, just as he rejected Liberalism and Democracy, on principle. To him they were mere catchwords. But Morris wished and hoped for Equality and for the nominal abolition of private property in the sense of individual control of the forces of production.

But both Saint-Simon and Fourier in France spoke for an earlier period of life than did Morris, and this is something which must be borne in mind. They had a totally different concept of empirical thought and of the motivation of the external world. They did not see, and could not, as Morris did see, that the evils of intensified industrialization and the erection of large-town proletariats would change all social conditions; they did not live through the revolutionary procedure of 1848, the imperialist wars of a slightly later period, or the establishment of the First and Second Internationals and the Paris Commune. They did not know of Trade Unionism or even of "Whiggery" as Morris knew them. Yet they passed on the torch of Socialism to whatever "constructive" Socialists of a later generation were willing to grasp it.

With the revolution of 1848 in France the names of three new exponents of anarchic, democratic and humanitarian communism force themselves upon our attention: Proudhon, famous as the first great Anarchist of modern times, Considérant, a disciple of Fourier, and Pierre Leroux, a "humanitarian communist," who influenced greatly the romances of George Sand.

Pierre Leroux, like Comte, began as a disciple of Saint-Simon, but unlike his master he hoped for Equality. To him the breaking down of castes and classes is the *sine qua non* for the continued progress of the world. With Equality would come human *solidarity*—a solidarity that is necessary because we of today are one with the generations who have made the past and with the generations who will make the future. Solidarity will bring into being a new religion of *Humanity*. Leroux exercised considerable influence upon later humanitarians and anarchists, so-called, and it may have been the similarity of his general views, in the abstract, to those of Morris which once induced Engels to refer to Morris as a *Gemütssozialist*. Justice, equality, and fellowship (*humanité*) were important principles in the eyes of both Morris and Leroux; but, unfortunately, there is no evidence to prove that Morris obtained his views from Leroux or that he ever heard of Leroux's work.

Proudhon, on the other hand, can in no sense be termed a Communist. He was an Anarchist in only one sense: *viz.*, that he believed the future progress of man depended upon individual initiative. While maintaining individualism, he, like Morris, insisted upon the abolition of injustice. He also was hostile to religion and to all centralized state power; indeed, he was the most formidable enemy of Marxism among the revolutionary thinkers of his time. And like Morris, in at least one stage of the latter's career, Proudhon held that all property is "theft."

With reference to Huxley (who had been one of the "inheritors" of the nineteenth-century tradition) Morris wrote in his last letter to *Justice* that he (Morris) was a personality and not a type, that he was careless of metaphysics, religion and scientific analysis, yet felt "a deep love of the earth and the life on it, and a passion for the history of the past of mankind. Think of it! Was it all to end in a counting-house on the top of a cinder-heap, with Podsnap's drawing-room in the offing and a Whig committee drawing out champagne to the rich and margarine to the poor . . . though the pleasure of the eyes was gone from the world, and the place of Homer taken by Huxley?"

Strangely enough, perhaps, and yet not so strange in the light of his whole life, Morris's thought displays clearly marked concordance with certain aspects of the thought of Immanuel Kant. Kant, in his *Idea of a Universal History on a Cosmopolitical Plan,* approached the problems of civilization in a manner new to the society of 1784. Although dealing with politics, he looked for justice in a civil society that would become universal. In that society there would exist a "confederation of states," among which and within which the fullest individual freedom and justice would prevail, although the limits of freedom would be strictly preserved. A universal society, he stated, is the only one in which the tendencies and the capacities of human nature, and of the individual consciousness, can develop naturally and healthfully.

This idea, that a loosely bound federation, as Morris called it, with extensive but not anarchical freedom, would *not* suppress individualism but rather encourage it, is here posited as one of the most important ideas of both Morris and Kant for the society of the future. Both Kant and Morris believed that in their own times, respectively, there was discernible a definite trend in that direction, but that it was as yet impossible to see clearly the future outlines of that state, or to trace the plan of its development. Nevertheless, they believed that such vision as one could command was enough to furnish us with reasons for thinking that such a development is not only possible but also *bound to occur*.

The foundation of Kant's conception of the future ethics rests, he tells us, on practical experience rather than upon mental and moral trends. But it would be useless, he felt, to attempt to determine the future course of development without a knowledge of the social laws which shape development, and he lamented that those laws have not yet been discovered.

This much of the vision of Kant's Cosmopolitical system is similar to that which Morris envisioned almost a century later. There is no evidence, however, that Morris either read or was influenced by the great German philosopher; and it is fairly safe to assume that Morris gained his conclusions independently as a result of his own experience and as a result of his studies in the realms of art and history. Perhaps even his poet's nature and intuition may have helped him.

In his essay on *Perpetual Peace* Kant assumed that a universal Republic might be the ideal form of social organization, but believed that humanity would probably have to rest content with a Federation of Peoples, loosely bound together, which would guarantee peace and co-operation while affirming independence, individual liberty, and civil equality.

Immanuel Kant differs fundamentally from those philosophers who have regarded human happiness as the *summmum bonum*. "Is enjoyment to be the sole test and end?" he asks. "Then who among you would choose any other known condition of life than what you now have?"

Throughout all these views there are similarities enough to indicate that Morris and Kant may have been somewhat alike in their "practical" outlooks. Indeed, it might have been possible that Ernest Belfort Bax, a student of German philosophy, may have had something to do with encouraging Morris's development of ideas of future social and political organizations—although, as we have seen, Morris had developed most of his ideas long before he met Bax. But it is improbable that any Kantian influence will ever be proved owing to the lack of adequate data; yet it would make a nice problem for investigation. Here, however, we have no further problem. *Non nostrum tantas componere lites.*

## CHAPTER II

---

### WILLIAM MORRIS AND THE BUILDERS OF THE FUTURE

THE common view of Morris, as it has come down to the workers of our own day in the English-speaking world, is that he was a great and noble poet and craftsman overflowing with humanity: a fine gentleman who loved the meanest labourers and associated with them on terms of equality: a man who gave from his own funds to those who were in need, and who spent the best years of his life in organizing the workers of Britain for the time when they might know "equality of condition." This much is true of him and of his Socialism. But to many modern workers he has been made to appear as a man who was in active and violent revolt against the capitalistic government: a man who, had the Revolution occurred, would have been found marching in the vanguard of the revolutionists, among the red flags and the clubs and bayonets of the proletariat: a man who was a proletarian leader in the State Socialist and sometimes in the State Communist sense: a man who favoured action and violence: a man who believed that the State—that all-powerful capitalistic factotum —owed to the workers the satisfaction of all their economic wants, and a man who believed that the workers must receive all the advantages of these things immediately, else there would be no equality. These latter views, as we have had occasion to observe, are not true.

It is of course true that Morris wished for equality of condition: that he wanted the proletariat to represent all the citizenry of Britain. But it is also true that he believed that men must prepare themselves for the obtainment of that equality—through education both in the arts and in the traditions of life—and that every man must be prepared to offer *due* labour and to accept the *duties* and the *responsibilities* of his position. He believed that by means of proper education the creative capacities of common man would be kindled anew and that when labour was made pleasurable and creative, with free play guaranteed for the initiative and for the creative capacities of every man, then, and then only, work would become wholesome and not toilsome.

It was, in brief, a doctrine of give and take—of sportsmanship and of fellowship—that Morris urged upon the workers of Britain. When these things were brought into being Morris believed that man would learn to know what he really wanted; and that, as the result of a new equality of art and of labour, men would turn to those activities in government and in society which would permit them to realize the beauties and the noble qualities of life. Then there would be brought about a new harmony in living. The necessity of rigorous laws enforced by carefully centralized bureaucratic State systems would disappear. Once again, as in certain glorious times long past, as, for example, in the Grecian and Swiss and Icelandic Federations, men would be free, and men would enjoy the practice of the "difficult arts of life." The disappearance of monopolies, both in politics and in economics, would be brought about; and the destruction of monopoly, Morris felt, "will be the greatest change for the best that has ever happened in the history of human progress."

Morris was a Socialist only in the etymological sense of believing that man must become a social animal. Yet social-mindedness did not exclude, in his system, individual qualities. Rather, he felt, individual qualities would tend to be encouraged by freedom of enterprise in working for the common weal, especially with sportsmanlike praise and friendly rivalry serving as the incentive to make men face work gladly.

But Morris was not a Socialist in that ultra-modern sense which decrees that a bureaucratic State should control, regulate, and own, in the name of its subject population, all the basic means of production and distribution, or all the creative enterprises which may cause the raising up or the debasement of its civilization. Morris was opposed to centralized ownership—whether in business or in politics—and to centralized control. He knew that any such impersonal factotum would be unable to nourish the mental and spiritual needs of the individual subject or the needs of the individual community. He believed that the common man, under such a system, would lose touch with the "common government," and *vice versa*, and that out of this situation there would arise a new tyranny as exclusive and as ignoble as the old.

Under Morris's system of Distribution and Decentralization, each community, or commune, would regulate its own affairs, but the people who belonged of their own free will and accord (*i.e.*, by self-determination) to the larger organization, or Federation of Communes, would participate in the regulation of transportation, education and other matters which might extend beyond the limits of each individual community. In brief, his system was Socialist only in that it placed the Social factors of civilization above individual competition for success. But that was merely an extension of humanity and of ethics beyond their present realm.

As a matter of fact, however, neither William Morris nor the early proletarian movement was a matter of much moment until more recent years. Just before the Great War of 1914, for example, Socialism and all other forms of revolt against existing political, social, and economic conditions seemed relatively insignificant. Only in the few years that have elapsed since the World War has the British Labour Party "loomed large." And although its rapid growth has attracted worldwide attention, little scholarly probing has been directed at its roots of growth —at those "small beginnings" which made possible its present potentialities.

That Morris had an unusually important part to play in the founding of the modern British Labour Party is indicated by a letter of Mr. J. S. Middleton, Secretary of the Labour Party, Transport House, London, who wrote that, while he "had never associated Morris's activities with those of Transport House," nevertheless he could find himself "able to suppose" that "we [*i.e.*, Transport House and the Labour Party] are historical heirs to his activities."[1]

Morris was not only a more practical Utopian, he was also a more practical reformer than were most of his associates. Moreover, he was a more practical prophet. The events of more than four decades that have passed since his death have proved him to be more nearly right than wrong in almost all his prophecies regarding the political, social, and diplomatic history of the rising generation. Many of his demands have been met to some extent, and "the century of education"—as he called the twentieth century—seems now to be upon us.

Yet the evolution of Morris's "Practical Socialism," as he called it, was a long and continuous development in his career, reaching back at least to his college days, and forward to the time of his death some forty years afterward. Even as a child he had felt the primary urges of justice, equality, and fellowship. As time went on, "the study of history and the practice of art forced him into a hatred of civilization" as it existed in his time. Those years of growing wisdom also enabled him to evolve a clear and original idea of the forces which, he was absolutely certain, made for the growth and the decay of societies and their cultures. It was his hatred for existent civilization and its forms of government, combined with his own philosophy of the primal importance of art in society, that made him not only an "Artist-Philosopher" of arresting significance, but also a "Practical Socialist" of individual and independent vision.

Morris's main hope for the future, a hope expressed both in his art lectures and in his Socialist speeches and writings, was that the people of England might return to their traditional forms, at least in art—which would bring about greater and

[1] J. S. Middleton to Cosmo Rowe, April 4, 1936.

better simplicity in social, political, and economic life, and higher and nobler degrees of justice and of fellowship, instead of the prevailing injustice, suspicion and competition. This hope, or vision, might be said to embrace a more ethical sense of personal and social obligations than that which commonly prevails among the very best of reformers. But it was in his complete concept of *the potentialities of Art* that Morris combined all those integral factors—the labour, the ethics, the politics, the economics, and the religion of a society—in the struggle for the advancement of the human race. He saw that the way of living in the world ought to be changed. That was why he advocated a basic but gradual revolution in the very foundations of society. Thus, he did more than rediscover the artistic conscience; he did more than merely scoff at the intellectual fog that had blinded so many artistic and emotional souls in the Victorian Age. He pointed out certain definite steps looking toward a Golden Age to come when emphasis would be placed upon good, honest work, beauty, simplicity, romance, fellowship, and equality for all men.

This was the real *Earthly Paradise* for which he had hoped all his life, and to which he looked forward in some dim future, when he wrote:

> And, O ye folk, midst whom my feet have dwelt,
> And whom I leave now, if so be, that I
> Hard anger in my heart at whiles have felt
> 'Gainst things that pressed upon me wearily,
> Yet now the kindness of time past draws nigh;
> And ye will be my folk still, when I go
> Unto a land where e'en your name none know.

# APPENDIX

# A PARTIAL BIBLIOGRAPHY OF
# PUBLISHED WORKS

## *I*

## *BIBLIOGRAPHICAL WORKS*

John Carter and Graham Pollard. *An Enquiry into the Nature of Certain Nineteenth Century Pamphlets.* London, 1934.

Sir Sydney Cockerell. *An Annotated List of all the Books Printed at the Kelmscott Press.* Hammersmith, 1898.

Harry Buxton Forman. *The Books of William Morris Described: with some account of his Doings in Literature and in the Allied Crafts.* London, 1897.

Gerald H. Crow. *William Morris, Designer, with Bibliography.* New York: The Studio, 1934.

May Morris. *William Morris: Artist, Writer, Socialist.* Oxford: Blackwell, 2 vols., 1936.

Aylmer Vallance. *The Art of William Morris,* with a Bibliography of the Original Writings, Translations and Publications of William Morris, by Temple Scott. London, 1897.

Charles Edwyn Vaughan. *Bibliographies of Swinburne, Morris and Rossetti.* Oxford: Horace Hart, 1914. Pamphlet No. 29 of The English Association.

*A Catalogue of MSS. and Early Printed Books from the Libraries of William Morris, in the J. P. Morgan Library.* London: Chiswick Press, 4 vols., 1906–1907.

*William Morris:* Some Books and Periodicals in the Cleveland Public Library. Cleveland, 1910.

*A Bibliography of the Kelmscott Press.* New York: The Critic, 1899.

*Bibliographies of Twelve Victorian Authors,* compiled by Theodore G. Ehrsam and Robert H. Deily, under the direction of Robert M. Smith. New York: Wilson, 1936.

Karl Litzenberg. *William Morris and Scandinavian Literature: A Bibliographical Essay.* Menasha, Wisconsin: Society for the Advancement of Scandinavian Study, 1935.

Stéfan Einarsson. *Saga Eiriks Magnússonar í Cambridge.* (Bibliography and Corrigenda.) Reykjavik, 1933.

## II

## *A CHRONOLOGICAL LIST OF THE PUBLISHED BOOKS OF WILLIAM MORRIS*

1858—*The Defense of Guenevere and Other Poems.*

1867—*The Life and Death of Jason.*

1868–1870—*The Earthly Paradise,* Parts I & II, III, IV, 3 vols.

1869—*The Grettis Saga:* The Story of Grettir the Strong, trs. by William Morris and E. Magnússon.

1870—*Völsunga Saga:* The Story of the Volsungs and the Niblungs, with certain Songs from the Elder Edda, trs. by William Morris and E. Magnússon.

1873—*Love Is Enough.*

1874—*Three Northern Love Stories and Other Tales,* trs. by William Morris and E. Magnússon.

1875—*The Æneids of Virgil done into English Verse by William Morris.*

1876—*The Story of Sigurd the Volsung and the Fall of the House of the Niblungs.*

1882—*Hopes and Fears for Art.*

1884–1885—*Chants for Socialists* appear in *Justice* and *The Commonweal* and are reprinted in pamphlet form by The Socialist League Office, 1885, and soon afterward by other organizations.

1885–1886—*The Pilgrims of Hope* appears in *The Commonweal* and three parts are later reprinted in *Poems by the Way,* 1891.

1886–1887—*A Dream of John Ball* appears in *The Commonweal* and is reprinted in 1888 in book form.

1887—*The Odyssey of Homer, done into English Verse by William Morris.*

1888—*Signs of Change:* Seven Lectures by William Morris.

1889—*The Roots of the Mountains.*

1889—*The House of the Wolfings and All the Kindreds of the Mark,* written in prose and verse by William Morris.

1890—*News from Nowhere* appeared in *The Commonweal* and was reprinted, March, 1891, in book form.

1891—*The Story of the Glittering Plain.*

1891—*Poems by the Way.*

1891—*The Saga Library,* trs. by William Morris and E. Magnússon.

1892—*The Saga Library,* Vol. II (*Eredwellers*), trs. by William Morris and E. Magnússon.

1893—*The Saga Library,* Vol. III ( (*Heimskringla*), trs. by William Morris and E. Magnússon.

1893—*Socialism: Its Growth and Outcome,* by William Morris and Belfort Bax.

1894—*The Wood Beyond the World.*

1895—*The Tale of Beowulf,* done out of the Old English Tongue by William Morris and A. J. Wyatt.

1896—*The Well at the World's End.*

### POSTHUMOUS PUBLICATIONS

1897—*The Water of the Wondrous Isles.*

1897—*The Sundering Flood.*

1902—*Architecture, Industry and Wealth.*

### POSTHUMOUS COLLECTIONS

1910–1915—*The Collected Works of William Morris,* Vol. I–XXIV, ed. by his daughter May Morris and Sir Sydney Cockerell, with Introductions by Miss May Morris.

1936—*William Morris: Artist, Writer, Socialist,* Vols. I–II, with an Introduction to the second volume by George Bernard Shaw. Written, compiled and edited by Miss May Morris, and including, besides her commentary, numerous rare and hitherto unprinted letters, lectures, articles, poems and fragments from the writings, published and unpublished, of William Morris.

## III

## *WRITINGS ABOUT WILLIAM MORRIS*

### A: BIOGRAPHICAL STUDIES

J. W. Mackail. *The Life of William Morris.* London, 2 vols., 1899.

Aylmer Vallance. *William Morris: His Art, His Writings, and His Public Life.* London, 1898. 2nd ed., rev., 1909.

May Morris. *William Morris: Artist, Writer, Socialist.* Oxford, 2 vols., 1936. NOTE: While much of this work is filled with bibliographical studies and with writings which supplement the *Collected Works,* many chapters contain both scholarly and reminiscent biographical material, as does Mr. Shaw's Introduction to Vol. II.

Oscar Lovell Triggs. *William Morris: Craftsman, Writer and Social Reformer.* The New Order Series. No. 1. Chicago, *n.d.* (*c.* 1902).

Arthur Clutton-Brock. *William Morris: His Work and Influence.* London, 1914.

Alfred Noyes. *William Morris.* London, 1908.

Elisabeth Luther Cary. *William Morris: Poet, Craftsman, Socialist.* New York, 1912.

The Countess of Warwick (Frances Evelyn Greville). *William Morris.* London and New York, 1912.

Georges Vidalenc. *William Morris.* Paris, 1920.

Frank Dawtry. *A Few Notes on William Morris.* Manchester: Labour's Northern Voice, 1936–37.

### B: CRITICAL STUDIES

Arthur Compton-Rickett. *William Morris: A Study in Personality,* with an Introduction by R. C. Cunninghame-Graham. London and New York, 1913.

John Drinkwater. *William Morris: A Critical Study.* New York, 1912.

Bruce Glasier. *William Morris and the Early Days of the Socialist Movement.* London, 1921.

Holbrook Jackson. *William Morris: Craftsman-Socialist.* London: Fifield, 1908. Revised and enlarged edition, London: Cape, 1926.

Elbert Hubbard. *A William Morris Book.* . . . Throwing a Side-Light, More or Less, on the Man and His Times. East Aurora, New York, 1907.

Gustav Fritzsche. *William Morris' Sozialismus und Anarchistischer Kommunismus: Darstellung des Systems und Untersuchung der Quellen.* Kölner Anglistische Arbeiten, herausgegeben von Herbert Schöffler. Leipzig: Tauchnitz, 1927. NOTE: One of the most pretentious and least accurate studies ever made under the guise of scholarly procedure.

John Spargo. *William Morris: His Socialism.* Westwood, Massachusetts: Ariel Press, *n.d.* (*c.* 1907).

Oscar Lovell Triggs. *Chapters in the History of the Arts and Crafts Movement.* Chicago: The Bohemia Guild of the Industrial Arts League, *n.d.* (*c.* 1902).

Aylmer Vallance. *The Art of William Morris,* with a Bibliography by Temple Scott. London, 1897.

Karl Litzenberg. *Contributions of the Old Norse Language and Literature to the Style and Substance of the Writings of William Morris, 1858–1876.* NOTE: A Ph.D. dissertation at the University of Michigan, and a very good one.

Karl Litzenberg. *William Morris and the Reviews: A Study in the Fame of the Poet.* Reprinted from *The Review of English Studies,* XII, 48, Oct., 1936. London: Sidgwick and Jackson, Ltd., 1936.

Karl Litzenberg. *The Social Philosophy of William Morris and the Doom of the Gods.* An essay in the University of Michigan Publication *Language and Literature,* X, 1933, pp. 183 *et seq.*

Karl Litzenberg. *William Morris and Scandinavian Literature: A Bibliographical Essay.* Reprinted from *Scandinavian Studies and Notes,* XIII, No. 7, August, 1935, Menasha, Wisconsin, 1935.

Karl Litzenberg. *William Morris and the Heimskringla. Ibid.,* XIV, No. 3, August, 1936.

Karl Litzenberg. *Allusions to the Elder Edda in the "Non-Norse" Poems of William Morris. Ibid.,* XIV, No. 2, May, 1936.

Karl Jakob Lüthi-Tschanz. *Gutenberg, Bodoni, Morris: Eine Vergleichung ihrer Kunst.* Bern: Büchler, 1925. (ed. limited to 250 copies.)

Anna Augusta Helmholtz. *The Social Philosophy of William Morris.* Durham: Duke University Press, 1927. NOTE: Apparently a Ph.D. thesis, quite the opposite of Doctor Fritzsche's in point of view, but apparently as inaccurate.

Paul Elmer More. *Shelburne Essays: Seventh Series.* New York, 1910, pp. 95–118. NOTE: As the considered essay of a well-known "man of letters" this particular piece on William Morris is not only unsound at the core, but illustrates almost every vice of superficial scholarship. Entire sections—and those very poorly selected— are little more than paraphrased passages from the biography of Doctor J. W. Mackail, which, by the way, is valuable mainly for its treatment of Morris's classical translations and his travels.

Frank Laurence Lucas. *Eight Victorian Poets*. Cambridge University Press, 1920, pp. 91–112.

J. Bruce Glasier. *Socialism in Song*. Manchester: The National Labour Press, Ltd., *n.d.* (*c.* 1919).

Holbrook Jackson, ed. *Three Papers on William Morris*. NOTE: These consist of: (1) *The Illuminated Manuscripts of William Morris*, by Graily Hewitt. *The Typography of William Morris*, by Holbrook Jackson. *The Typography of William Morris*, by James Shand. Printed and presented to the members of the Double Crown Club by the Shenval Press, 1934.

Herbert Pundt. *Dante Gabriel Rossettis Einfluss auf die Gedichte des Jungen William Morris*. A dissertation at the University of Breslau, 1920. A 2 pp. summary printed, Breslau, 1922.

Graham Stanhope Rawson. *William Morris's Political Romance, "News from Nowhere."* A dissertation at the University of Jena, 1913. Borna-Leipzig: Noska, 1914.

George Saintsbury. *Corrected Impressions: Essays on Victorian Writers*. New York, 1895, pp. 178–97.

Arthur Glaton. *Urbana Scripta*. London, 1885, pp. 132–55.

Sir William Blake Richmond. *Leighton, Millais and William Morris*. A Lecture. London, 1898.

Alfred Noyes. *Introduction* to the *Everyman* Edition of *The Early Romances of William Morris*. New York and London, 1907, 1910, 1913, 1920, 1925.

Henry Halliday Sparling. *The Kelmscott Press and William Morris, Master-Craftsman*. London, 1924.

Vida D. Scudder. *Social Ideals in English Letters*. Boston, 1923. (Miss Scudder seemed to have studied Morris only to the extent of attempting to read, unsuccessfully, his two "Socialist romances"— *A Dream of John Ball* and *News from Nowhere*—and what she has to say on the subject of Morris indicates blatant and totally ignorant misunderstanding of his entire position. A very shallow and totally erroneous study.)

H. C. Marillier. *The Morris Movement*. Privately printed, *n.d.*

J. W. Mackail. *William Morris and His Circle*. Oxford, 1907.

Ney Lannes McMinn. *The Letters of William Morris to the Press, 1868–1895*. A dissertation at Northwestern University, 1928.

John Drinkwater. *Prose Papers*. London, 1917. Essay entitled *William Morris and the State*.

Stopford Brooke. *Four Victorian Poets*. New York, 1908, pp. 205–300.

Amy Violet Hall. *William Morris and Main Street*. A master's essay at the University of Washington, 1922, pp. 73.

Mrs. Townshend. *William Morris and the Communist Ideal*. Fabian Tract No. 167, London, 1912, pp. 23.

Thomas M. Parrott and Willard Thorp. *Poetry of the Transition, 1850–1914*. New York, 1932.

G. D. H. Cole. *Revaluations*. New York and London, 1931.

Granville Hicks. *Figures of Transition*. New York, 1940. NOTE: The essay on Morris seems to have been based upon the thinnest sort of secondary reading, without much comprehension of the fact that Morris's Socialism was not the Socialism of the nineteenth century.

Chauncey B. Tinker and Carl P. Rollins. *William Morris as Poet*. Stamford, Connecticut: Overbrook Press, 1937. (Printed for the Yale Library Associates.)

## IV

## MISCELLANEOUS PAMPHLETS CONCERNING MORRIS AND HIS TIMES

John Drinkwater, Holbrook Jackson and H. J. Laski. *Speeches in Commemoration of William Morris*. The Bath's Hall, Walthamstow, Saturday, 24th of March, 1934. The William Morris Centenary Celebrations Committee.

Geo. Ed. Roebuck, ed. *Some Appreciations of William Morris*. Issued by request of the Borough Council. Publ. by the Walthamstow Antiquarian Society, January, 1934. Containing "The Earthly Paradise" by Alfred Noyes, and prose contributions by May Morris, Lascelles Abercrombie, Sir Reginald Blomfield, Robert Blatchford, C. Delisle Burns, Gordon Bottomley, G. K. Chesterton, G. D. H. Cole, A. Compton-Rickett, G. G. Coulton, John Drinkwater, B. Ifor Evans, Hamilton Fyfe, Holbrook Jackson, the Reverend Honorable Edward Lyttelton, J. W. Mackail, Compton Mackenzie, Sir Eric Maclagan, H. C. Marillier, F. S. Marvin, Francis Meynell, Herbert Read, G. Bernard Shaw, Viscount Snowden, Sir John Squire, H. M. Tomlinson, Hugh Walpole, and Frances Evelyn, Countess of Warwick.

"A Plain Tory." *Justice for England, or, How to Fight Socialism.* By "A Plain Tory," author of *Tory Democracy.* London, Swan Sonnenschein, 1893.

John Carruthers. *Socialism and Radicalism:* A Lecture Read before the Hammersmith Socialist Society, London, 1894, pp. 16, price 1 *d.*

Socialist League Pamphlets, published by "The Office of 'The Commonweal,'" e.g., *Revolutionary Studies,* price 2 *d.,* London 145, City Road, E.C., 1892.

## V

## *BOOKS OF RELATED VALUE*

G. K. Chesterton. *The Victorian Age in Literature.* A volume in the Home University Library. London and New York, 1913.

F. J. C. Hearnshaw. *The Development of Political Ideas.* New York and Garden City, 1928.

Holbrook Jackson. *The Eighteen Nineties: A Review of Art and Ideas at the Close of the Nineteenth Century.* London, 1913. New ed., London and New York, 1927.

Henry Wood Nevinson. *Essays on Freedom.* London, 1913.

Henry Wood Nevinson. *Changes and Chances.* London, 1923.

Henry Wood Nevinson. *Fire of Life.* With a Preface by John Masefield. New York, 1936.

John Paton. *Proletarian Pilgrimage.* London, 1935.

John Paton, *Never Say Die.* New York, 1936.

G. B.–J. (Lady Burne-Jones). *Memorials of Edward Burne-Jones,* 2 vols. London and New York, 1904. New ed., 2 vols. in 1, 1906.

Godfrey Elton. *"England Arise!": A Study of the Pioneering Days of the Labour Movement.* London, 1931.

Walter Crane. *William Morris to Whistler: Papers and Addresses on Art and Craft and the Commonweal.* London, 1911.

H. D. Traill. *Social England,* Vol. VI. London and New York, 1897. (See especially Miss May Morris's contributions on the state of Victorian Art.)

R. C. K. Ensor. *England: 1870–1914. (The Oxford History of England,* Vol. XIV). Oxford and New York, 1936.

R. H. Gretton. *A Modern History of the English People, 1880–1922.* Book I, 1880–1898. London, 1912. New ed., 3 vols in 1, New York and London, 1930.

Arthur Clutton-Brock. *Essays on Art*. London, 1919, pp. 132 *et seq.*

Max Beer. *A History of British Socialism*. London, 1920, Vol. II, *passim*.

Ramsden Balmforth. *Some Social and Political Pioneers of the Nineteenth Century*. London, Swan Sonnenschein, 1900, pp. 179–86.

George Henry Blore. *Victorian Worthies*. London, Oxford, 1920, pp. 302–22.

William Dana Orcutt. *Master Makers of the Book*. New York and Garden City, 1928, pp. 207–28.

A. M. W. Stirling. *William De Morgan and His Wife*. New York, 1922, *passim*.

Douglas McMurtrie. *The Golden Book*. Chicago and New York, Pascal Covici, 1928; Later rev. and enlarged ed., New York, Covici, 1937.

H. C. Marillier. *History of the Merton Abbey Tapestry Works, Founded by William Morris*. (A pamphlet.) London: Constable, 1927, pp. 37.

James Mavor. *My Windows on the Street of the World*. New York, 1923. Vol. I, pp. 193–202.

Alfred Richard Orage. *Readers and Writers*. London, 1922, pp. 136 *et seq.*

Richard Le Gallienne. *The Romantic Nineties*. New York and Garden City, 1925, pp. 121–27.

Robert Lynd. *The Art of Letters*. New York, 1921, pp. 150–55.

Walter Hamilton. *The Æsthetic Movement in England*. London, 1882, pp. 58–61.

Ford Madox Ford (Francis Hueffer). *Memories and Impressions*. New York, 1911, *passim*.

Chris Healy. *Confessions of a Journalist*. London, 1904. Chapter I, entitled "William Morris and Prince Kropotkin," pp. 1–18.

Frederick J. Gould. *Hyndman, Prophet of Socialism*. London, 1928, *passim*.

Ada Earland. *Ruskin and His Circle*. London, 1910, pp. 108–25.

James Douglas. *Theodore Watts-Dunton*. New York, 1906, *passim*.

Ernest Belfort Bax. *Reminiscences and Reflections*. London, 1918, *passim*.

Wilfrid Scawen Blunt. *My Diaries*. New York, 1921. Vol. I, *passim*.

Peter Latouche. *Anarchy!* London, 1908, pp. 187–90.

APPENDIX

Edouard Guyot. *Le Socialisme et L'Evolution de l'Angleterre Contemporaine.* Paris, 1913, pp. 379–424.

H. M. Hyndman. *The Record of an Adventurous Life.* London, 1911, *passim.*

H. M. Hyndman. *Reminiscences.* London, 1911.

H. M. Hyndman. *Further Reminiscences.* London, 1912, *passim.*

Rosalind Travers Hyndman. *The Last Years of H. M. Hyndman.* New York, 1924.

Beatrice and Sidney Webb. *History of Trade Unionism.* London, 1894, ed. of 1923.

Bernard Shaw. *Early History of the Fabian Society.* Fabian Tract No. 41. London, *n.d.*

E. R. Pease. *History of the Fabian Society.* London, 1916. See particularly Shaw's Notes, and Appendices.

Charles Booth. *Life and Labour of the People in London,* 1886–1890. Ed. of 1902.

Charles Booth. *In Darkest England.* London, 1899.

Sidney and Beatrice Webb. *Industrial Democracy.* London, 1897.

R. Mudie Smith. *Sweated Industries.* A Handbook of the Sweated Industries Exhibition of *The London Daily News,* London, 1906.

*The Exhibition of the Royal Academy,* 1884. Vol. I.

H. M. Hyndman and William Morris. *A Summary of the Principles of Socialism.* London: The Democratic Federation, 1884. (I assume this to have been Hyndman's work.)

W. R. Lethaby. *Philip Webb and His Work.*

Philip Webb. *Cartoons for the Cause, 1886–1896.* London, 1896.

Friedrich Engels. *Condition of the Working Classes in England.* Ed. of 1892.

*Briefe und Auszüge aus Briefen von . . . Friedrich Engels, Karl Marx, u.a., an F. A. Sorge u.a.,* Stuttgart, 1906.

Karl Marx. *Capital: A Critique of Political Economy.* Trs. from the fourth German ed. by Eden and Cedar Paul. New York and London, 1930, 2 vols.

Charles Fourier. *Théorie des Quatre Mouvements et des Destinées Générales.* Paris, ed. of 1841.

Charles Fourier. *Théorie de l'Unité Universelle, 4 tomes.* Paris, 1841.

Charles Fourier. *Le Nouveau Monde Industriel et Sociétaire.* Paris, 1829.

Karl Marx and Friedrich Engels. *Communist Manifesto*. London, 1848.

Peter Kropotkin. *Fields, Factories and Workshops*. London, ed. of 1900.

Peter Kropotkin. *Mutual Aid*. London, ed. of 1902.

Robert Owen. *Theory of the New Moral World*. London, 1836.

Brougham Villiers. *The Socialist Movement in England*. London, 1908.

Sidney Webb. *Socialism in England*. London, 1890.

Matthew Arnold. *On Translating Homer*. London, 1861–62.

Matthew Arnold. *Study of Celtic Literature*. London. 1867.

Matthew Arnold. *Mixed Essays*. New York, ed. of 1902.

Matthew Arnold. *Culture and Anarchy*, ed. with an introduction by William S. Knickerbocker. New York, ed. of 1925.

Thomas Carlyle. *Carlyle's Reminiscences*, ed. by James Anthony Froude. London, 1881.

James A. Froude. *History of the First Forty Years of Carlyle's Life*. London, 1882.

*Letters of Jane Welsh Carlyle*, ed. by Froude. London, 1883.

Thomas Carlyle. *Chartism*. London, 1839.

Thomas Carlyle. *Past and Present*. London, 1843.

Thomas Carlyle. *Sartor Resartus*. New York, *n.d.* (Scribners), ed. with an Introduction by H. D. Traill.

John Ruskin. *Complete Works*. New York, ed. of 1898.

Edward Carpenter. *Towards Democracy*. London, 1883.

Edward Carpenter. *My Days and Dreams*. London, 1916.

W. Stephen Sanders. *Early Socialist Days*. London, 1927.

*Letters of Queen Victoria*, Vol. I, Third Series, ed. by George Earle Buckle.

Stewart D. Headlam. *The Socialist's Church*. London, 1907.

George Howell. *Trade Unionism: New and Old*. London, 1891.

H. M. Hyndman. *England for All*. A pamphlet, 1881.

H. M. Hyndman. *The Coming Revolution in England*. London, 1882.

H. M. Hyndman. *The Social Reconstruction of England*. London, 1883.

H. M. Hyndman. *The Historical Basis of Socialism in England*. London, 1883.

G. D. H. Cole. *A History of the British Working Class Movement*, Vol. II. London, 1926.

*VI*

## PERIODICALS OF RELATED VALUE

*The Labour Leader,* ed. by Keir Hardie. From 1888 *et seq.*

*The Clarion,* ed. by Robert Blatchford. From 1891 *et seq.*

*The Anarchist,* I, No. 4, 1909.

*The Labour Monthly,* March, 1934. William Morris *vs.* the Morris Myth, by R. P. Arnot.

*Labour's Northern Voice,* 1936–37. A Few Notes on William Morris, by Frank Dawtry.

*The Wheatsheaf,* October, 1936. Artist and Prophet, by J. R. Williams.

*The Literary Guide,* April, 1934. William Morris: Freethinker and Utopian, by W. Kent.

*John O'London's Weekly,* March 10, 1934. William Morris: Poet and Craftsman, by Gerald Bullett.

*John O'London's Supplement,* March 10, 1934. Gerald Bullett.

*The Clarion,* March 24, 1934. Craftsman and Rebel, by Henry W. Nevinson.

*Bodleian Quarterly Record,* 1932, No. 2, pp. 71 *et seq.*

E. Bernstein. *H. M. Hyndman's Erinnerungen. Archiv für die Geschichte des Sozialismus und der Arbeiterbewegung,* 1914, IV, 105–15.

*Royal Society of Arts Journal,* 1934. The Life and Work of William Morris, by Paul Bloomfield.

*Revue Britannique.* William Morris, by G. Bonefont. Paris, 1896.

*Die Neue Zeit,* 1896. William Morris, by Walter Crane, pp. 133 *et seq.*

*The Nineteenth Century,* Jan., 1893. Modern Poets and the Meaning of Life, by Frederick W. H. Myers. (Quoted by Vallance.)

*Primitive Methodist Quarterly Review,* 1892. William Morris, by F. Richardson, pp. 414 *et seq.*

*The Craftsman,* I, No. 1; I, No. 2, October, 1901; April, 1902. Articles by Irene Sargent on Beautiful Books; Life, Art and Influence of Morris; Morris and Burne-Jones; Morris and Company, Decorators; William Morris: His Socialistic Career.

*The Craftsman,* May, 1903. William Morris as I Remember Him, by Arthur Stringer, pp. 126 *et seq.*

*Notes and Queries,* 9th Series, December 22, 1900. William Morris as a Man of Business, by George Young Wardle, pp. 495 *et seq.*

*The Adelphi Magazine,* October, 1933. Marx, Morris and Keir Hardie, by "R.R."

*The Architect,* Feb. 19, 1915. William Morris as a Craftsman, by H. J. L. J. Mason, pp. 172 *et seq.*

*Arts and Decoration,* November, 1919. The Modernity of William Morris, p. 61.

*Oxford and Cambridge Review,* 1909, VII, pp. 37–60. The Prose Romances of William Morris, by M. M. Pattison Muir.

*Adelphi Magazine,* 1932, No. 4, pp. 774 *et seq.;* V, 19 *et seq.* The Greatness of William Morris, and The Return to Fundamentals: Marx and Morris, both by John Middleton Murry.

*The Socialist Review,* 1920, pp. 322–25. A Proletarian Epic (The Pilgrims of Hope), by John Bruce Glasier.

*P. M. L. A.* of the Modern Language Association of America, 1896, pp. 220–57. The *Nibelungenlied* and *Saga* in Modern Poetry, by Gustav Grüner.

|*The Socialist Review,* 1921, pp. 245–49. William Morris and Bruce Glasier, by Mary Agnes Hamilton.

*Philobiblon,* 1934, VII, 172 *et seq.* William Morris, by Rudolph Koch.

*Quarterly Review,* 1911, pp. 482–504. The Poetry of William Morris, by Percy Lubbock.

*Scandinavian Studies and Notes,* 1923, No. 7, pp. 151–68. The Treatment of the Völsunga Saga by William Morris, by George Tremaine McDowell.

*Cambridge Review,* Nov. 26, 1896. William Morris, by Eiríkr Magnússon.

*The Studio,* 1934. Morris Centenary Number, March, 1934.

*The Saturday Review* (London), October 10, 1896. With the North-West Wind, by R. B. Cunninghame-Graham, pp. 389–90.

*Arena,* December, 1906, pp. 613–17. William Morris and Æsthetic Socialism, by Thomas Dickinson.

*Scandinavian Studies and Notes,* 1934, No. 13, pp. 17–32. Eiríkr Magnússon and His Saga Translations, by Stefán Einarsson.

*Journal of the Society of Arts,* 1898, pp. 618 *et seq.* The Life Work of William Morris, by Frederick Startridge Ellis. (Mr. F. S. Ellis.)

*Contemporary Review,* March, 1934, pp. 315–23. William Morris, His Influence and Reputation, by B. Ifor Evans.

# INDEX